The ✠ Old ✠ Sod ✠

The Odd Life and inner ✠ work of William G. Gray

ALAN RICHARDSON ✠ MARCUS CLARIDGE

SKYLIGHT PRESS

This edition published in Great Britain in 2011 by Skylight Press,
210 Brooklyn Road, Cheltenham, Glos GL51 8EA

First published in Great Britain by Ignotus Press, 2003.

Designed and typeset by Rebsie Fairholm
Cover photo by Lee James, from the original 1974 Rollright Ritual photoshoot,
reproduced courtesy of Helios Books.

Printed and bound in Great Britain by Lightning Source, Milton Keynes

www.skylightpress.co.uk

ISBN 978-1-908011-12-1

Contents

ABOUT THE AUTHORS

Marcus Claridge is a godson of William Gray and spent much time in Bill and Bobbie's company as he was growing up. He was initiated by Bill in his Temple in Bennington Street, Cheltenham, and is currently Warden for the Sangreal Sodality in Britain. As well as his esoteric interests in the Western Tradition he is also active in furthering its wider cultural elements. He practices Western Martial Arts such as broadsword and quarterstaff, and is percussionist for Fires of Love, a leading early music group in Scotland. He lives in Edinburgh with his partner Angela and daughter Freya.

Alan Richardson, the son of a coal-miner, was born in Ashington, Northumberland. He drifted into the Northern Counties College in Newcastle on Tyne and left there without any worthwhile qualification, then spent a few years wandering around America, attending universities in Kentucky and West Virginia – and totally failing to graduate from either. He has had many jobs, a few enemies, odd adventures in many dimensions, done many stupid things which still make him shudder, and written lots of books on magic which have sold dozens of copies.

AUTHORS' NOTE

A number of people have helped us in this biography even if they haven't always approved of our approach or attitude. It is a testament to their integrity and honesty that they still co-operated. Obviously their opinions, pro and con, do not necessarily match ours. Anyone who might want alternative viewpoints to the enigma that was William Gray should track down appropriate sources via the Web. Likewise, Bill made some savage comments about the Society of the Inner Light as it was in the 1960s when he joined, but that was only his personal view. Although neither of the present authors are members, past or present, we must insist that it remains today a group of the highest calibre, and interested readers might like to decide for themselves through the details in the appendix. The term 'Old Sod' means different things in different countries. As we shall explain, we use it here with absolute affection. Bill himself, in a letter to Alan Richardson dated 12th September 1989, was fully accepting of the term, and the sense in which it was to be used.

William G. Gray at the Rollright Stones. Photograph by Geoff Dearn.

Introduction

"OK so I'm an old sod, an old bastard, a thousand different kinds of shit if you like, but I am a human being who loved the esoteric Tradition I tried to serve... Perhaps I didn't do very well with what I'd got but I did my best..."

[letter to Alan Richardson, 19th Sept. 1989]

William G. Gray was a *real* magician, a kind of primeval spirit who worked his magic as an extension of the Life Force, not as a sop to ego. No-one who met him had any doubt that he was in touch with supra-human sources of wisdom, or that from his home in a dowdy back-street of Cheltenham he was bringing through energies from other dimensions that would one day influence us all. He reeked of psychism like he often reeked of incense, could give you the uncomfortable feeling that he could see right through you and beyond, and had been to places in spirit that we could scarcely imagine. He had powers of low-key prophecy which he often demonstrated, which were often accurate, and he turned some of the convoluted magical systems that had endured for centuries inside-out and upside-down, thus making it simpler for the rest of us to work with Light. Many of the books on magic and the Qabalah which appear today owe a huge if unrecognised debt to his pioneering writing. If nothing else, he was a true original in everything he did. In some ways he was larger than life, and many people were fearful of him. In other ways he had exasperating and unapologetic human quirks which could make him seem very small, depending on where you stood – or sometimes rather appealing if you didn't get blasted by his ire.

Anyone who ever met Bill Gray must laugh at the books churned out by the self-styled witches, magicians and urban shamans who, a generation later, imagine they are High Priests, mighty adepts, or 21st Century *brujos*. What empty figures they are in comparison, clutching their amulet-filled power pouches or dream-catchers, communing with their power animals while riding their dainty silver broomsticks through crystal-singing candy-floss Otherworlds where everything is eternally positive and ineffably, irritatingly, *nice* – and always with at least one eye on achieving a few sound-bites on local TV.

As Bill might have said when asked if they raised any real power: "Raise power? That lot couldn't raise so much as a good fart between them."

Yet if there is anything evolutionary about the current urge to revitalise the present by looking at the patterns of the past, and the increasing notions that there are harmonic energies within the Earth and ourselves that can be worked with – whether through green eco-movements, the Celtic Revival or the Wiccan arts – then it is due in no small degree to the work that was done by an old bastard who lived near the bus station in a faded town in Gloucestershire.

At least Bill Gray could raise power. Power that could make your eyes water and your fillings ache, and seep out into the world to change it. That's what *real* magicians do. Whether he could always handle it with love or wisdom is another issue. He made many enemies. Even his friends often winced at his antics. Yet now, almost two decades after his death, both friends and enemies remain united in their recognition of the fact that – whatever his mortal faults – he was a one-off, and that holy magic flowed through his veins like blood.

Bill was hard. He could intimidate. A real sod at times. He wrote brilliant letters, but when it came to books he often fell out with his editors. Yet they tolerated a lot because they knew that he was in a different league to the other writers on their lists who simply made it up as they went along. Underneath the dense and often abrasive prose, with the alliteration he felt would help get concepts embedded in the reader's mind, it was quite obvious to them that here was a new level of insight into the theory, practice, philosophy and sheer experience of Magic, and how it impinged upon the world. Here was a *real* magician.

He seemed to know everything, although he rarely bought a book or plundered the library.

"Do you know why Aleister Crowley spelled magick with a 'k'?" he asked Alan Richardson once, and the young man perked up because he had read exactly that only days before and saw a rare chance to impress the old mage.

"Actually Bill I do. Not only did he want to distinguish the medieval, supernatural and spiritual art of Magic from mere conjuring, but the 'k' referred to the Greek word —"

But Gray wouldn't let him continue. He had already worked it out himself, intuited it, and proceeded to explain at great length because the lecture was in his head just waiting for an audience. And although it wasn't *exactly* what Crowley had said, it was impressively close. All to do with sex.

So for those who are new to the topic, what do we mean by magic, as practised by *real* magicians – regardless of which spelling they use? And why, of all things, did we call his biography *The Old Sod*?

Bill himself wrote of magic:

> Definition of Magic is largely a matter of individual opinion… Fundamentally it remains what it always was: Man's most determined effort to establish an actual working relationship through himself between his Inner and Outer states of being. By magic, Man shows that he is not content to be simply a pawn in the Great Game, but wants to play on his own account. Man the meddler becomes Man the Magician, and so learns the rules the hard way, for magic is concerned with Doing, while mysticism is concerned with Being.
> [*Magical Ritual Methods*, Helios 1969]

Compare this with Crowley's:

> From the nature of things… life is a sacrament; in other words, all our acts are magical acts. Our spiritual consciousness acts through the will and its instruments upon material objects, in order to produce changes which will result in… new conditions of consciousness.
> [*The Confessions of Aleister Crowley*, Bantam Books 1970, page 110]

It was once an art. It was an integral part of religion. As Bill further explained:

> The word Magic… had root connections with greatness (*Maj*) and mastery (*Magister*), and providing this might be understood in the sense of spiritual development and self-mastery, it seemed a reasonable description of the Path I intended to follow. Orthodox religions of all descriptions rejected Magic as a dangerous rival, yet Magic was inclusive of religion… Religion was collective whereas Magic was individual, and I was all for individualism… I would find my own faith through whatever I might learn of Magic and its practical purposes.

As to the title *The Old Sod*…

It was partly because he really could be, in the British vernacular, an old sod. That is to say, an extremely awkward character; a bit of a bastard.

However it is a term that can be used with admiration and very deep affection also, akin to Americans calling someone an old fart. Second, it also refers to *sod* as a clump of earth, and has allusions to the pioneering Earth Magic which underlay a lot of his inner work. Bill was aware of both of these usages and grudgingly accepted them. But it never seemed to enter his head that it also referred to his role as the founder of the Sangreal Sodality – the latter word meaning a confraternity of like-minded souls. And beneath these there is perhaps a fourth reason: by calling him this, we could keep him at a slight distance, and not get sucked into the sort of fawning that so often mars the art of biography. We owe the man and his magic a huge debt, and want to repay this as fully and honestly as we can, but we were not *totally* blinded by his light.

Did Bill have any dark secrets? Well he certainly looked into and possibly explored many dark and secret areas of the psyche, but that is the path of anyone hell-bent on the getting of wisdom. William G. Gray could be and was a mighty magician, but he was also human, with many of the prejudices of his class, age and locale. He lived in Cheltenham for god's sake! – and that alone explains much.

Next, to get the current (and tedious) spiritual and political correctness out of the way, Was he sexist, homophobic or racist?

Sexist? No. Not at all. Although hardly what you might call a Ladies' Man, he could get on extremely well with women, and some – younger ones in particular – often found him immensely charming and loveable. Whatever his faults, none of the younger generation of women ever took him to task for being sexist, although his contemporaries might disagree.

Homophobic? No. We knew a number of gay people in common, who were involved in magical activities, and he never once took issue with their sexuality. In fact he didn't really understand gay issues much, and the only weak part of his classic *Ladder of Lights* is when he gives some absurd advice to gay men and lesbian women as to how they might 'get straight'.

Racist? Well, yes. No denying it. His use of the term 'Nigerian' as a euphemism for the obvious became tiresome very quickly. Yes he *was* a racist – although he modified the term in his later years to 'racialist', and this is something that must be looked at in some detail. But right from the start it is worth bearing in mind that one of his most respectful and meaningful encounters in South Africa was with Credo Mutwa, the famous Zulu medicine man, author of *Indaba my Children* and *My People*. They got on famously, expressed mutual admiration, and he spoke of it later with great pride. So the issue is not that simple, and we shouldn't brand and reject him with the bald word 'racist' without looking at the whole issue.

For various reasons – legal, moral, literary and magical – we decided that it wouldn't really be advisable to publish Bill's autobiography verbatim. So we took the best bits in which he explained things in his own inimitable way, and turned the rest of it into a third person biography in which we could use the memories and comments of those who had known and worked with him. But as he wrote to Marcia Pickands, one of the inheritors of his Magic:

> For god's sake don't make me out to be any kind of 'Master-Figure' with any kind of 'powers' or faculties other than those of human understanding. I have simply written what I have seen by the Inner Light afforded me. If this helps others well and good, and if it doesn't I'm sorry but it's all I've got. What I've written is for *others to make their own way with* and do a lot better than I possibly can. The more they can do with it the happier I'll be.
> *[29th July 1986]*

Right then Bill, we won't make you out to be any kind of Master-Figure as you term it. But you *did* have talents that went a little further than everyday human understanding; you *did* have an enormous impact on a wide range of people, either directly or indirectly; you weren't *quite* as modest and self-effacing as the above quote might imply; and you could be so bloody difficult that we, who sort of idolised you, will let you have your say in all the important things relating to Magic, but also take this chance to make you listen. Just for once. Blast us to buggery if you want, but be aware that we've written according to the inner light that you sparked within us. We are determined to make that light grow. If readers can use it to find their own Holy Grails through the inspiration of your work and example, then we will be more than happy.

CHAPTER 1

The Child Who Became a Priest-King

"There is no doubt whatsoever I must have been more than the traditional handful. From what I remember I was an absolute horror. I was badly behaved, disobedient, untidy, and I wet the bed with both force and frequency."

William G. Gray was born old. He was one of those babes about whom knowing grandmothers furrow their brows as they look into the cot and say, tersely: *He's been here before...*

Of course he had.

In that curious philosophy of the Qabalah, which Gray made his own, there are certain aspects known as Magical Images. These are symbols connected to certain realms of consciousness. One of these realms is known as the Sphere of the Sun, and this is where you can find all the Solar Gods and Heroes in all mythologies and religions. Now there are three interlinked Magical Images for this sphere, and they are known as The Child, the Priest-king, and the Sacrificed God. All the great heroes and solar deities function in at least one of these phases, and sometimes all three.

Bill Gray never lived the sort of life which might enable him to achieve the exalted and eternal status of the Sacrificed God, but he certainly worked through the first two. And he had certainly been here before. If he was not entirely the sort of Wonderchild around whom legends are woven, everyone involved in his birth knew that there was something – well, *different* about the twelve pound baby boy who plummeted into the world like a fallen and very disgruntled angel.

William Gordon Gray was born in Harrow, Middlesex, on the 25th of March 1913, at ten minutes past two in the afternoon. In those days only station clocks were synchronised electrically, and therefore reliable, and so his mother (who later became an astrologer) felt so strongly about checking the exact birth-time that she sent the father out to set his pocket-watch by the nearby railway clock at noon.

When she had recovered a little from the ordeal of producing such a large baby boy, the mother asked the midwife if there were any marks on her child's body. After assuring her that the child was in perfect shape, with all the bits in the right places, the midwife eventually admitted that there was a lozenge-shaped birthmark on his lower left side.

"Oh," remarked the mother, "then he's who I think he is. That's where he was stabbed to death last time."

The 'last time' in question referred to her past life, in which a Venetian soldier-merchant had tried to rape her, and she had stuck a knife into his side. In the present life the intended victim found herself giving birth to her attacker.

The midwife, who was also the woman's sister-in-law and thus knew something of the new mother's quirks, went quiet for a moment before offering: "What an odd thing to say. You *are* a strange girl, Christine…"

The strange girl, however, was fey enough to realise that she had just given birth to someone who was quite unusual, and who had been here many times before – not always happily – but usually with effect.

It was a second marriage for both parents, and there was a considerable age gap between them. He was 44 and a divorcee with two daughters living in America, and she was a young widow of 27 whose daughter by a previous marriage had died in infancy. His full name was John McCammon Trew Gray, and hers had been Christine Ash, *née* Christine Chester Logie. A tablet to her great-uncle Lemuel Chester is still to be seen in Westminster Abbey, where he became a Recorder, and he is one of the very few Americans commemorated in the national British shrine. At the time they met, John had been manager of a theatrical touring company and Christine one of the actresses. They married in Philadelphia on August 26th 1910.

Interesting that Bill should have derived from a theatrical background. *Real* magicians are all, to a very great degree, good actors. Conversely, the great actors are all, in their own ways, very good magicians; and in later years Bill did a lot of amateur dramatics himself, while the ham actor often shone through in his conversations.

As far as his son could see, John Gray had no interest in esoteric topics whatsoever, being if anything of Low Church persuasion. (Throughout his life Bill always used the term 'Low Church' in a disparaging sense, as though it were synonymous with third rate.) Yet it was not that, like the vast majority of the public of that era, John had had no exposure to esoteric thought. In fact he had been theatrical manager to that extraordinary woman Katherine Tingley, the social reformer and Theosophist leader at Point Loma in California – of which more later. Although she did her best to acquaint him with the general principles of that lush and exotic religious hybrid, he could never take it seriously as a mode of life – although he did rate the charismatic Ms Tingley as the best business woman he had ever met. And even if he wasn't drawn to esotericism himself, it seems he could not really escape it because his older brother Will became an American citizen and married a Theosophist concert pianist named Florence Shinkle.

Mind you, perhaps his father sensed more about his son's 'otherworldliness' than Bill realised at the time, and was simply afraid of things within himself that he did not fully understand. In this odd business of Magic, like often attracts like and deep calls to deep, whether both parties are consciously aware of it or not. Decades later, not long after the older man's death, John Gray 'came back' to commune with his son, who was intrigued to see him looking totally different to how he remembered him when alive. The wraith said, very seriously: *I'd like you to go and get your eyes tested.* Now anyone else might have been astonished or deeply moved by such an visitation, but this sort of thing was clearly old hat to Bill by this time. Being the awkward sod he was, Bill immediately asked his father's ghost why he was so concerned about his well-being now, when he hadn't been very interested in it whilst he was still in this world. One can only imagine that the shade of John Gray shrugged. "What struck me especially," wrote Bill, "was how much younger and smarter he appeared. However I did take the advice and it was discovered that I needed spectacles for close work very much indeed. They made quite a difference to my Life."

Of course spirits tend to return at the age of their greatest vigour – if they know their business. That odd moment was probably the closest that father and son had ever been in *that* life. In fact, because of his father's apparent lack of interest in things magical, Bill tended to portray him as rather a dour, uninteresting character when in fact the man had an extraordinary life, and certainly – once – had enough charisma and sex-appeal to attract a young actress 17 years his junior. Fragments of surviving letters from father to son c.1940 show that John Gray actually had enormous interest in and concern for Bill, and expressed this with sound advice and humour. He even advised him to live with his current girlfriend before even thinking of marrying her – which was radical for those days. Bill never seemed to understand that you could know bugger all about magic and still be a great soul – or at very least a good and wise man.

But Bill's mother Christine had the advantage (in his eyes) of being officially a Roman Catholic, even though she practised her faith light-heartedly, intermittently and somewhat haphazardly, while managing to reconcile it with her very marked psychism and obvious belief in reincarnation. In her youth she had been educated by American nuns working under the Paulist Fathers, who apparently had rather advanced views for their times. She would have been known at that time as something of a Bohemian, and seen by her peers as a free and occasionally wild spirit. A close friend of the poet Ezra Pound, whom she called 'Ray', she used to play chess with him on a regular basis, and once kicked the board across the room to stop him winning – as he always did. They exchanged many letters over a long period of time, but she destroyed these as being 'too personal'.

She once bemoaned the fact that the so-called permissive society of the time had absolutely ruined the excitement and joy of pursuing forbidden pleasures. When sin was such a simple affair as seeing a glimpse of proscribed human flesh, drinking a glass of spirits, or smoking a cigarette in public, one could do any or all of these things with a delightful air of depravity totally unknown to liberated people. Christine felt that when sin became not only permissible but advisable she lost a lot of interest in life. Once, in her late teens, she dressed in the most sophisticated fashion with a picture hat and wickedly dangling earrings while wearing a lot of make-up and then going alone to a likely dive where she hoped to meet dangerously interesting characters. Sitting by herself with a glass of absinthe before her, she noticed two such men at the next table scrutinising her carefully. She thought maybe they might mistake her for Clara the Crook or Connie the Conwoman. One man spoke quietly to the other who shook his head and said audibly: "Naw. Lady novelist looking for copy." She was so furious at the failure of her scheme that she went home forthwith and hurled both hat and earrings to the floor.

Not by any stretch of the imagination could Bill have been called a 'mother's boy', but she was the primary influence on him, and they became best friends in later years even though she had woefully little to do with his upbringing. She might have not have a been a 'great mother' in the mythological or even slang sense, but reading his anecdotes, you can't help thinking what a lot of fun she was.

She was also *extremely* aware of how much this world interlocks with others...

Once, when she was ill and being looked after by a retired nurse, she became distinctly conscious of an Otherworldly being in the room

Christine Gray

with her, trying to help. Intrigued, Christine asked the being how it was possible for him to be there in communication with her while at the same time she remained aware of everything else happening. Smiling, the being offered to demonstrate. Then, as the nurse entered with a spoon in her hand and said brightly: '*Now come along dear, it's time to take your...*' everything suddenly seemed to freeze solid everywhere, yet the Otherworlder remained chatting cheerfully away while the old lady remained motionless, her poised spoon still pointing in Christine's direction. "She said it seemed like hours to her when all of a sudden the spell appeared to break and her nurse said '...*medicine!*' and pushed the spoon into her mouth, adding: '*Now you have a good sleep dear,*' and left the room. The Otherworlder then went on to explain the elasticity of time and how it might be expanded or contracted in conformity with consciousness. In other words what could seem like millions of years to a microbe would only be moments for an ordinary human, and what would be an entire lifetime to that human would only be micro-moments to a Consciousness operating on a Cosmic scale..."

The midwife was right: Christine Gray was a *very* strange girl.

When the First World War broke out in 1914 Gray senior falsified his age in order to enlist in the Army and 'do his bit' for this country, as they said then, all supremely confident that it would be well over by Christmas. He joined the Ox and Bucks Light Infantry, going first to France as a sergeant, then later when he was commissioned, to India, where he took charge of a Turkish prisoner of war camp in Elephanta Island, off Bombay.

As far as Bill could recall, in his last years, his mother never really forgave her husband for his patriotic fervour, because it meant a financial failure from which they never truly recovered, and they came to live increasingly separate lives. But reading his story with what might be the cynical eye of the outsider, it often seemed as if John Gray's enlistment was less to do with patriotism, and more to do with keeping out of his wife's way. Certainly, neither of them seemed to have an overwhelming desire to look after their own son, and used the War as an excuse to farm him out with relatives.

Christine Gray's response to this effective marital desertion was to off-load her son and get a job. It never entered her head that she might try and bring up young Gordon, as she called him, by herself. So she worked for a time as a secretary for the British War Office, and then later when America entered the conflict she transferred to the London American Headquarters, where, as Bill recalled, she was *much* happier among her own kind.

Since the parents had split up for the duration of the hostilities, young William Gordon Gray was sent to live with his ailing grandmother and his Aunt Lella (the midwife who had delivered him) at Ramsgate. So poor unmarried Lella had the double responsibility of looking after her elderly mother and her extremely difficult nephew.

People of our era, acting out of what they imagine to be spiritual impulses, often tend to make a fuss about finding the Child Within. They see it as a means of winning back innocence and hope, and rejuvenating that which they feel has been lost or stolen from their adult lives. No such cosy image for Bill Gray however. When he was in his seventies, he talked quite happily and openly about the little monster he had been, an image which he never wanted to restore.

"There is no doubt whatsoever I must have been more than the traditional handful. From what I remember I was an absolute *horror*. I was badly behaved, disobedient, untidy, and I wet the bed with both force and frequency. In case anyone thinks that adults were to blame for not correcting such bad behaviour, it should be remembered that those were far from normal times. One adult was in her dotage, and the other in a more or less continual state of stress. They could only afford a single servant, and these left with distressing regularity, sometimes because they quarrelled with Aunt Lella, and sometimes because they could not stand me."

On the rare occasions when Bill saw his father on leave, he was never punished by him in any way, because no normal man in those times who expected each visit might be his last wanted to leave an unfavourable memory in the mind of his only son. Likewise, his Uncle Harry, a major in the Seaforths, would sometimes give the difficult child a sharp lecture, but he also had a dislike of actually striking his brother's child.

Bill had no memory of his mother visiting during the War, so his immediate female influence was confined to elderly women with a Church of England background. They were, however, highly literate women who taught him to read and write long before school age. Grannie would often read the Bible to him, and tell him stories of her travels, especially in Russia, where her husband had spent some time as Chaplain to the British community in St Petersburg. Every Easter she would say to her grandson solemnly: *Hristos voskrese matushinka* which meant *Christ is risen, my little one.*

Bill was to claim that the First World War was little more than a dim memory, although he had clearly retained an impressive amount of detail. He could recall that certain foods were rationed, and remembered being pushed around by Auntie Lella in a child's push-chair from shop to shop, enduring long queues at each. He remembered too her shock when she asked a milkman the price of eggs, and being told: *Heggs mum, his ninepence each HIF you can get em.* But his clearest memory of all was the Zeppelin.

"I was asleep when Auntie dragged me out of bed while she wrapped a blanket around me and spoke excitedly of what I was going to see. Then she carted me out to the upstairs balcony which was strictly forbidden to me, and told me to look at this glorious sight carefully and remember everything so that I could tell my eventual grandchildren. What I saw looked like a huge silver cigar floating in the glare of searchlights over the sea not very far from the shore, nor so very high either. From our house in Brockenhurst Road we had an almost uninterrupted view of the sea over the cliff tops. AA [anti-aircraft] shells were bursting with noisy flashes in the direction of the Zeppelin as the gunners did their best to destroy it. Suddenly one of them hit it somewhere centrally and a huge sheet of flame exploded from one end to the other, lighting up the town with a momentary glare of blazing light. Following that flare we could distinctly hear the cheering coming from the throats of everyone watching. The airship broke into two sections, the foremost plunging directly into the sea while the rear part seemed to slip more slowly with a side-to-side motion until it too hit the sea with a horrible kind of hiss…"

Strange to think that, just along the coast, watching the same event and cheering as heartily as his asthma would allow, was a man whom many people felt Bill Gray came to resemble physically when he reached the same age: Aleister Crowley. The Great Beast himself, a cult figure even today who was, in the eyes of vast numbers of the counter-culture, the Logos of the Aeon. Or, in purely philological terms, the man who put the 'k' in Magick, and who has become synonymous with that ancient art ever since. Strange to visualise the pair of them being joined by the same night-sky images of light and darkness; the middle-aged magus all unaware of the oddly magickal child just along the coast who was sharing the same burning vision – although they would both meet up before too long.

Eventually of course the war ended, leaving Bill with memories of people rushing out of their houses into the streets and banging frantically on tea-trays or anything else that would make a racket. They sang and danced noisily, while perfect strangers kissed each other and mobbed old wounded soldiers in their hospital blues with cigarettes, drinks, or gifts of money. The euphoria seemed to continue for several days. Churches were packed and so were the pubs. Though familiar with the former it was to be many years before he encountered the latter, though he never gave them good or regular custom.

And it was shortly after the war ended that Bill met his mother consciously for the first time.

"It was rather comical. My aunt and grandmother had discussed her in my hearing quite frequently and with some disapproval. They had several points against her. First she was a Roman Catholic and therefore

Bill with his Aunt Lella and Grannie

not quite a proper Christian to their Evangelical minds. Secondly, she had been an actress, and good Victorian ladies knew the sort of reputation *they* had. Third (and probably worst) she smoked, and it was rumoured she had even done so *in the streets*. Open vulgarity to the Victorian mind was considerably worse than concealed immorality. Consequently I was loaded with preconceived opinions when at last I was sent into a drawing room to meet my mama.

"I saw a strange and smartly dressed woman with pince-nez glasses standing by the fireplace smoking a cigarette. When she saw me she smiled, held out both hands and said with a strong American accent 'Hello Gordon.' Uncertain of quite what to say and rather taken back by her approach I retreated warily and spoke very firmly: 'I don't approve of women smoking.' It was so obvious how I had learned those words that she burst out laughing and replied 'Oh Gordon, don't be such a little prig!' At which I felt totally disconcerted and ran from the room altogether. I am uncertain who or what brought us together at our next encounter. This must surely be one of the oddest passages between a mother and her six year old son on record. We subsequently became the closest of friends."

Close friends they might have become, but Christine Gray seemed to lack certain motherly qualities. Even though the war was over, she and John did not take their son back into their fold. Instead they left for

London, hoping to establish a small Oriental importing business. Bill was left behind with his increasingly frail maternal grandmother and the often despairing Aunt Lella.

He spent most of his time reading. Someone in the family had presented him with a complete set of the *Children's Encyclopaedia*, and he read every word avidly. "My favourite trick was to read up well on some subject that interested me, then question an adult about it hoping to catch them out in some small inaccuracy, when I would display my superior knowledge with a burst of juvenile erudition, expecting praise for my exposition. I was a precocious little pest, and a voracious reader of everything I could get hold of…"

It was a technique that many would-be polymaths develop. Aldous Huxley, for example, would choose a particular essay from a dense and learned tome, memorise it, and then later, in company would bring the conversation around to that very topic and mesmerise his listeners with his apparent omniscience. Likewise, in adult life, visitors to Bill would often find their general conversation bent in a particular direction so that their host could give them an apparently spontaneous lecture of the highest quality. There was no deceit involved, beyond an urge to expound and the will to find an audience. Plus Bill could talk – really talk. The child was not so very far removed from the man: the older soul was always present in the child.

It was around this time that he began to stumble into magic. He did so through the arts of play, which are not so very different to the techniques of magic itself. Solitary children often develop powerful imaginations from, as he put it, "…an intense need for companionship with compatible consciousness. They often invent imaginary playmates which seem more real to them than actual adults, and sometimes project these alter-ego personalities into inanimate physical objects such as dolls or puppets of some kind. In other words the thing becomes a practical symbol for a state of consciousness in the human mind and the two interrelate. This is in fact the basis of workable magic, and I learned it very early in life." He was also helped by the model theatre that his father constructed for him, using the tiny dolls to act out his fantasies before imaginary audiences, and thus understand the principles of psychodrama that underlie the techniques of ritual magic.

On top of this, at about the same time, Lella became ill and was taken to hospital, so he was taken into care by his Uncle Will and Aunt Florence – the Californian concert pianist and dedicated Theosophist "…of the Annie Besant persuasion".

At that time the Theosophical Society was split between the extraordinary Annie Besant, who championed young Krishnamurti as the new World Leader from the main base in Adyar, and the equally compelling Katherine Tingley with her headquarters in Point Loma, California, who advocated a 'Back to Blavatsky' movement in an attempt to return the society to its occult roots, and away from the dubious Messianic impulses which she felt had overtaken it.

Florence lectured her nephew for long periods, but even at that age he was uneasy with her 'dollar-dedicated' personality, which felt that self-advantage was the only possible goal in life worth following. In her eyes, any manoeuvre to outwit or exploit the gullibility of fellow humans was good to learn, because this was a dog-eat-dog civilisation where it was every man for himself. Despite this, his Aunt Florence spoke about Theosophy with almost missionary zeal, and she herself could have seen no contradiction between her general attitude to life, and Theosophy's approach to the lives which follow and precede this one.

"She talked to me at great length concerning its principles and implications. It was true I did not understand all her references to root races, sub-cycles and the reputed Masters guiding human destinies from Tibetan secret centres, but I got an instinctive feeling there might be at least *something* in what she spoke of, even if it was a somewhat alien something which seemed to strike a warning note to my receptive mind. It was not a hostile note, but one which seemed to say: *This is not quite what you are looking for, but it points the way in that direction. So listen.*"

So he did. Despite his doubts, Bill always had a soft spot for Theosophy:

"My experience in those days led me to associate the general run of British Theosophists with elderly ladies of both sexes and genteel behaviour whose ideas of Nirvana centred around mysterious Oriental Masters who directed the destiny of all mankind from a secret spot in Tibet. On the whole they appeared to be 'naice' people but very ineffectual and somewhat on the timorous side. Endless talk without any action that I could detect. No real dynamism. Nevertheless the Movement itself had opened up channels of communication amongst people which were previously closed to the average person, and provided alternative viewpoints to be explored by those who found conventional religions too limiting or constrictive."

In his later life he never claimed to have made any kind of mind-to-mind contact with Himalayan Masters, but, although he was firmly committed to what might be termed the Western Mystery Tradition, he never quite rejected the possibility of their existence. They were, indeed, not quite what he wanted, and far too 'naice' for him. By the time he had matured magically, he found other sources of wisdom that were attuned to specifically Western psyches.

It was then, however, at the age of eight, while his young mind was tantalised by images of supra-human beings and levels of consciousness far beyond the mundane, he was inflicted by Masters of a very human kind. Quite simply he was sent to school, and experienced for the first time what it was like to mix with boys of his own age. To him, the other children might have come from another planet. To them, he was an oddball to be teased or treated with suspicion and distrust, because his speech was so adult and out of date. He totally failed to understand their schoolboy slang or behaviour, was utterly useless at games, and – worse – he never joined in with their attempts to outwit the school authorities. In short, he was the ideal butt for their juvenile pranks.

He was saved from this torture by the death of his grandmother, and by his formidable Aunt Florence. She didn't need wisdom of a Himalayan Master to realise that John and Christine Gray had been a little backward in coming forward, as regards taking a proper responsibility for their own son. She insisted that, for once, they do something about the boy. So Bill found himself living with them at last, in Forest Hill – and that was another shock to the system.

"My father would give me … pocket money, enquire after my schooling, and depart with a polite handshake. [We] had a courteous but distant relationship for the whole of our lives together. I could never talk to him about intimate matters because he would put up immediate barriers the moment I mentioned anything of a controversial nature. He made it so plain that he did not want to know about or discuss such topics that I soon realised it was useless pursuing the subject and gave up attempting to communicate with him in specific directions. Otherwise we remained on a fairly friendly footing."

His mother, as we have noted, was very different. If the entity we think of as William G. Gray derived from anyone, it was from her.

"It was at this time that my life long interest in the occult showed signs of budding, encouraged by my mother's empathy and general guidance. She did not belong to any organised esoteric concern at that period, and her knowledge was natural and instinctive rather than academic and systematic. Her clairvoyance and what are now called ESP faculties were purely a matter of heredity through her Scots blood, and were once taken for granted among Highlanders who called it simply 'The Sight'. She treated it as quite normal and natural even if erratic and not always trustworthy. Her version of Inner Life was a fascinating mixture of myth and magic blended with her own interpretation of Catholic Christianity which varied considerably from the official and orthodox presentation."

One important thing she did was take him to Mass. Important that is, not from the religious aspect as such, but because the old Tridentine Rite completely captivated him as no Evangelical Church of England service had ever done:

"Although I did not understand a single word of the Latin, I felt entirely at home with the ritual as if I had taken part in it many times. Instinctively I recognised the force and power present in that place at that time. I could literally feel it for myself as a physical influence affecting all my senses. Granted that the officiating priest was the subsequently well-known Father Corbishley SJ, but the impression made on me by that mystical experience was indelible. The unusual effects of the ritual equipment such as the incense, candles, colours, and choral chanting, stirred me to my very depths and awakened an insatiable desire to know what it all meant and why it had such an appeal..."

It was not long before he insisted on becoming an official Catholic like his mother. She was not wildly enthusiastic because she felt that he should wait until he was older, and had developed more fully, but he proved so keen on the idea that she eventually gave way and he was duly re-baptised by Father Corbishley.

"Then I felt that I had started to climb the ladder of my lifetime, one of its most important rungs being priesthood. There was a strange feeling of familiarity about this process as if I already knew what it meant and had been through it all before somewhere."

What mainly attracted him was the apparent position of a priest in relation to ordinary people. To be able to interpret God in a believable way. To deal with supernatural forces he could feel himself during religious rituals. For him, the priest was much more than merely mortal, and seemed like a human of the highest kind exalted by special spiritual authority over the heads of everyone else for some particular purpose decided by Deity Itself.

"At least now I had an objective in life," he wrote, "and I resolved to find it one way or another."

CHAPTER 2

The Opening of the Way

*"From that moment to this I have never worried
about what others might think of me."*

William G. Gray must have seemed particularly odd to his peers. As a young boy, aged nine, he never had the interests or concerns that come with 'normal' childhoods, nor yet was he troubled by the sort of worries that bedevil other children. *They* might have agonised about sweets, favourite toys, best friends, cold parents, school bullies or teachers they feared, but such things had little or no impact on Bill. His progress through childhood was rather like that of a weary old soul trying to master a clumsy vehicle that would enable him to drive through difficult countryside in order to return home. His childhood memories contained nothing in the way of boyhood chums or schoolyard enemies. He seemed oblivious to the fact that his parents really didn't seem to want him around. Apart from the theatre his father had made him (which he remembered not so much as a toy but as an extension of his 'intuitive approach toward psychodrama and ritual'), there were no cowboy outfits, air rifles or catapults, no bicycles, pets, rough games, sweethearts, birthday parties or Christmases.

It was obvious that being a real magician was, through choice, a very solitary path.

In fact the one thing that *really* troubled Bill was that his overt interest in esoteric topics had been forced to an abrupt halt, and he found himself – literally – in a completely New World. One that was colder, stranger and infinitely less appealing than the inner realms he had started to explore, and which he knew in his bones had once been entirely familiar to him. It was not that he had lost interest in his magic; it was because of sheer lack of communication with the people he now found himself among. People who had no inkling of, or sympathy for, the upwelling of the magic within him. "There was no-one to talk about it" he lamented, "no books to read about such topics, and not a single soul to tell me anything except myself..."

And the cold new world which gave him so much trouble was Canada.

He went to live in Canada because his mother had become increasingly and seriously ill with chest trouble. Eventually, after many family meetings and uncharacteristic appearances of his father, it was decided that Bill and his mother should go to Montreal, where Christine's sister had married a well-to-do stockbroker. The plan was that his Aunt Leslie would arrange for her sister's treatment at a sanatorium, and also look after her nephew in addition to her own two children. "Close relatives" wrote Bill solemnly, "took such responsibilities very seriously in those days, regarding them as a normal factor of human living."

To any normal boy this might have been an exciting if worrying series of events, but he seemed strangely untouched by all the huge changes that suddenly occurred because, even now, he had realised that the *true* life of his kind was the internal, spiritual one.

It was his first experience of ship travel. And what did this strange, difficult 9-year-old boy remember about this wondrous voyage across the Atlantic? The storm waves? The infinite sky and vast horizons? The engine room? The whales? The glimpse of distant icebergs? The exotic human life on all the decks?

No, what he chiefly remembered was the separate Divine Services for all denominations (the Captain naturally conducting the C of E gathering in the main saloon) and the elderly Catholic priest saying his Mass with its equipment confined to a drawer he had borrowed from a desk and placed on a convenient chair. Bill found himself disappointed that he was not sufficiently familiar with the liturgy to serve as an acolyte, but at least, he wrote, with an almost audible sigh of relief, he participated in the prayers.

Sometimes, you can't help worrying about the boy.

After another long trip up the St Lawrence the ship eventually docked at Montreal, and they were driven in a bright yellow Bramson taxi to a large apartment block on Pine Avenue West.

His Aunt Leslie turned out to be one of the oddest women he had ever met. She seemed absolutely unemotional, completely correct in everything she did, and had a frosty formal manner which forbade any attempt at intimate or close relationship. He just could not love her, no matter how much he might be grateful for her undoubted hospitality.

Her husband Bruce, however, was a very large man who quickly gained young Bill's eternal respect, since he made it quite clear at the start that he would tolerate no bad behaviour in the household, and who usually made the punishment fit the crime. For the first time in his life, the difficult child experienced 'masculine discipline applied firmly with intelligence and purpose'. By his own admission, he needed this desperately. For example, when once he picked up the family cat by the tail, he quickly found himself suspended by the wrist in mid air. When he protested, Uncle Bruce remarked quietly: "I'm only doing to you what you just did to her. Don't you like it? Well neither did she, so don't do it again or you'll feel worse." The lesson went well home because it was only thoughtlessness on his part which had made him handle the cat so badly. "It never occurred to me that an animal could experience like a human being until that moment."

When his mother was sent off to the sanatorium at St Agathe de Luat, her son was given a place at the Stanstead Wesleyan College, even though – with astonishing presumption – he had asked for a Catholic education.

After some tests it was realised that Bill had, what he termed, a 'non-numerate mind'. In fact throughout his life he was never any good with figures. "Somehow my mind would always work in words and reject numbers as alien concepts." He realised even then that every worthwhile profession was likely to be denied him in later years because he did not have the sort of brilliance at mathematics that was a prerequisite. Yet he hoped, both admirably and rather sadly, "to get by with what I had."

However, because of his literary ability alone they assigned him to a class in advance of his years, which provoked the usual schoolboy antagonisms. Once again, he faced the hostilities of his contemporaries, but this time mainly because of his Britishness. English people were intensely unpopular at that period in Quebec. The French was spoken with – to him – a peculiar patois. He never mastered any of it, and only acquired a rudimentary knowledge of conversational French with extreme difficulty. Nevertheless this was to come in useful when he went, eventually, to Egypt.

He was consciously aware that the inner path he had started to walk seemed to have petered out. Catholicism, which he felt held the answers he was looking for (and was certainly an impulse from a previous life) was not very impressive in that part of Canada at that time.

"The garishness of the decorations [in the local village church] irritated me, and the strong smell of Galoise cigarettes pervading the incense puzzled me until I stumbled across local youths smoking and playing cards with their caps on during a service while hidden from view on steps leading to the gallery. Then there were two sermons, one in French and the other in broken English. I was amazed at the antics and contortions of the priest who literally bounced about in his pulpit like a rapid rubber ball... As maybe a final touch the holy water in the public stoup was absolutely filthy. All in all I was not very happy with the French Canadian version of Catholicism. I was really in a dissatisfied condition with myself and what seemed my lack of progress."

So Bill Gray did at that time in his young life what he was to do throughout it: he saw the whole thing as a kind of spiritual lesson. He could not put his awareness into actual words at that age, but he *felt* it through, rather than thought it through, and expressed it many decades later as:

"The simple truth is of course that human life should be a balanced exchange of energy between one's internal and external state of existence until neither become necessary for self-expression... Absolutely everything has an 'occult' or 'hidden' side to its nature which can be used to serve one's primal life-purpose, which is self-discovery in the hope of eventually finding the *TRUE SELF* ...."

So Bill's isolation came to be a practical lesson in itself, as he continued with the problem of living as a Canadian schoolboy. Years later he realised that the wisest thing anyone genuinely interested in esotericism can do from time to time is to cut themselves completely off from external contacts of every obvious kind and literally *force* the flow of true Inner experience to express itself from the very depths of one's being. In other words, you do not need books, deep conversations, ceremonies, groups, debates, ritual artefacts or any external objects in order to connect with genuine inner sources of wisdom.

So to his mind he was not just a lonely little boy: he was a trainee magus. Boyhood was just one of the disciplines he had to master on the way.

"Genuine esoteric teachers... will often disconcert would-be students by insisting for a time that they abandon their enthusiastic occult practises, make no attempt to develop their *psi* faculties and confine themselves to pure meditation and attend to the business of everyday living, with as much competence as they can muster. ... Old-time ascetics used to claim that when Divinity could be discerned in the dirt beneath ones fingernails, the devotee would be ready to encounter *IT* in the elaborate Temples of Earth."

In due course Bill at least managed to acquire a semi-Canadian accent, and found that the attitude of the other lads altered somewhat for the better, even though they never forgot that he was an alien. He was somewhat perturbed, however, by the fact that all these pre-teenagers wanted to talk about was baseball or sex – both of which rather baffled him at the time. Not surprisingly, he had never cared for team games, and sex was still a marvellous mystery which he hoped to uncover later on. "As a straightforward biological urge to be satisfied with a few bodily movements alone, the subject had no appeal for me. There had to be intense emotional outpouring and great personal love involved as individual beings before I could believe in sex as a worthwhile practice."

Perhaps his mother was right: perhaps he *was* a bit of a prig. Or maybe, at heart, he was a romantic. Whatever, he refused to join the pissing competitions, or take part when they played with their penises *en masse*. There was no criticism involved, and certainly no homophobia. Indeed, as far as he was aware none of them showed any signs of homosexuality, and all seemed normally heterosexual. But he did come to wonder if the American passion for baseball might be interpreted as a public sex-substitute with its penis-like bat, hurled balls, and a frantic scrabble around a vagina-shaped pitch.

Looking back on his years in Canada, Bill had many detailed memories that are more anthropological than personal. It was as if he was a visitor there whose sole duty was to absorb as much as he could without getting involved with the natives, or disturbing their own evolution. And absorb he did:

"Their houses were built from wood some seven feet from the ground around a central chimney and boiler in what they called the basement, which was actual earth level. A main front porch was reached by steps to a widish veranda extending for the whole front of the house and closed in by a fine wire mesh for excluding mosquitos in the Summer. In winter false windows were screwed over the real ones and masses of spruce branches cut from the closeby woods were arranged around the lower part of the house to keep the heavy snow away. The house was heated by the faithful boiler located beneath the floorboards and fuelled from an enormous woodpile at the immediate back of the house which had been cut and stacked by the menfolk of the family during the summer. That boiler had to be kept going for the whole winter which lasted from mid October till mid April in Quebec.

"During the long winter the menfolk were expected to cut slabs of ice from the frozen lake which would then be stored in an ice-house for use during the year. That was a fairly deep pit in which the ice-blocks were kept insulated by sawdust obtained from the Summer woodcutting. The primitive refrigerators of those days known as ice-boxes were a sort of kitchen cabinet: with the large zinc tray on top and the outlet pipes extending down the sides and back, the whole thickly insulated by sawdust packing. The ice went into the tray and when it melted down the sides was emptied by a drain-tap occasionally. Being of course non-electric it cost nothing to keep except the efforts needed to supply the ice."

And then there was the deeply symbolic moment when he encountered a radio for the first time. Symbolic because he would eventually regard Hermes as one of his favourite gods – Hermes the messenger-god with winged heels, carrying information from one realm to another. And also because such devices were important parts of his later career in the Army, when he joined the Royal Signals Regiment.

"One of the male country cousins had built a one-valve set with an early form of loudspeaker which was really a large earphone with an upright horn attached. There was a whole tray full of dry batteries and accumulators to activate the thing. It was of course the wonder of the entire district and endless neighbours came to hear its tinny sounds with incredulous gasps, scarcely believing that these arrived via the impressively long aerial wire suspended between the rooftop and a tallish pine tree. The contraption absolutely fascinated me with its strange magic and I resolved to find out how it worked if I possibly could."

But again there were also events that he looked back upon as giving important and immediate lessons in his own personal development, rather than symbolic auguries of his future path.

A country cousin of his cured him of his self-consciousness for life in a very simple way. She wanted a few ferns for her garden and asked him to get them for her from a nearby woodland. When he objected to this errand on the grounds that he did not want to be seen carrying ferns in his arms by the local people, she said very practically: "Gordon, I think it's time you learned something for your own good. People in this world are so wrapped up in their own affairs that they can't bother to think of much else. They certainly aren't going to take notice of an ordinary little boy carrying a few common ferns which don't mean anything in particular to them anyway. Try it and see for yourself." So he duly went out and dug the ferns and sure enough came back through the main street of the village without anyone paying the slightest attention to him. He concluded: "From that moment to this I have never worried about what others might think of me."

Well that was only partly true – as we shall see. Nevertheless that ostensibly trivial event was actually an extremely important lesson to him, and one that helped give formidable substance to the man he wanted to become.

Meanwhile, his mother had made a dramatic improvement in her health. When she had left Britain she had been almost skeletal. Yet when Bill met up with her again on her discharge from the sanatorium she had become enormously stout – a 'monstrous mama' as he described her. "With her weight however she gained the traditional cheerfulness of a plump person and made many jokes at my expense. My prominent ears and large feet fell easy victims to her humour and she teased me unmercifully about them, inventing little rhymes as she did so… Mother could versify impromptu with considerable speed and ingenuity."

Mother also decided that it was time to go back to Britain, and her husband had found a flat in Southampton where his shipping company was based. The plan was that Bill would follow her on a later vessel when he had finished his school term, travelling over on a liner in which one of his cousins worked as a social hostess.

"I did not look forward very much to rejoining my parents who were both almost strangers to me by this time, yet with no other alternative before me what else could I do?"

He scarcely saw his cousin during the whole voyage, and arrived back in England safely enough wondering if he should recognise his parents when he met them again.

"My mother's comfortably fat form waving from the dockside convinced me that the military looking man with the walrus moustache beside her brandishing a cane cheerfully was indeed my father. I found another temporary home at last."

He had also entered the period in his still very young life when he would have visions, experience hauntings and mediumship, practice his first *real* magic, and come face to face with a friend of his mother's who had also spent a lot of time 'wandering in the wastes' and who was known variously as the Master Therion, the Great Beast, Logos of the Aeon – or simply dear old Aleister Crowley.

CHAPTER 3
The Rising of the Light

"[My teacher] would always stress the difference between psychic abilities which might be quite spectacular yet were a purely temporary phenomenon, and what he called the 'spiritual realities' which took perhaps many lifetimes to acquire but would be a permanent part of one's being. He told me that in the old times when the Mystery Schools of initiation found a very promising pupil who showed signs of precocious talents, they would deliberately refrain from encouraging these further than a certain point, and then send the student out into the world to make his own way amongst ordinary mortals for maybe a prolonged period."

His father had found a flat for them at East Park Terrace in Southampton, and although Bill was united with both his parents at last, it was a very awkward time for him. His parents had long since ceased sleeping together and he had to share the bedroom with his father, whom he didn't know at all.

The old man worked very hard to strike up a relationship with his odd son and tried to coach him at maths, in order get him a scholarship at the local Catholic school. His own schooldays had been spent at King's School, Canterbury, mainly run for the sons of clergy, and although Mrs Gray had all but severed her connections with the Church, it was felt by all that Catholic schools gave the best available standards of education. John Gray told Bill how, at his old school, the boys were beaten for failing to construe their Latin exercises correctly, and he himself was slightly deaf in one ear for life as a result of a blow delivered by an irascible master. He added with some secret glee how his schoolmates loved to approach one very deaf master muttering "Tickle your arse with a feather Sir?" and then when he queried what they had said would roar: "PARTICULARLY NASTY WEATHER SIR". Whereupon he usually agreed with them and went on his way. Bill found that amusing, at least; however his maths still failed to improve.

His father really did try to forge a bond with this complete stranger who was his son, but the best that Bill could admit in later years was that they formed 'an odd mutual relationship'.

Yet it was not just the actual room-sharing which irked him at that time, unhealthy though that was. It was the fact that the room seemed to be haunted.

"For some reason I did not understand, I found myself taking a great dislike to one corner of the room which had nothing particular in it except some ordinary coat-hooks on the wall. It felt evil and frightening, yet I knew instinctively that whatever it was could not leave that location to harm me, and so long as I stayed peacefully in bed at the opposite end of the room I was perfectly safe. Eventually this antipathy grew so strong I questioned my mother about it and she in turn tackled the landlady, with whom she had formed an alliance. The story that emerged was that the previous tenants had been a married couple, the husband of which would occasionally return very much the worse for drink. One night he came home in such a condition, and somehow his wife managed to infuriate him so much he attacked her and very nearly strangled her to death in that particular corner of the room. Naturally the woman was terrified and made as much noise as she could, which attracted the attention of other tenants who kicked the door in and separated the pair just in time.

"Had the woman died, I could easily have been persuaded it was her ghost haunting the place. She did not die however, and her husband was so horrified at what he had nearly done that he swore off drink permanently and I was told they were both living happily together not very far away. This convinced me that in some way intense human emotions, such as in this case anger and fear, release energies which influence the vicinity for a long time afterwards and can be sensed by perceptive people. Many of our so-called ghosts are, in fact, nothing but replays of past events with no more actual entity to them than a video tape or any type of recording. That does not mean that they may not be frightening to anyone unaware of their nature. Once I realised this I was never bothered again by that bedroom."

This is the sort of experience that marks out the true magician: the ability to perceive, interpret and – if necessary – communicate with entities and energies beyond the material world. Most of the modern self-styled magi around today simply cannot do that sort of thing. Make no mistake: they are making it up as they go along, deriving everything from the writings of those *real* magicians who have gone before them, and are connected to nothing more than the mellifluous sound of their own voice – which usually emerges from no higher place than the arse.

And make no mistake again: to young Bill Gray, and a few others like him, such abilities were as natural as breathing.

By this time he had made his first communion, become an acolyte, and still had many thoughts of the priesthood, although he was beginning to feel the pull of a spiritual force a lot older and deeper .

"What I felt strongest of all was an overpowering urge to KNOW the realities of spiritual matters. To experience them for myself and realise them just as certainly as I realised my own body or any materialised matter in existence."

The priests he met only gave evasive or standard replies based on scriptural texts which he was supposed to accept without question. His mother used to tell him that whenever some vital point such as "Is there an existence apart from death?" or "Is there really a God?" came up, she would specify clearly that she did not want quotes from scriptures or any other assumed authority whatever. What she was asking for was that particular individual's actual experience with the subject in question. She was not prepared to listen to their beliefs or opinions, but only to their involvement with whatever it might be. That sounded reasonable enough to Bill too, and after that he frequently applied the principle with useful results.

Throughout this time he had but one main aim in mind, and that was to compose – eventually – an ideal magical ritual which would comprise every essential item of the Tradition and also justify his own continued existence. "All my efforts were unsatisfactory which is not surprising due to my lack of experience at that period, but at least the clumsy start I made then planted a seed which germinated and bore fruit many years later. We often make the mistake in magical work of supposing nothing whatever has happened as a result of expended effort, whereas we have actually started something which will not mature for a long time in calendar terms. Not even an idiot would expect instant oak trees or babies, so why should anyone expect their equivalents in different dimensions of existence?"

Like so many before and since, he found some of what he needed at the Public Library. In those days members were issued with two tickets, a fiction and a non-fiction one. A fiction ticket could be used for a non-fiction book, but not the other way round. This was to encourage erudition among the literate labouring classes, but he found it a godsend, since he could bring back two serious books at once. There was not a very large section dealing with occult subjects, since all books were selected by what was called a 'Reading Committee' who were virtually censors who decided what was fit to be read and what was not. They also had to work within the financial limits of public and local funding. Therefore there would be masses and masses of books dealing with the 'useful' arts such as gardening, cooking, housecraft, mechanics, child-rearing etc., while relatively few on the 'liberal' ones of philosophy, religion, folklore and the like.

There were however a fair number of books on psychology and what were classed as 'metaphysical' subjects. He read those several times and discussed them with his mother, whose views tended to be very practical and common sense. She would never accept anything purely because somebody notable had said so, but only if she herself considered it to be reasonable or advisable in the light of her own life-experience. For example she firmly believed in reincarnation because of an early experience which stayed with her all her life: Somehow she knew that she was an old sick woman dying in Paris. Suddenly a nurse appeared and she tried to say something like 'Who sent you? I can't afford a nurse. I can't pay you anything, I'm sorry.' But all she could produce was a sort of gurgle and she thought 'Oh my God, I must have had a stroke, I can't even speak now'. Then she noticed how happy the nurse looked as she bounced a baby up and down. Christine was horrified and tried to say 'What are you doing with that child? A sickroom is no place for a baby, so take it away at once'. Then she realised that the nurse was speaking a foreign language and appeared to be lifting her up. Again she tried to protest that she was much too heavy for such a slight woman to lift on her own, but only more gurgles came and she was aware of her movements coinciding with those of the mysterious baby. All of a sudden the terrible realisation came to her that she was looking in a mirror, and that the baby was *herself* in a new body. Her nursemaid was indeed bouncing her up and down before a bedroom glass. "She said that a brilliant light seemed to hit her on the top of her head, then there was a sort of upward rush and she remembered nothing else until later. Suspecting whom she had probably been at that period, it seems like a remarkably rapid rebirth."

That rapid rebirth took place on December 25th 1886. In fact she suspected that she had been Noémi Cadiot, the estranged ex-wife of the influential French magus Eliphas Levi, who had married him when she was only 16. Moreover, after checking various dates, Bill himself came to believe that Levi made an equally rapid reincarnation as his teacher, the enigmatic ENH, whom we will meet shortly.

Eliphas Levi was the pen-name of the French occultist Alphonse Louis Constant (1810-1875) who was the son of a Paris shoemaker. He took the name from the Hebrew equivalents of his first and middle names. He entered the theological college of Saint-Sulpice and was ordained Deacon in 1835. Here he became deeply disillusioned with what he experienced, and although he was scheduled to be ordained Priest in 1836, he had by this time met and fallen in love with an un-named young girl. Although nothing ever came of the relationship, he realised that he could not live without human affection and – to his eternal credit – abandoned his vows before his ordination. After hearing of his apostasy, his mother committed suicide. Following this, Constant, who by all accounts was a man of great personal charm, spent a period associating with revolutionary socialists, including Flora Tristan, grandmother of Paul Gauguin and M. Ganneau, the 'Mapah.' In 1846, he married the 16-year-old Marie-Noémi Cadiot, who left him seven years later.

After their separation he moved for a short time to England, where he met with Sir Edward Bulwer Lytton, and where he performed his famous evocation of Apollonius of Tyana, bringing that ancient spirit to tangible and visible appearance. On his return to Paris he took on a number of pupils, and became increasingly famous and influential through his unique writings.

He had been deeply influenced by the works of Francis Barret, whose work *The Magus* (1800) was something a watershed in the genre. His own books include: *The Dogma and Ritual of High Magic* (1861), *A History of Magic, Transcendental Magic,* and others, most of which are still available today in reprints. He was possibly the first occultist to associate the 22 trump cards of the Tarot with the 22 Hebrew letters – which is an area of Magic that Bill came to specialise in.

Like many real star-crossed magicians plus your average everyday megalomaniacs, he clearly had a sense of his own destiny. When he was initiated into the masonic Grand Orient of France, in 1861, he told the assembled and astonished brethren of the *Rose of Perfect Silence* lodge: "I come to bring to you your lost traditions, the exact knowledge of your signs and symbols, and consequently to show you the goal for which your association was constituted." He didn't last long in that lot. It was at this period that he was thrown in jail three times for his writings, the authorities citing his attempt to create a political uprising. In jail he met several socialist radicals, and members of occult organisations. Occultism and socialism was a heady mix then, and he gained a strong and loyal following as he travelled Europe, continuing to write and teach until his death in 1875. It has been argued that Levi's writings revived magic in the 19th century. It is certainly true that most of Levi's magical texts were followed by The Hermetic Order of the Golden Dawn, founded in 1888.

So if Christine Gray did still have echoes of Noémi Cadiot within her psyche, then it was hardly surprising that she should have had such an intuitive knowledge of Magic in her own right.

But in *this* life, at that time, Bill's father did something else which really troubled his mother greatly. He gave up his reasonably well paid seagoing job and took a much lower paid position with the shore staff. He did this because he was weary of endless travel and wanted some kind of family life at home. His wife had been hoping that he would stay at least another couple of years at sea in order to save enough money for another venture – or so she said – but he was adamant, and so the family income was sharply reduced once again.

Bill's mother was a capable typist but there was no real money to be made doing that, so after a great deal of thought she decided to use her very genuine psychic abilities and become a professional fortune teller. She had frequently done this on an amateur basis with a great deal of success, so now it was only a question of putting it on a different footing.

In those days the Witchcraft Act had not been repealed and altered to the Fraudulent Mediums Act, so clairvoyants could technically be prosecuted under the 'who shall pretend to tell fortunes' clause. In point of fact however, it was almost never invoked and the Grays only knew of a solitary case in which a consultant astrologer who was a friend of Christine's was proceeded against by the police, who were acting on a complaint by an unbalanced ex-client. It was only in a magistrate's court and the friend insisted on conducting his own defence, which was mainly in the form of refuting the charge by producing witnesses and signed affidavits to prove how much he had helped clients by his expert advice and counsel. He called so many to testify that, far from *pretending* to supply astrological advice, he showed that had in fact done so with the best possible effects. The magistrate dismissed the case out of hand and the defendant was swamped with work for many months to come. He had given himself the finest free advertisement possible. However, as a safeguard, Christine Gray displayed a prominent notice saying 'FOR AMUSEMENT ONLY' since there was nothing to prevent anyone telling fortunes as entertainment and charging a legitimate fee for doing so. Most professional clairvoyants did the same thing at that period.

Although she made a show of reading palms and telling the cards, her real skill lay with interpreting the inner impressions she received from the clients themselves. Even later when she became a qualified astrologer herself, she would read the charts far more by instinctive clairvoyance than by careful calculations. Observing all this, her son saw how amazingly accurate she could be, yet she confessed that she never quite knew how she arrived at her conclusions. Nevertheless, however remarkable she might have been on behalf of others, she could never predict her own future successfully. Or maybe she had already seen it and simply refused to allow it to reach her objective mind.

Sometimes, being in the very presence of psychic individuals can trigger off things in the people around them, like tuning forks resonating to a sound. The fact that his mother was giving free rein to her innate psychic talents must have unlocked Bill's own powers, for it was at that time he had a vision which stayed with him all his life. Sixty years later, when he reminisced about this to one of the present authors, his eyes still went soft with delight, and a portion of him seemed still to exist in his other dimension beyond time and space.

"I was ill at the time with measles, but the clarity and intensity of my experience was quite beyond all doubt. I knew that I was not in this world at all, but in a state of being very far removed from normal earth-life. It was all very wonderful and enjoyable not because of any scenery or surroundings, but entirely because of the ambience created by the consciousness of those who existed there. I can only describe this as a palpable, mutual, and completely experiential type of sheer Love. There is really no other word for it. Everything and everyone was part and parcel of each other and we all realised this together. There was no such thing as a stranger, everyone was on equal relationship with each other, and although we were all separate individual selves we knew quite well that we were only bits of a whole being. The feeling of completeness was indescribable. An absolute certainty of being one's Real Self in the truest sense of the word. I never wanted to quit such company.

"There were objective surroundings in fact, but everything appeared to be made only by the energy of thinking something into existence and it was manufactured out of pure light. 'Houses' seemed to be mostly dome-shaped and the energy stored somehow at their summits. They were not 'furnished' as we understand that word, but their interiors simply assumed the colours and textures intended by the residents. Complete comfort and ease was always assured, and we felt completely supported by each others thoughts alone. I knew without being told that there were other types of construction to be found if necessary. For example a library of unimaginable dimensions containing every book ever written by human authors, and a theatre of comparable size capable of producing every possible play or simulative situation. I had also no doubt there must be a Temple wherein types of worship unknown on earth would be performed with perfect grace and effectiveness. The wonder of it all astounded me…"

Then came the most terrible sense of disappointment and dismay, brought on by the realisation that he had to return to his own world because he was not yet fit to stay on there. He had only been a privileged visitor, and had to return to the material world and earn his entitlement to what he immediately saw as his rightful home. He knew that ahead of him lay the task of "structuring myself so as to accord with its spiritual condition".

What Bill experienced has since been recorded many times among those people who have had what are now termed Near-Death Experiences: the dreadful sadness of discovering that they will have to return to their bodies and continue living their ordinary lives on earth. But what helped make it all worse when he did return to his body was the awful feeling of physical weight, and the amount of effort required to make the simplest movement.

"Definitely however the worst feeling was that of separation, even if only temporary, from the marvellous mass of which one should be a full member."

It is hard to describe real visions: they occur at such levels of supra-consciousness that we have to struggle to describe them via simile and metaphor. Furthermore it is unwise to try and judge visions. Of course we can spend many hours analysing them in Freudian, Jungian or even (in this case) Swedenborgian terms, but that is a largely sterile exercise. Anyone, with practice, can stimulate mere pictures in the head, but the real mystic or magician learns to distinguish between what is effectively a kind of junk mail littering the mind's hallway, and genuine entry into other realms. What Bill *saw* were not mere pictures in the head, but experiences in other dimensions which involved all the senses, with full and indeed enhanced consciousness.

Bill had this powerful inner experience when he was only 10 years old. Really, he was *very* different to most of us.

"I did not have many visions of this kind but when they came they were deep enough to be indelible. I remember another in which I was attending some kind of service in the Great Temple which is reached at the top of an exceptionally long stairway which has to be climbed step by step. There appeared to be so many acolytes crowding around the sanctuary that I could not see what was going on. As I was trying to obtain a better view, they all leaped momentarily into the air and the whole congregation broke into a hearty laugh. I was absolutely horrified. Laughter in a Church was unimaginable to me, and I cringed before such blasphemous behaviour. My immediate neighbour, an older man with a shortish brown beard in very plain clothing put a friendly arm around my shoulders and said in the friendliest manner with a smile: 'Why, don't you know that laughter is one of the highest forms of worship?' Though I was not inclined to believe this at the time, life itself has long since proved the surprising truth of that simple affirmation."

When writing to Alan Richardson about this in 1989, he added:

"Oh yes, I've just remembered one remark that was made to me there which impressed me... A man was speaking, and he said (these are the exact words) 'I can't tell you how wonderful it is not to have to be one person any longer. Why do you know, *within reason*, I can be almost anybody I like.' The *within reason* was heavily accented. Don't ask me what was meant by that, I've no idea."

To him, this experience did not take place in some sugary heavenworld whose structure was dependent on Christian myth and imagery. It was something that happened on another planet entirely. To him, Earth was nothing but a little dot in a solar system in a galaxy with a hundred million solar systems, in a universe with a hundred million galaxies – and this is before we even begin to consider the infinity of other dimensions. He believed, for example, that the Atlantean visions that came through so strongly to Dion Fortune and her initiates probably related to something that happened on a different world, and when speculating on the likely catastrophes facing the Earth he once said, as if with an insider's knowledge: "Well, just look what happened on Mars..."

For the next few years life consisted of a routine comprising school and Church, and reading whatever esoteric matter he could obtain, plus plain growing up toward adulthood. Though he still had the Catholic priesthood in mind, his inclinations had definitely become a lot fainter, and his mother showed a marked relief at that. When he suggested to her that he practice Magic instead, she gave it as her opinion that he was not only far too young, but should actually be studying something of a more practical nature to enable him to earn a living. In fact she had no objection to the practice of Magic *per se* (she knew Crowley after all) but she felt that there would plenty of time for that when he had made some kind of way in the world, in some rewarding profession. The time was coming when he would have to leave school, and if he could not get into university because of his mathematical failings, then he had to sort something else out soon.

Bill still wanted to practice Magic.

His mother then pointed out the obvious difficulties. The practice of Magic called for an ambience and equipment that he just did not have. Where would he have his temple? What would he use for robes? Incense? How would he organise his rituals? What about his father?!

Yet for every point she raised he offered a solution.

He proposed to construct his temporary Temple in the kitchen from spare curtain materials and bedspreads hung like a tent from lines secured with large drawing pins. Its entrance would naturally be the door. He made his robe himself from cotton. The incense was made of gums and herbs gathered from the local common. For the rite itself he relied on the very small amount of information he had gleaned from books plus his 'instinctual imagination'. As to his father... well he would wait until the old man had gone visiting friends and would work the rite then.

What would be the purpose of the rite? Well he would ask for opportunities or actual gifts of money for his mother, who greatly needed either at the time.

As best as he could recall many years later, the only two books he had as guides were *The Romance of Sorcery* and *Sorcery and Magic*. Neither gave any detailed techniques or procedures but they did provide a general ideology. In particular they described the use of waxen images for focusing the invisible forces, and Bill created these with Plasticine. Since they also emphasised the energy of the four traditional Elements he included these by using a small flowerpot full of earth, a cup of water, an empty cup for air, and a very smelly little paraffin oil lamp for fire. On top of this, for some time he had been concocting a species of incense from pine gum, oak bark and other aromatics including lavender and potpourri taken from his mother's store. He even made a sort of thurible from cut-down coffee tins to burn the incense in with charcoal from firewood. Finally, he made five crude little figures from the Plasticine and set them on a small tray. The central one represented his mother, and the four others with outstretched arms were supposed to be people bringing gifts or favours.

Eventually the great day arrived, and when he had draped the kitchen into a semblance of an Arabian tent and arranged his furnishings as he thought fit, he summoned his mother to examine his efforts.

"She did not seem vastly impressed and remarked that I could scarcely expect a very select class of spirit to work in such ramshackle surroundings. To this I replied airily that I would invoke only a most superior order of Angels who would be far too noble to notice their earthly environments. She told me a long time later that she had actually been amused and impressed at the appositeness of my answer, but she did nothing then except to wish me success with my undertaking and left me alone to get on with it.

"I cannot at this distance of time remember the exact details of the ritual that followed. I can remember praying that all the angelic powers proper to the four Elements should concentrate on prospering my mother's purpose and bring her good fortune from every quarter of the earth. I can remember also scattering these symbolic elements over their figures on the altar, and waving my makeshift thurible around until its smoke made me cough uncontrollably for a while. I can remember pointing at them with a wand cut from a hazel tree in the garden and willing as intensely as I could that what I asked for would come true. I have a vague idea that I called on the few angelic names I knew and politely requested them to help my worthy cause. Although nothing appeared or manifested, I did become aware of a strange presence in the place as if I were being watched by an invisible observer. Nothing more than that, and it faded away before the end of my ceremony. Exactly what I might have contacted I have no idea now, but I know *something* spiritual was stirred by my amateur attempts at magic."

This was not, perhaps, great magic but it was certainly *real* magic. And this from a young boy who even then knew that the outward trappings of ritual magic are simply a means of linking with inner realities. As he later defined it: 'Real esotericism is not just dressing up in handsome robes and manipulating symbols for the sake of so doing. It is knowing how to apply the meaning of such symbols to Life itself for the purpose of altering or directing its energy in accordance with intention.'

His analysis of what happened that afternoon was quite straight-forward, and typically Gravian in terminology:

"What I had been doing without being aware of it then was actually what might be termed *prayerplay*. Active direction of inner intention with the assistance of external symbology. In fact this is, and always has been, practical magic. It most probably derives from the extremely primitive practice of making hunting movements while beseeching superior and unseen powers to assist such efforts in earnest. Of course it is the actual consciousness involved which causes the desired effect providing it connects properly with such levels which are normally beyond range of ordinary human awareness. The employment of external symbology in special patterns generally extends this range sufficiently to permit some degree of that vital contact. This is precisely what I had done by sheer instinct or ancestral memory which are really identical."

Did the magic work? Even Bill was not sure. Although his mother's immediate financial position did indeed improve somewhat from that point, he came down with a serious case of mumps within a fortnight, and no other child at his school was known to have had it. If a carrier was responsible then other children would definitely have been infected. Bill became unusually ill with the mumps and was absent from school for several weeks. To him, it seemed the price he had to pay for his performance, and he resolved to be more cautious on the next occasion.

Occasionally he attended lectures at the local Theosophical Society, where he was amused to see the feud which existed then between Theosophy and Spiritualism. It was the tendency among almost all of the occult movements at that time to descry Spiritualism as fraught with error and illusion, and Theosophy with its psuedo-science tended to take a particularly superior attitude in this respect. This was despite the fact that Theosophy itself had evolved from the spiritualist experiences of their founder Madame Blavatsky – a formidable medium if ever there was one. This was probably a jealous reaction against a movement which, only a couple of decades earlier, had swept the Western world and dented the rationalism of the Victorian Age. Even today, in the fluid Western Esoteric Tradition which Bill Gray helped shape, there is still a tendency to think of Spiritualism as something that is intellectually inferior and downright misguided – no pun intended. Bill himself was not always sympathetic toward Spiritualist mediums. As he expressed it:

"I did not doubt for one moment that there were indeed higher orders of life than human in existence, and that it could be possible to communicate with these once a satisfactory method of doing so had been worked out. I just saw no convincing evidence whatever that Spiritualists had done this with any real degree of success. If they were indeed in touch with defunct fellow humans, then these certainly did not seem to represent a very intelligent or even interesting class of consciousness... I was not interested in contacting so-called 'spirits' which could do nothing except preach stupid little sermons full of platitudes and impractical advice. I wanted only to encounter those who were able to impart evidence of their existence by the value of their communications..."

At risk of enraging the troublesome ghost of William Gray... this is pure shite. He was probably miffed that he never got any messages; he was probably hurt that no spirit on the Other side paid him any heed. Unfortunately it is spiritual snobbery of a kind that is endemic among magicians. Anyone can sit alone in a room invoking gods and come away feeling smug and in touch with the higher forces of the universe. But how many magicians can stand up before complete strangers several times a week, put their talents on the line and bring through messages of what might be termed 'adequate accuracy' for no reward other than the emotional and spiritual uplift of the listener? A few could, and did: Ernest Butler, Debbie Rice, Dion Fortune, to name but three. Even Dion Fortune, toward the end of her life, intimated that the real secrets of magic could be found in the heart and essence of Spiritualism. Anyone who has ever had their heart opened by a message via a medium will know that while the information might seem trivial in the extreme to the outsider, it can touch the very deepest part of the individual receiving the message. Theosophy in contrast might, superficially, show a far greater intellectual depth than anything in the Spiritualist philosophy, but many of the teachings transmitted by 'Masters' like Kuthumi and Morya and the rest of the trans-Himalayan supermen are just as open to derision, rarely more than psuedo-scientific, sometimes unbelievably crass or just downright wrong, and played no little part in providing spurious justification for the race-supremacy of Heinrich Himmler and his ilk.

No apologies Bill.

However he was amused by the fact that Theosophists and Spiritualists seldom missed a chance to get in digs at each other, and would sometimes attend each other's meetings for the express purpose of doing so.

"I remember when one very elderly and decrepit looking Theosophist was speaking of the dangers involved with trance mediumship. He quavered: 'After all, my friends, if I had a beautiful and valuable house, I would hesitate a long time before allowing some total stranger to enter it. He might do it a very great deal of damage.' As the speaker paused for effect a broad Yorkshire voice said from the back of the hall: 'Aye, and happen he could put in a few good repairs on thee lad!' Even the lecturer smiled faintly among the spontaneous laughter."

Apart from this, his mother knew some interesting people in her own right. Among her astrological acquaintances was Brother XII who was then well known in occult circles. His real name was Arthur Wilson and he was a maritime captain by training but a Messiah by inclination. He was at that time getting together a group of people whose ambition it was to avoid the coming war which he forecast for some four years ahead of its actual date. The idea was to buy an island off the west coast of Canada and found a community which would survive the slaughter and its aftermath. Being wealthy people they were able to do this, and he set himself up as leader. It was not long before he ditched his wife in Britain for the acting Secretary of the group and issued a statement that the two of them were going away to make a baby together which would grow up to be the Saviour of the World. Since both of them were rather past the breeding age it would have been a miraculous child indeed. In the end however, he converted the community funds into bearer bonds and sailed away in company with his mistress, an Alsatian dog, and a crew member in the expensive yacht ostensibly owned by himself. Since this contained the only working radio, it was some time before the mainland was contacted. Much later, after they had virtually run out of food, they were found under false names somewhere in the South Seas where they were on the point of killing and eating the dog. After that they disappeared entirely, yet his wife and Bill's mother remained good friends for many years.

Another notable was Victor Neuburg, which Bill always wrote as 'Newberg' because he simply heard the name and spelled it phonetically. If Bill had ever been familiar with any of the current histories of modern Magic he would have known this, but he actually lived the books rather than read them.

"I liked Victor Newberg," he wrote. "He was one of the gentlest men I ever met. My mother was great friends with his female companion whom she always called Saga, meaning a wise woman with special esoteric experience. The two of them would usually visit together, and mother told me how Saga had managed to remove Victor from Crowley's influence. … Seemingly Crowley could hypnotise Victor with ridiculous ease and especially liked to do so before company in order to impress them with his evident 'powers'. He would make Newberg behave like a dog, barking and grovelling at his master's feet. Then he would order poor Victor to empty his pockets of money and hand it over immediately. Since his father was usually generous there might be as much as five pounds on his person. Crowley would throw back about half a crown contemptuously saying: 'Get yourself some fish and chips. We're going to the Savoy with the rest.' And forthwith do so. In those days it was perfectly possible, and there could even be change left over."

When Bill met Aleister Crowley through his mother, the old wizard was already notorious, feted and abhorred in equal measure, but not quite the icon that he became in the decades after his death in 1947. Even so, he was already synonymous with the very word 'magic', though he spelled it with the 'k' which hinted at the dark and essentially Tantric secrets behind his methods. Victor Neuberg was by all accounts a delightful man whose personality and poetry was admired by no less than the young Dylan Thomas, but the sad fact is that, historically, he was never more than one of Crowley's many shadows.

If anyone in the 21st Century were to do an analytical survey of contemporary magical/mystical/occult/spiritual movements, they would have to conclude that their essential philosophies, style and techniques were derived from a mere handful of people who inter-reacted with each other over a century before. It's the sort of game you can play in pubs or (more likely) wholefood restaurants. *Where did modern Wicca come from? What are the real origins of the Celtic Revival? Who influenced the present attitudes toward sex and spirituality? Name five people who might be responsible.* Three names which would probably come up on most lists are Aleister Crowley, Gerald Gardner, and Dion Fortune.

Between them they opened the doors of the Age. And Bill Gray met all three.

"Once or twice Crowley himself appeared, but his visits were brief and I only met him for moments. With his reputation I believe my mother was afraid of what might happen to little boys' bottoms, though I am sure she need not have worried. Crowley was not a natural homosexual and only practiced it mostly with Victor Newberg because he believed in its magical possibilities, and Victor was so easy to victimise. All I remember Crowley saying to me was something like: 'So this is your Great Magician is it? He doesn't look very dangerous to me. Wouldn't you like to be as wicked as I am?' Not quite knowing what to make of this I muttered something about my uncertainty and mother turned it to a joke by saying 'Oh he can be wicked enough when he wants to be.' Whereon Crowley stared at me very solemnly and almost intoned his famous phrase: DO WHAT THOU WILT SHALL BE THE WHOLE OF THE LAW, making this his exit line. I never met him again, nor did I ever discover what he and mother said to each other. Later I saw the book he gave her, a signed copy of 777. All she would say was that he was not a very nice man, and some time afterwards she burned the book because she felt it was a bad influence coming directly from him. But by that time I had copied it out for myself."*

* I believe that Christine had been a member of the Ragged Rag-Time Girls, the touring company that Crowley had been involved with in travelling through Russia. [AR]

At that time also Bill, who himself played an unwitting but significant part in the creation of the modern Witchcraft movement he often mocked, also saw Gerald Gardner.

"One of the people I met was a Rosicrucian from the Pythagorean Crotona Fellowship which had some kind of a community near Portsmouth. He was an interesting man who told me a number of points concerning their fraternity. Their leader, who termed himself an Ipsissimus, had written a play which they intended to produce, and he lent me the script. It purported to be a morality play between the forces of good and evil, and the central character was a pseudo-monk called Liveda, which of course is 'A Devil' spelt backwards. Young as I was, I could see what an appallingly bad play it made. Full of quotes, false sentiment, and awkwardly constructed sentences, it would bore and annoy most audiences rather than edify them. Nevertheless The Rosicrucian Players as they called themselves did actually present the play to a very small audience at Portsmouth... I gather the part of 'Liveda' was played by Gerald Gardner of later witchcraft fame, and he did the best he could with a very poor part. As one might expect, the Ipsissimus and his 'Grand Secretary' were conducting a power-struggle between themselves, and as a demonstration of her feelings she once attended a local Fancy Dress ball clad in her full robes and regalia of office. This of course should have earned her immediate expulsion from any authentic esoteric Order, but I believe she continued in office with no other reprimand than a severe rebuke."

And then there was 'Dion Fortune' (pen-name of Violet Firth), who was Womanhood's answer to Aleister Crowley and the Shakti of the Age. Whatever Crowley did for magic from the masculine point of view, with as much publicity as he could muster, DF as they called her, did very quietly and secretly from the distaff side. She was born in 1890 and died in 1946. She was an initiate in the Hermetic Order of the Golden Dawn and saw it in its zenith, then later formed her own Fraternity of the Inner Light, where they worked the magic of the West: of Atlantis, Ys and Egypt; of the Celts and Scandinavians; of King Arthur and the Holy Grail, and explored all of those obscure by-ways that might now be termed 'Native British'. Although there was a Christian Mystic section for the less able, she specialised in the magic of the Great Goddess figures. Her main temple was at 3 Queensborough Terrace in London, but she also had a small centre right at the foot of Glastonbury Tor. Her books such as *The Mystical Qabalah, Applied Magic*, and the very odd *Psychic Self-defence* have been much copied but never surpassed. Her novels *The Sea Priestess* and *Moon Magic* are utterly beautiful in their prose and almost hypnotic in their magical effect upon the reader. Most witches, crafting their art in the early days after the War, stole ideas and attitudes from her writing; every magician owes her a debt for the sheer clarity of exposition on obscure Hermetic topics they might never have grasped otherwise. Every woman who has ever challenged the patriarchy of modern times should give her no small degree of gratitude for paving the way.

How could young Bill Gray not have been attracted by such a woman?

"Since my paternal Uncle Will was then living in London at Kew while working from an office in Watling Street, I found it convenient to visit him occasionally for a few days while I explored the esoteric possibilities of the metropolis. I soon became very familiar with the Underground which was then both cheap and frequent in all directions. On one such excursion I decided to make a call on Dion Fortune whose London address I had obtained from the *Occult Review*. Getting there was an easy matter, but meeting the lady in question was quite another affair altogether. The female dragon on the doorstep was enough to discourage anyone, but after some argument I was admitted and told rather rudely to wait the presence in a somewhat chilly sort of library. Mysterious gongs or bells occasionally sounded in other parts of the house, and once someone opened the door, peered round it at me and went away again without a word. I thought I detected a faint smell of incense as the door closed. There were no clocks in the room and I did not then possess a watch, but it seemed to me a long time was passing.

"Eventually the door opened briskly, and Dion Fortune entered accompanied by a different type of dragon who simply sat, in a distant corner of the room staring at me silently. 'Well young man,' said DF, 'they tell me you are a most persistent person who refuses to go away when requested. I don't have much time today, so tell me as quickly and clearly as you can what you are looking for.' She sat in the chair immediately facing me and waited for my reply which I had rehearsed to myself in advance. I explained that I was dedicated to occultism, greatly desired to learn everything there was to know about it, had heard she was running an organisation which dealt with it, and how could she help me. She immediately asked the single question I had feared. 'How old are you?' Whereupon I had to confess I was just fourteen and expected to leave school very shortly. She then told me briefly that her Society did not accept members under the age of twenty one, and she certainly could do nothing whatever without my parents' written consent, nor would she indeed ever think of accepting an under-age candidate. In any case there was a longish study period required before anyone was considered for membership. Those were the rules and she had not made them to be broken by herself or anyone else on any account. She was sorry and wished me well, but that was that and when I was older and more experienced I could always apply again. She would await that date with interest and good afternoon to me. So saying she quitted the room quickly, and the hitherto silent woman rose and beckoned to me with the single word 'Come', then led me to the outer door which she closed after me without another sound. Although everything had been absolutely correct, I felt utterly rejected."

Remember that this was a fourteen-year-old boy who had thrust into her office and demanded to work Magic with her. Other fourteen-year-old English boys of that or any other time would be interested in football, aeroplanes, derring-do and girls, in roughly that order, but William G. Gray wanted nothing less than access to the hidden secrets of the Otherworld. It was not that she rejected him, but more a case that she earmarked him for a lot of work on her behalf in later years. As we will see, he would meet her again both on the inner planes after her death, and on the material plane after she was reborn.

So he had still failed to find the sort of group which could help him evolve in his chosen direction. In fact, he never managed to find one, and mused in later life that because of the internal politics in any occult group, many sincere esotericists refuse to join fallible earthly organisations, and consider themselves companions of an 'Overorder' which exists beyond and behind the confines of this world entirely. Rightly, he always poked fun at high-sounding esoteric titles and claims. Referring to the personal jealousies, enmities and 'oppositional opinions' which mar any group, he lamented: "It never seems to strike any of them that *all* views may be correct according to the angle from which a central Truth is seen."

Sound advice, surely, but advice which Bill himself in his prime never heeded. He fell out with almost everyone.

Bill became an inveterate letter writer as a teenager, and this continued throughout his life. His letters were always written as he spoke, and he showed a style and wit which were often lacking from his published books, the formidable personality coming through writ large, so to speak. Intrigued by something he had read, he was also prompted to contact a character who used the name 'El Eros'.

"He was Randall-Stevens, a First World War fighter pilot who had dedicated his life to the futile task of trying to prevent another conflict.

His books consisted mainly of automatic pencil sketches he believed were transmitted by his ancient Egyptian spirit guide accompanied by scripts from the same source. They were actually somewhat sententious and dealt with the myth of Atlantis and the mysterious continent of Mu, but they were also impressive and to some degree plausible. At any rate there was no doubting the man's sincerity. Although we never met in person we corresponded for quite a while and he sent me his books to study. He believed that the evils of our earth were fomented by a spirit he called Satanaku, and he wrote of the endless struggle between the forces of Light and Darkness. He was mostly mythologising his own experiences of the War into spiritual terms. Since he departed for the Channel Islands to start his group in Guernsey, I lost touch with him and ceased communicating."

At that time there was a hoary but essentially true saying in occultism that when the pupil is ready the Master will appear. Remember that the term 'Master' didn't have the rather unsavoury connotations then that it might have today. It meant an enlightened being, an Adept, or true Initiate of the highest kind. Everyone worth their salt in those days wanted to find a Master. And it was through his mother that he eventually found his own.

Christine Gray had been taking in the *Occult Review* regularly, which was an excellent monthly periodical published by Riders that kept readers in touch with current occult affairs. Its contributors were mainly scholarly and reliable writers dealing with their specialist subjects as clearly and concisely as possible. It carried an extensive correspondence section with letters from people well known in occultism at the time such as Dion Fortune, W. L. Wilmshurst, Walter Gorn Old, Oliver Lodge, and occasionally Aleister Crowley. One particular letter caught Bill's eye however, for this dealt with Rosicrucianism from a viewpoint he simply could not agree with, and he felt impelled to sit down and write a refutation. His strong inner feeling, which he duly sent off to the magazine, was that the *real* Rosicrucians were a purely spiritual Fraternity operating on a higher level of life than the physical world, and any organisation on earth claiming such a title could only be ambitious imitators – however well intentioned. To his delight it got published.

In due course he received a single reply sent via the magazine. It bore a London address and was signed by a man whom, decades later, he would only describe as ENH. This was the man whom Bill would regard as his Teacher. As he remarked himself: "That letter began my longish relationship with the initiate who influenced my whole esoteric life to an untold degree and inspired me into courses of conduct I would not otherwise have taken. Most exponents of the occult in their writings usually acknowledge their debt to some 'Master' or senior soul who guided and taught them at least the elements of esoteric lore and procedures. This is where I have to make obeisance to the memory of my mentor and spiritual father in what are still called in some circles the Holy Mysteries."

ENH were the initials of Emile Napoleon Hauenstein. Born in Vienna in the Spring of 1877, he had lived most of his life in Britain and had at one time been associated with 'Papus', the noted French occultist Gerard Encausse who had founded the Qabalistic Order of the Rosy Cross, and who also wrote dense classics on the Tarot and allied topics. Additionally ENH had been at one time a Martinist, 'or Christian type of Masonical mystic' and was also a member of that American based 'Rosicrucian' Order known as AMORC – the *Ancient Mystical Order of the Rosae Crucis*. Years later when ENH had become profoundly disillusioned with the fundamental commercialism of AMORC, Bill was rather smugly aware that as a boy he had seen through the money-spinning racket right from the start, and sensed that it was "really nothing more than a sales organisation acting for the profit of its promoters" whereas his wise old teacher was completely taken in. To add insult to disillusionment he had supplied AMORC with a lot of material from his previous association with Papus which they then commercialised without any credit to him whatsoever.

Although ENH was still officially married to an Englishwoman, she had lived in Colney Hatch, a home for the incurably insane, for many years. For a while he had worked as a top chef in a high class London hotel (Bill thought it was the Dorchester) but later he rented a shop with living quarters quite close to Piccadilly, which sold newspapers, magazines, and a limited number of books. He lived with his grown up daughter Dorothy whom he had raised largely by himself, and who managed the business, although it barely supported them both.

"For quite a while we kept in touch by correspondence only and got to know each other that way first. I naturally bombarded him with questions, most of which he would parry with skill while encouraging me to think along lines he considered would serve my best spiritual interests. At first he discouraged my suggestions of coming to London and meeting him personally. He insisted that as soon as he considered the time was ripe we would indeed meet. Before then, he insisted, my mind and soul must reach a condition of preparedness, otherwise it would not obtain any benefit from closer contact with him. Meanwhile he gave me simple exercises to do and a programmed series of thinking tasks to perform.

Although most of them seemed deceptively easy they were in fact a very clever training course in Western esotericism. It was the order and sequence of the pattern he presented them in which held the secret.

"For example, he told me to obtain a child's set of alphabetical letters and try dropping them on the floor frequently to see if sense can possibly come from the fortuitous combination. No matter how many times this was done there would never be anything except accidental meaning to the untidy heap because no consciousness and intelligence had been intentionally applied to their arrangement. That was what made sense of everything, and knowledge of what how and when to combine units of awareness together was the first and fundamental objective in the occult. Correct control of consciousness must be the primary aim of every initiate, and I was making no real effort to control mine at all but just letting it run wild wherever I fancied. When I was able to exercise deliberate and intentional authority over my awareness and direct it effectively where I willed, then it would be time for us to meet. In the meanwhile here were my next set of exercises. And so our communication continued.

"Like myself he had been a boyhood Catholic, and like myself again had thoughts of the priesthood but decided against this because he could not accept that the Roman section of the Christian Church alone had absolute authority over all human souls and could send them Heaven or Hellwards at choice. He believed that every soul itself had that option and responsibility and it was up to us entirely which fate we would embrace for ourselves in the end. He strongly believed in reincarnation, saying that we had been connected in many personal lives and would be so again in the far-off future, but none of that was so important as doing our best in the NOW which was forever. He taught that I should never accept anything without question, but should make myself into a living question mark which applied to everything in existence. Only that way would I ever learn how to live.

"He pointed out in particular that all the occult symbols which fascinated me without knowing exactly *why*, were in fact individual letters of an "occult alphabet" and it was for me to discover how to put them together so that they all made spiritual sense out of sheer consciousness alone. The symbols fascinated me because of familiarity from previous lives, but until I could comprehend what they all stood for as a whole they would be no more valuable to me than my scattered letters on the floor. As with ordinary alphabets, one needed to follow some definite system which was capable of making sense from the right combinations. That was all esoteric organisations really were. Systems of working calculated to make spiritual sense out of special symbols. For example out of the same letters a Frenchman would combine them to communicate in the French, a German the German tongue, and so for the rest of mankind. All saying the same thing with different combinations of the same units. Esoterics were doing no more than communicate with the universal consciousness of pure symbolism. That was the importance of mathematics which I seemed to have missed. Figures meant the same to a German as they did to a Frenchman or an Englishman, and that was why old time Qabalists calculated their consciousness with numerical values. ENH insisted in making me see the reason behind and within everything he wrote of, and revealed many purposes behind otherwise baffling problems.

"Eventually of course we did meet, and having found his London flat for myself, I experienced a stocky middle aged man of neat appearance, clean shaven with very thick eyebrows and the most piercing eyes I have ever encountered in my life. What rather surprised me was the heaviness of his Austrian accent. Although his command of written English was faultless and his writing extremely neat and legible, his speech was deep-toned and more of a growl than otherwise. His handshake was unusually firm and powerful. He too called me Gordon as my family did. He offered me tea, sent his daughter to make it, and then we sat down to talk. Mostly we discussed the subjects of the letters he had sent me and the possibilities arising therefrom. It was the first of many such meetings and experiences.

"One thing he would never do was answer a question outright. He would question me instead and guide the conversation from one point to another until I had supplied an answer myself when he would probably prod me in the ribs and say triumphantly 'There you see? The answer was in yourself all the time. You KNEW. All you had to do was use your intelligence and ask. Everything is in yourself if you only realised it. So now you know where to look, DO it and then you needn't ask so many damn-fool questions. Now you know what Jesus meant when he said 'Ask and you shall receive.'' Again and again he would drive me back inside myself to seek a solution for whatever problem perplexed me. He could be quite sarcastic too, and would often hold me to ridicule for some unwise remark I had made or obvious absurdity I appeared to believe with insufficient grounds.

"He seemed to have read all the books I had ever heard of on occult topics, yet he kept insisting that no amount of book learning was worth a modicum of practical experience. Nevertheless he was very much against my pursuing my ideas of practical magic at that period. He pointed out that I was too young and needed to concentrate on making a living and

ENH, photographed in 1932

laying the foundations of a career. He spoke of Qabalistic teachers who would only accept students at the age of forty when they had succeeded at some kind of business and usually brought up a family who were then supporting themselves. No reputable teacher he said would encourage a young man to avoid his legitimate responsibilities in this world and become a burden on others for the sake of selfish spiritual advantages which could only be temporary or illusory if obtained under such conditions.

"When I mentioned the young *chelas* of the East and monastics who began early vocations, he pointed out that we were neither. We were modern Occidentals with an inherited way of life and totally different spiritual standards which were there to be respected and not avoided. We were incarnate to uphold and honour our Inner Tradition and its Holy Mysteries, not deny or destroy it. Modify and modernise it we might and should, but only for the sake of improving or enhancing it into a better condition than that in which we first encountered it. Did I even know I *had* a 'Holy Tradition'? What did I suppose it was? When I had to confess myself uncertain of what he was talking about, he began to explain the principles of what he meant.

"Mankind, he said, was created by the Great Consciousness most people call God by one name or another for a particular purpose, and we were all of us some part of the Great Entity which is really a Single Self. In this world we were classified according to whatever part of that Purpose we might be, just as our bodies are composed of many different types of cells each of which should fulfil its special function adequately if human bodies are to remain healthy. This process has been continuing for very many generations during which each type of entity has built up an inheritable behaviour pattern which characterises its proper function. The spiritual structure of such a pattern therefore becomes a distinct Inner Tradition of its own which differs from others only because of its nature. Although it should be instinctive, this is what we should find and follow with intelligence and conscious intention. Thus there were several major Traditions in this world, and a number of sub-traditions which were important to know about.

"For example the Eastern and Western Inner Traditions were not identical and served different functions of the same Primal Purpose. Our particular proper place lay within the Western Tradition by birth and breeding. Thereto belonged our true spiritual loyalty although there was a choice of many Paths or sub-traditions we might take along our line of advance. He himself for instance had chosen the Christian and Rosicrucian system, but a Jewish and Qabalistic one would have been equally valid. All genuine Paths led to the same goal which he termed Liberation into Light. Now did I understand what he was driving at? If not, I should go away and meditate about it. The important thing about correct meditation was first to establish contact with a higher level of intelligence than my normal state of consciousness, guide it to a specific source of teaching and then listen carefully to what it had to tell me, or rather just absorb the influence as it came to me and try to interpret it later into terms I could understand with my ordinary awareness. So my instruction continued for session after session."

ENH was amused when Bill told him of his meeting with Dion Fortune. 'What did you expect?' he chuckled. 'Should she make you Grand Master on the spot?' He went on to explain that all bona-fide esoteric Orders applied the same ruling of not accepting under-age candidates for initiation, and he felt it would be exceptionally rare to find any members of that age-group. Twenty five and upwards was the general figure, and his own Order complied with that convention. However, he went on to say, there was no ruling to prevent individual relationships between practising members and younger aspirants providing there was no objection from their parents or any good reason for preventing such a friendship.

In their case there was none, because ENH had already written to Bill's mother and she had been delighted that he had found such capable and friendly sponsorship to guide him on his path. Already he had found an affinity between himself and ENH which he could never find with his own natural father who seemed to have no interest whatsoever in his esoteric endeavours.

In terms of the actual spiritual mechanics of what passed between ENH and William Gray, we can listen to what Jacobus Swart wrote many years later as he tried to summarise the odd way that Bill himself came to 'teach' people:

Bill pointed out a common error with early-stage people on the Paths to Inner Mystery, which is that they frequently expect wonderful "teachers" to come and instruct them verbally by lectures, and other imparted information, which will make them Masters ahead of their time. It may take several incarnations to convince them that great spiritual truths cannot be imparted by words, however "magical" such words may be... Their best "teachings" are imparted by influence alone. Just by ambience alone, so to speak. Proximity. Do not ask me exactly how it is done because I do not know, but you might as well ask why any two people should love each other. There has to be what used to be called "rapport," or some reciprocal connection between them on a non-physical level. So there is some kind of contact between them which will facilitate an exchange of energies.

One of the authors recalls the same technique clearly. As a schoolboy, this young and eager student of the occult would truant from sports sessions to sit between Bill and a chainsmoking Bobbie at their breakfast bar, trying to field conversation from both sides and ducking the superlatives they hurled at each other. Bobbie taught him the rudiments of astrology, but despite all teenage wiles, Bill was difficult to draw on occult topics. Even in later years, spending evenings together in the paraffin-reek of his cluttered study, Bill was expert at turning questions back. To be sure he would loan a book, offer his latest script for perusal, or hold forth on a topic of his choosing; but as a pupil, all the motivation, the answers, the direction had to come from oneself. On one level this could be the most frustrating process. At times one would feel like crying out, "Look Bill, please just tell me what you think I need to do or to learn and I'll go and do it!" He would of course have just looked at you with an enigmatic smile and moved onto other things. It somehow makes a mockery of some of the so-called teachers of the occult today, promising the secrets of the magi in a £50 afternoon workshop. Yet anyone who experienced this contact with Bill will say the same – there was an indefinable something that changed in oneself just through spending time with him.

Jacobus went on to define this as an actual force flow, an 'Inner Sexuality' causing Energy to pass from one soul to the other, which carries the teaching deeply down to the subconscious depths where it 'comes to life'. He went on to say: "A printed or written page does not have any energy of its own to transmit. Therefore there is intellectual appreciation, but little else. Even in oral instruction it is not the actual heard words which put over the 'teaching', but the unspoken Inner Intentions directed or 'mediated' towards the pupil by the teacher. It is the *Inner* contact which constituted the real 'teaching' purely by its presence and persistence."

So if we were to see the actual teachings of ENH written down we might find them disappointingly thin, best categorised as 'Sound Common Sense'. What we might not feel is the curious ambience, the odd magnetism that all real magicians have, which can make even the least sensitive person aware that things were going on at other, deeper levels, no matter how banal the conversation was in intellectual terms.

After leaving school Bill went from one temporary job to another, sometimes being sacked for unsuitability and sometimes quitting of his own accord because he disliked the conditions so much. Although it was relatively easy for a young person to find a job at that period, permanent prospects were not good. So, as he often did then, he took his troubles to ENH.

What he wanted to know was simple: should he or should he not join one of the Armed Services? And if he did, would this be inconsistent with his esoteric activities? As might be expected, ENH put everything in its proper perspective.

After admitting that he had quit Austria to avoid its normal compulsory conscription, ENH went on to say that he could not see any spiritual objection to serving one's country in a defensive capacity. After all, he added, every kind of animal had been provided with some natural means of defence against predators, and each one of them was fully entitled to fight for its own life and the survival of their species. Surely no one in their right minds would deny that ? In essence, the old teacher said that Bill must do what he had to do, so long as he did it well and nobly. All things, all experiences, could be regarded as spiritual symbols, and that he should learn to look *through* these symbols rather than at them, in order to link with the energies beyond.

So what about shit? asked Bill. Could that also be a spiritual symbol?

Indeed it could, replied ENH without blinking. Was it not the waste matter in our bodies which had to be expelled for the sake of our health? If so, did it not signify all its equivalents in our souls which must also be eliminated if we were to be spiritually healthy? And did it not make excellent fertiliser when dug into the soil?

"Real esotericism was not just dressing up in handsome robes and manipulating symbols for the sake of so doing. It was knowing how to apply the meaning of such symbols to Life itself, for the purpose of altering or directing its energy in accordance with intention. For example a Magical Sword was not the physical symbol handled in Temple practice, but its qualities as applied to a human being. Flexibility, sharpness, keenness, brightness, pointedness of action, and everything else to be thought of in connection with a well-balanced blade..."

All the outer trappings of High Magic were useless unless they were synchronised with appropriate inner activity. Thus there would be no point in lighting a candle unless one sought self-illumination at the same time. Nor would there be any point in sending up clouds of incense unless fervent invocation accompanied the action also. This sort of thing may seem obvious to the ritual magicians of today, but this was about the year 1928, and such things had not then been formulated so clearly or publicly. This was *real* magic. This was the sort of thing he had to put into practice.

So basically ENH convinced Bill that all true magic took place inside, and had nothing to do with the glamorous outer trappings that are so beloved of the popular imagination. He could, therefore, learn all this as a soldier equally well as if he were a hermit, once he knew the way. In fact, Bill had hardly been a soldier for a year before he managed to add another magical layer to his reasons for joining up and, if necessary, risk his life for King and Country:

"There seems to be a psychological urge in young men to make them deliberately risk their lives for seemingly no reason, but I believe there is a deep-down instinct to do so in order that the Gods (or Goddess) will have an opportunity to select the best for breeding purposes. In other words if the Fates spare their offered lives, then they are meant to go on living and are fit to breed. If their lives are taken, then they were never meant to mate and carry on their race. Thus it is an atavistic impulse bred into our genes from the very dawn of our civilisation. After they become older and have probably started a family, the instinct alters into one of wanting to live so as to care for that family until it can look after itself. That was why the act of sacred self-sacrifice on the altars of any Temple had to be absolutely voluntary in order to be valid."

So with the approving words of ENH ringing in his ears William Gordon Gray did what so many Britons have done for over a thousand years: he packed up his belongings, said his goodbyes, and went off to War.

CHAPTER 4
The Coming Forth By Day

*"The word Magic however had root connections
with greatness (Maj) and mastery (Magister),
and providing this might be understood in the
sense of spiritual development and self-mastery,
it seemed a reasonable description of the Path
I intended to follow. Orthodox religions of all
descriptions rejected Magic as a dangerous rival,
yet Magic was inclusive of religion... Religion
was collective whereas Magic was individual,
and I was all for individualism. So that was
the definition on which I based my choice of
conscious courses. For the future I would find
my own faith through whatever I might learn of
Magic and its practical purposes."*

Well, it was not so much War that he went toward – at least not yet – but
Egypt, although he had to make a slight detour via Catterick Camp first.
Even young Priest-kings have to learn the fundamental Army lessons of
how to polish boots, march in step, and kill with a bayonet.

Bill was accepted for admission to the Royal Corps of Signals,
which was supremely apt given that his whole life was devoted to
communicating between this world and the infinite realms within
and beyond. Once given his Army number – RCS 2321415 – his basic
training at Catterick took the same route that army training has done
for nearly two centuries. The day was divided into periods of digging,
foot drill, gymnastics and cleaning – all muscle tasks calculated to build
up healthy and efficient bodies. They were not given time to think, and
everything was done to assess their amenability to discipline and their
capability to adapt to commands. Again and again it was pointed out
that to keep a single modern infantry soldier in battle, it needed about
six or seven specialist technicians to supply his immediate needs. He
realised then that the fighting soldier is only the tip of a very long spear
pointing at potential enemies.

Once the elements had been mastered he was transferred for technical training. Since his was telephonic and radio maintenance, this consisted of theoretical lectures and actual workshop practice.

"The latter came in very useful many years later when I handcrafted all my required solid symbols. It was mostly insisted on by old-time esoteric Orders that their members make as much as possible of their magical symbols with their own hands."

By 'solid symbols' he meant the Sword, Rod, Cup and Shield which symbolise the Elements of Air, Fire, Water and Earth respectively, and which in turn relate to qualities within the psyche. When he lifted the Cup, for example, he was using a key to unlock all the corresponding qualities of Feeling, Dreams, Ancestral Memories, Holy Grails and so on. It is every magician's task to work out his own system of 'correspondences' so that mundane objects become mental keys which can open the doors of inner worlds. Not all magicians use these particular techniques of course, but many do.

Yet the striking thing about his memories from that time is that although they are rich in detail about the working day, there is almost nothing about his relationships with fellow soldiers beyond the fact that they wanked a lot, and gave him the nickname The Professor, or simply Prof, because of his knowledge of obscure subjects. He became fond of that nickname. Yet unlike other military memoirs there are no adventures on the town, no hilarity on the assault course, no drunken escapades, no desperate attempts to lose his virginity. Everything was an adjunct of his magic. Everything was used as a symbolic link with inner realities.

"My early training in theoretical electronics and the principles of radio gave me considerable insight into the probable behaviour of intangibles and influences behind our physical universe. All one had to do was extrapolate them into different dimensions of existence and they spoke for themselves with a meaning which only a mystic might comprehend. The bi-polar nature of electrical energy told me of the Divine duality of Life through male and female biology. All the physical facts I was learning about the make-up of our unseen Cosmos had their spiritual equivalents among the metaphysics I had previously been considering. Little by little I began to realise I was only looking at occultism from a different level. One could trace the same symbolism expressed in other ways. The caduceus became a graph used to illustrate alternating electricity. The hexagram showed positive and negative fields combined to produce power. The Cosmic Cross was a dynamo. The Pentagram was the rotor of an electric motor. The spiral an electromagnet. The Rod was a resistance, the Sword a conductor, the Cup a condenser, and the Shield an insulator. Once I began to relate the electromagnetic nature of our Universe with the Mystery Teachings which concerned me so deeply a whole new and fascinating field of enquiry opened up for me and I began to follow it as far as I could."

And he now understood that real esoteric Temples were not physical locations at all, but conditions of consciousness which one had to create around oneself.

He quickly realised that life in the army was not so very different from the monastic life he had yearned for as a boy, and which he had lived in for at least a couple of previous incarnations. At a time when every 'spiritually correct' mystic and occultist was claiming Cathar past lives, he confessed to one of the present writers that he had clear memories of having been part of the great Crusade which had ridden south to wipe them out! He unapologetically remembered a time when he had been a Dominican on the other side.

"In fact there are many parallels between any army and a monastic religious community. Both are collections of a single male sex, both are authoritarian and run according to set rules, both are bound to obedience and fulfilment of orders given by superiors, both have clothing in common and must keep this in good condition, both have periods of duty interspersed by alternative behaviour, both sleep in dormitories and eat in common, both are subject to discipline as decreed by an accepted ruler, both have a shared language, one sacred and the other profane, while both again are conscious of facing an opponent which the monk knows as the 'Devil', and the soldier as the 'Enemy'. Where they diverge entirely is in their relationship with women. The monastic idealises the Feminine Principle in the person of the Virgin and relates with her by spiritual service, whereas the soldier regards the same Principle as something to be served with sexual intercourse on physical levels of life alone. Together they constitute the twin Pillars of the Temple supporting the entire edifice with Purity and Passion."

Again, when he was given leave, there was no attempt to go back to Southampton and see his parents, nor did he have (or even want to have) riotous weekends with the lads. Instead we glimpse the anthropologist again, taking an opportunity to study the strange species on this new planet he had landed on. Once, he found himself in a pub in Richmond, having a quiet drink at lunchtime, when he encountered a *very* curious local wedding custom which he had never met elsewhere:

"Suddenly a party of very cheerful women entered with lots of laughter and giggling. The landlord evidently knew them quite well. They were actually a wedding party with the bride, and the groom had gone to another pub with his male friends. It was a bright winter's day, and a good fire was going near which I was sitting. The women were crowding round the bar with their drinks. The landlord went out and returned with a bright rosy apple, at the sight of which there were audible reactions from the gathering. It was given to the bride who took a single bite from it and passed it to the next woman who did likewise. Eventually everyone had taken their share and there was a lot of looking at me and whispering with the landlord. He took the gnawed apple and came over to me. 'I wonder if you'd mind taking the last bite and then chucking it in the fire,' he said. Intrigued, I did so and questioned him about the happening, but he told me it was just a local practice and he had no idea of its origins or significance. From that day to this I have never heard of it elsewhere. I can only assume that it is symbolic of the Edenic myth and willingness to share the 'guilt' of Eve for temptation of Adam. A man taking the last bite and burning the core would signify male acceptance of a share in such 'sin' and its consequences in hell fire. Possibly there was supposed to be a kind of curse on whoever took that final bite which was why the landlord did not tell me. Anyway the women sent me over a drink to compensate for my co-operation."

It would be wonderful to learn what that custom actually signified. Was it really, as Bill supposed, something deriving from the Old Testament and filtered down through surviving post-Victorian values? Or could it have been a fragment of pagan tradition lurking among the womenfolk of Yorkshire? Moreover, it would be interesting to see whether Bill's subsequent life was in any way predicted by that burnt core.

On another occasion he went slumming in London to see for himself the extent of the homelessness problem there, which was just as prevalent in the 1920s as it is today. He wandered around the Embankment and made acquaintance with several of the down-and-outs, noting how they lived, showing curiosity rather than compassion, but no little admiration also. At Charing Cross underground he saw how the derelicts, as they were then termed, would climb the projecting cornerstones to sleep on the warm roof of the station, and showed surprise at the young men with heavy lipstick, rouged cheeks and darkly pencilled eyebrows, who 'did it' for a tanner a time. And he railed against the Salvation Army at that time which owned enormously expensive properties along Victoria Street yet failed to do anything effective for the poor wretches they were meant to serve.

But mainly he still sought contact with like minded souls – which is a prime concern for any human being, whether involved in occultism or not. As he had done in Southampton, he sought out the local branch of the Theosophical Society, rather hoping that it might help him find the sort of occult group which would appeal to his own tastes.

"In other words an ordinary TS gathering which the public were welcome to attend was sometimes used as a sort of recruiting office for concerns interested in serious esotericism. The most unlikely looking people would often act as 'talent scouts' seeking genuine spiritual contacts. They might often be individuals with an ability to detect human auras since those are more than difficult to falsify and they provide immediate clues to their owner's character. I have never had such an ability myself for it depends on the actual construction of the eye itself. Apparently the deep brown iris with short sight seems the most sensitive, while my grey eyes with normally long sight are the least suitable. There is certainly a genetic factor involved with so-called psychic vision which is frequently no more than a natural ability for seeing further into the light spectrum than average mortals. Literally some can see further into brick walls than others as the saying goes."

The bit about the eyes is fascinating. But the idea that members of mysterious Orders went trawling for likely recruits at TS gatherings is pure bollocks. The real magical orders in Britain operated from private houses, using spare bedrooms, sitting rooms or sometimes hired the local Masonic lodge. The adepti – the *real* adepti – all had full-time jobs in the outer world. When they were not invoking ancient gods and goddesses, or squabbling among themselves, they were too busy raising children, paying the mortgage and generally trying to satisfy their bank managers. The last thing they were inclined to do was to trudge around such places using their psychic talents to find recruits. The 'old Orders' as Bill envisaged them were just not as awesome or as omniscient as he might have wished, despite the very real energies that they worked with, and brought into the world.

Nevertheless, at that time, he did manage to meet several helpful souls who invited him into their homes to discuss much deeper matters than the average Theosophist, although none of them seemed to belong to the sort of esoteric group he often pined for – and which didn't exist outside of his own wishful thoughts.

Quite simply young Bill was lonely. He wanted to meet congenial souls. He was too young for the Golden Dawn, as manifested by Dion Fortune's group, and felt that the Spiritualist circles were certainly not what he needed. What else was left but the Theosophical Society and the echoing depths of his own soul? He wanted to make eye contact with someone across a crowded room who would make his spirit soar and bring him to life, light, love and learning. We have all wanted that, at some time. But there was no-one who met the criteria, or showed the sort of inner stature he yearned for.

What saved him was Egypt.

Magically, he *had* to go there...

Eventually he became due for foreign service, and naturally he wanted Egypt because he felt such an affinity with the place. India had never attracted him in the slightest despite all the tales of great Masters and wonderful gurus, but Egypt seemed to call with a mysterious summons that echoed in his answering soul. It spoke wordlessly of a past that he could only sense with indistinct and uncertain memories. He did not for one moment suppose that he had been anyone of historical note or even social significance in those far-off times, yet he had the strong feeling that he had been then as now, a serving soldier – but in the Roman Army instead of the British.

When the list of postings went up on the Company notice board he read it with a certain amount of apprehension in case anything had gone wrong. He need not have worried. There was his name under the draftings to Egypt Signals, and he could scarcely wait to inform his parents and – of course – ENH. He did not feel that he was being sent abroad, but back to a land where he and ENH had once had important experiences together, and that this time he would have to discover whatever it was that he had failed to find previously.

Naturally, he asked his Teacher for a clue as to what this indefinable but strongly felt 'lost' thing might be, but the wily Austrian said no more than that everyone has to look for his Holy Grail by himself. When Bill came right back and asked him whether he had ever found *his* Grail, ENH merely smiled and said that he had never lost it in *this* life. Intrigued, the young soldier wanted to know what the Grail actually was.

"[ENH] said that if he told me I would never believe him and therefore might miss it entirely. 'I can give you only one clue,' he said. 'The key to the Grail Castle is in yourself. It's up to you to find which lock to turn it in. It may take you the rest of your life to discover that.'"

Equally naturally he got his mother to consult his horoscope and read the tarot cards. They both predicted a fairly fortunate outcome to his time overseas, and although she saw warfare around her son she insisted that he would not be personally involved even though danger might come quite close. She did warn him about visiting underground or confined spaces, and also predicted a minor love affair which would not result in marriage. After that, there was nothing more for his mother to do except kiss him goodbye and wave him farewell from Southampton dockside.

"Egypt seemed to have changed a lot in two thousand years," he wrote. "Roads, railways, telephones and high-rise blocks of flats had moved it into our modern world. Some things were just the same though. The sand, the flies, the filth, the date-palms, the heat, and of course the muddy Nile..."

Their barracks were just outside Cairo at Abbassia, a short tram ride from everything he might need. His young life blossomed in this hot climate. He learned how to swim. To speak and read a little Arabic. How to accompany the armoured cars and support them with radio. Like every new soldier before and since, he marvelled at the anachronisms within the British Army and the general ineptness of the officer class. He earned a little money in his spare time by acting as an extra in costume dramas that were always being filmed with the pyramids as a backdrop. And he even found himself a sweetheart, a lively and attractive Albanian girl called Helen, who spoke almost no English and so his French had to improve quite markedly. Although she had no inkling of his esoteric interests, he really was charmed by her natural and unaffected beauty, as well as her 'exuberance and almost impish sense of fun'.

About time too. You can almost hear the cockles of his heart (whatever they are) warming to her memory. Until then there seemed to be no human warmth or softness in his life, as it all seemed to be Ideas, Bigger Ideas and more bloody Magic. He always liked women. Liked them enormously in fact, and probably got on with them better than men. But he could seem a bit austere. Here at last he started to have a perfectly normal, light-hearted, male-female relationship.

But of course, apart from all the details and practices necessary to adapt to a new country, as well as learning the ancient arts of courtship, mating, and how to protect himself against Venereal Disease, it was inevitable that that the very first thing he *had* to do at this point was visit the Pyramids.

"The tram journey from Cairo cost a whole ten piastres or two shillings of English money. I could scarcely wait for my first visit of very many during my stay. The journey began at the crowded commercial centre of Cairo, passed among some beautiful private estates and gardens, and eventually travelled along the flame-tree lined, dead straight, five mile long avenue which had once been covered with salt so that the Empress Eugenie of France could visit the Pyramids by sledge when she had come to Egypt for the opening of the Suez Canal in the previous century. The Pyramids are visible on their plateau from one end of this magnificent avenue to the other. They grew more awe-inspiring with every inch of my approach. I could scarcely bother to look towards my left at the splendid house which the film actress Pearl White had taken to live in with her ex-dragoman Egyptian lover. The train terminus was at the bottom of the plateau where I got down and waved away all offers of guides, camels, donkeys, and other types of transport. My feet were good enough to take me up the shortish climb to the base of the Great Pyramid. When I got there it blotted out everything else on the landscape, and at close quarters it and it alone *was* the landscape."

This was just a quick exploratory visit. He went back many times over the next five years, and took many photographs of the inner chambers. Although he was as astonished as anyone by the skills needed to build the Great Pyramid, and the sheer technical achievement, his senses told him that the blocks had been manoeuvred into position by men pulling ropes. Aware of the old tradition that Egyptian priests had uttered magic words that floated the blocks into place, he insisted that these were in fact 'work shanties' which the workmen sang with emphasis as they hauled on ropes or did anything with rhythmic effort. The stones, which had been cut from the Noquattan Heights across the Nile, had been floated over to the Pyramid site on huge flat rafts when the annual inundation took place. Although the water may only have been a couple of feet deep at the edges, that would still have been quite sufficient, he felt, to move the blocks.

He also took issue with the Ancient Egyptian belief-systems, as regards the building of pyramids and the mummification of kings:

"So long as their bodies remained intact so would their personalities survive, but should these decay entirely then they might be reincarnated but without their former rank and importance. Naturally a king or noble could not face the thought of being reborn a slave or anyone of no social significance whatever, so every precaution was taken to prevent this horrid happening. Apart from his body being preserved and carefully set into safety, his most precious possessions would be buried with him, and symbolic servants too, plus every artifice ambitious priests could think of in the way of special commemorative services and periodic prayers for his spiritual well-being in Heavenly happiness. They overlooked one all-important factor. The progress of evolution. Theirs would be a permanently ancient Egyptian heaven with no further developments or improvements to increase their experience. While other humans were advancing and expanding their spiritual growth through continuous lessons learned by living, those once wealthy and important people would remain statically bound to out-of-date beliefs imprisoning their consciousness in comfortable cages of their own creation."

If the entity now known as William Gordon Gray had reincarnated many times since it had last visited Egypt, then the original pharaohs were still existing in an Otherworld where nothing changed, nothing moved on. To him, whose whole life and magic was concerned with evolution, this was the most dreadful and wasteful concept imaginable.

"Once outside the Pyramid again I sought the Sphinx. It was invisible from that level, and I thought if I had been here before I should be able to find it again somehow. Instinctively I walked around the Western face of the Pyramid and bore to my left. After a few minutes walk I was rewarded by the sight of the Sphinx's head and upper body and eventually came to the edge of the pit in which it was crouching. I looked at the vast beast with wonder and it regarded me with what I thought might be surprised remembrance. Somehow I believed it had been elaborately painted when we had met previously…"

In fact for thrill-seekers, Bill's experiences with the Pyramids on the Giza plateau and further south at Sakkara are disappointing. He took lots of photographs. He scrambled about a lot. Did a lot of amateur archaeology. Never once was he assailed by discarnate souls or ancient deities, although on one occasion he had been brought close to panic by an eerie, dragging footfall which came closer and closer to him in the darkness of a minor pyramid. Until that moment he hadn't believed that human hair could actually stand on end, but his did then. It turned out to be a cat with a broken leg, which had followed him. In fact the most magical experience (that he confessed to) was that the Sphinx had seemed to recognise him.

Compare this with Aleister Crowley, who in 1903 spent the night in the King's Chamber of the Great Pyramid with his new wife Rose, determined to impress her with what a great Magician he was. By the light of a single candle placed on the edge of the coffer, he began to read the Preliminary Invocation of that grimoire known as *The Goetia*, and soon realised that the chamber was filling with the soft light that he immediately recognised as the astral light. Soon, it was aglow 'as if with the brightest tropical moonlight. The pitiful dirty yellow flame of the

candle was like a blasphemy, and I put it out. The astral light remained during the whole of the invocation and for some time afterwards...'
[*Confessions*, Bantam Books 1970, p.391]

But Bill's magic was never about thrill-seeking. Surely, if his visions were all about projections from the unconscious, wish-fulfilment, cryptomnesia or whatever, then great inner dramas would have unfolded themselves before his astonished gaze. In the event, nothing of the sort happened. If nothing else, it is a testament to the fundamental honesty of his vision.

After a year he was transferred to the newly formed Signal Section of the 11th Hussars, which had become an armoured car regiment. There he was exasperated not only by the antiquated attitudes of the officers, but the poor equipment they were supplied with. He may seem an antiquarian figure to us now, in the early 21st Century, but as a young man he was a technocrat, and as a magician a definite modernist. Yet at least he did feel that he was getting somewhere, magically.

"At last I was beginning to make progress with my occult ambitions. I did indeed contact someone I suspected was an active member of a mystical association which I had previously assumed no longer lived upon this earth. Again because of confidentiality I will nominate this special Soul as S, and say no more than that she was a White Russian born of very noble blood who had suffered terribly when her country turned to Communism and her family had been butchered ruthlessly when their estates were confiscated. She escaped herself because she was elsewhere at the time and members of her organisation managed to get her out of the country and eventually into Egypt."

Bill was a man who admired ideas so much that he rarely described physical characteristics. A yellowing photograph in Bill's collection shows a woman of middle years, with gentle features and what would obviously have been full and rebelliously wavy dark hair cut severely to the nape of her neck. It is signed, 'In memory of a very sweet friendship from "Sarah", Cairo, 11th May 1938'. Those enigmatic inverted commas around her name are her own, and all attempts by the authors to uncover her identity have been fruitless, but she comes across as a far more intriguing character than ENH. The best Bill offers is that: "She was very much older than I, was working as a secretary to a large insurance company, and her English was faultless." Did he fall just a bit in love? Certainly – but only with her mind and its magic. That's all Bill ever wanted.

"Sarah"

It is an admirable but often exasperating trait of occultists that they keep secrets when the need for keeping them has long since passed. Despite being asked direct questions by the present authors and Jacobus Swart, he never would reveal the identity of S, or give the name of that organisation which he had assumed 'no longer lived upon this earth', although he mentioned that she also belonged to another group which was dedicated to overthrowing Communism and restoring the Monarchy to Russia. Nevertheless the pair did come to some understanding concerning the esoteric circles with which she was connected, and said that he might serve his apprenticeship with her, after which he could be sponsored for initiation into the probationary grades of her Order. Such apprenticeship had to be for a year and a day, but could last longer than that. She tried to explain that her Society was nothing that one *joined* but simply *belonged* to because it was part of one's genuine Inner state of being. True spiritual status was not something that you could be given by wonderful ceremonies and initiations, but was something that you have to *become*, of your own accord. 'That is why they talked about *achieving* the Grail in the old days,' she said.

So once again, with this in mind, he started out with some simple mental exercises to do and attitudes to adopt. But all this was interrupted because the Hussars were suddenly ordered to Palestine, where trouble was breaking out between the Arabs and the Jews.

The actual task of the Hussars was to provide an armed escort for Jewish motor convoys carrying cargo between the settlements and trading townships such as Tel Aviv and Haifa. It was a brief interlude, occasionally fraught with danger from snipers and bombers, and he was only too glad when they were ordered back to Egypt again, where he could resume his burgeoning social life.

Yet although he was glad to return, he was seriously beginning to doubt that there *was* such a thing as 'Esoteric Egypt'.

"Where, I wondered, were the mystics and Masters who were supposed to teach world-shattering spiritual truths which would move mankind in the direction of Divinity? Where were the visionaries and dreamers who would open up inner worlds for the perception of their pupils? All [Egypt's] inhabitants seemed interested in was sex and money just like their Western counterparts."

The advice given by S. in this respect was that he should 'lengthen his time-sense until an entire lifetime seemed only seconds long, then shorten it, so that seconds lasted an eternity' – rather like his mother's experience when the nurse brought her medicine and time seemed to stop. She mentioned the Muslim legend of the water-jar, which tells of Mohammed asking the Archangel Gabriel to explain eternity, whereupon that Being deliberately tipped over the Prophet's water-jar and Mohammed made a grab at it to steady the vessel. Without explanation he found himself as a young man walking along the road to Damascus. When he arrived at the city he knew no-one there, and after some wandering found an elderly merchant who offered him temporary hospitality. After a little while they became firm friends, and the old man having no sons of his own took Mohammed as a partner into his business, and eventually as a son-in-law who produced several grandchildren. The whole family lived happily together until the old man died and Mohammed inherited the business. One day, as he was sitting outside the shop, his elbow caught his water-jar and he made a quick move to steady it whereupon he found himself back in his original position with the Archangel smiling at him and saying 'Now you know.'

S. went on to explain how it could be possible to live more than one life at a time by shifting consciousness from level to level as necessary. The art of this was called 'interlockment' by those capable of it, but it had to be gained very cautiously because if one condition became confused with the other the result could be insanity in both directions. Each existence had to be lived along its own lines without any mix-ups, otherwise there would be nothing but trouble everywhere!

Of course he asked her all the usual questions such as: What would happen if one linked two existences together, one of which was healthy and the other sick, or one was male and the other female?

She asked him in return how he supposed the Eternal One lived, who was all lives at once composed of every contradiction in Creation. She also mentioned the multiplicity of human nature itself and the complex nature of our consciousness which has to deal with great numbers of specific mental and spiritual attitudes.

By this time S. had begun to remind him so much of ENH that he began to wonder if they were members of the same... well, he was not sure *what* to call it. As best as he could define it, it would amount to a sort of worldwide confederation of souls which had reached a common state of spiritual awareness, and consequently shared each other's active essence so to speak. "Maybe Jung might call this the Great Universal Mind, but it was a distinct possibility which would explain many mysteries…"

At last the time for him to leave Egypt arrived. He was somewhat sad because he had enjoyed the experience very much, and had been quite happy there. He would miss the friendship of S. most of all, though he was rather looking forward to reunion with ENH again. And then there was little Helen, who was far from cheerful at the prospect of their permanent separation.

"It was the only time I ever knew her weep gently against my shoulder. I could not comfort her at all whatever I said. She only sobbed: 'Non non, je le sais, c'est pour toujours. Nous sommes tout a fait fini.' Although she did manage to put on a braver face for the farewell party, there was not much to be done otherwise."

Poor Helen, she never stood a chance with her handsome Hussar. There she was, broken-hearted, probably hoping against hope that he might propose marriage or ask her to come to England, yet while her tears were still wet on his collar he was listening intently to S. while she told him about something called the Qabalah, and a potent diagram known as the Tree of Life that would change him and his magic forever…

CHAPTER 5
The Tree of Life and Qabalah

*"Why does it all have to be in bloody Hebrew?
We're not Jewish! Why can't you use bloody
English, eh?"*

Bobbie Gray, in conversation with her husband

      —

At this point we must have what Bill himself might call a 'holy hiatus': a pause in the narrative to explain something about this system that S. talked about. Quite simply we cannot go far in looking at the mature William Gray without considering the philosophy of the Tree of Life and the Qabalah. Sometimes spelled Kabbalah, Cabbalah, or – awkwardly – Quabbala. Bill used all of these spellings at various times. None of them are wrong, because the actual word from the Hebrew (which does not use vowels) is QBL. This is a verb which means 'to receive'. It is a reference to those esoteric teachings passed on 'from mouth to ear': whispered secrets which no non-initiate must hear.

Although there were still important things happening to him in the outer world, the seeds of this odd, old and very influential philosophy had already been planted by ENH and S, and were growing in the darkness while the rest of his world plunged toward War.

There is a famous diagram in which the Tree of Life is superimposed upon the human body. This is almost a supreme image for Bill Gray himself: you cannot consider him without understanding this magical glyph that was built so firmly into his psyche. Those readers who are familiar with the QBL might like to skip this chapter. Those who are not, and who want to learn something about the Hermetic path that Bill trod, cannot really afford to ignore it.

The QBL, then, was an esoteric doctrine passed on from initiate to initiate, a mystic lore that was said to be capable of explaining the secrets of the heavens above and the earth beneath. It was supposed to have been transmitted from God, through the angelic orders to Adam. Noah, Moses, David, Solomon, and finally to Rabbi Simeon ben Yohai, who wrote the teachings down during the second century of the Christian Era.

Its main books were the *Sepher Yetzirah*, or 'Book of Creation,' and the *Zohar*, or 'Book of Splendour,' which was written in Spain by Moses de Leon in the 13th Century.

The theoretical Qabalah contains elements from ancient Egyptian, Babylonian and Greek philosophies, spiced up with the mysticism of Philo and the early Christian Gnostics, with the doctrines of reincarnation, transmigration, and the enduring realities of Good and Evil, Light and Darkness thrown into the mix.

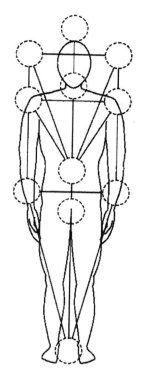

If the theoretical Qabalah proved irresistible to the mystics, then the practical Qabalah proved itself a manna to the magicians. And it is that diagram known as the *Otz Chaim*, or Tree of Life, which provided the framework upon which all else was hung. One commentator described it as the 'Mighty and All-embracing glyph of the Universe and the soul of Man.' Surprisingly, despite the bombast, it is exactly that.

Dion Fortune wrote what is still the best book on the topic in *The Mystical Qabalah*, although this is almost matched by Gray's own *Ladder of Lights*, which more than lives up to its subtitle of 'Kabbalah Renovata'.

According to the revelation, all life preceded via a series of emanations beginning from *Ain Soph*, which we might describe as Absolute Nothingness. This was the condition of the universe before Man, before God, before anything. From that Absolute Nothingness came the single point of pure white light known as Kether, which is that state of consciousness that we might crudely (very crudely) describe as God.

It was from this first sphere, or *sephirah*, that the universe began to manifest itself in the numerical sequence shown overleaf, so that Kether (1) is at the level of absolute spirit, and Malkuth (10) is the realm of densest matter. It is in Malkuth, the earth-sphere, that we find ourselves. The Tree provides us with a ladder by which we can attempt to climb back up to our Source.

The spheres themselves are clearly arranged on three columns known as Pillars. All the positive, upbuilding energies in the universe are linked with the right-hand column, and all the negative, breaking-

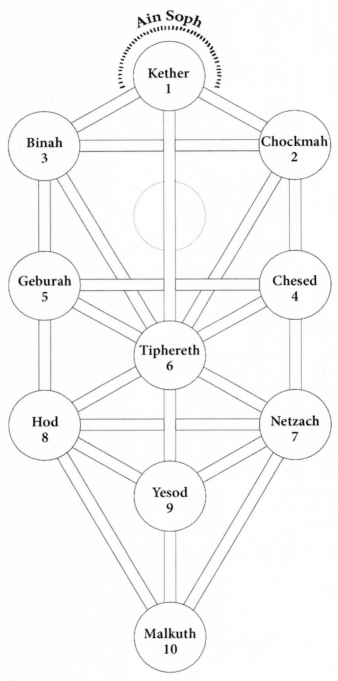

Tree of Life

down forces placed on the left. In this sense, however, 'negative' was never regarded as evil in itself, any more than it is evil to knock down buildings (or psychological edifices) which are dangerously decayed. It is wrong to associate Good with Positive and Evil with Negative. Being always positive, always saying 'yes,' can create just as much evil within the world as its unbalanced opposite. The balance, then, is represented by the middle pillar.

Within these columns we can resolve the universe for ourselves, if we are uncompromising enough: Yes/No/Maybe, White/Black/Grey. Sometimes, as all magicians know, the best way to deal with the world is to retreat into the basics, and nothing else.

By analysing the spheres, however, we can add some subtleties to the way that these three qualities express themselves.

We can best imagine the Tree as a kind of filing system which is divided into ten compartments, and into which everything – *everything* – can be placed. Our initial problem is simply that of having the exact nature of this system explained to us, because after that it begins to explain itself.

Had there been 26 compartments then this would present no problem at all, for it would be based upon the alphabet. Into the compartment 'L' for example, would go leopards, lemurs, light, locusts and love. While it would be simplicity itself to store such data the exercise would be meaningless on any spiritual level: it is no good looking for love and finding lice, lugworms and loquaciousness. That won't teach us anything. But with the system used by the Tree we can not only store away our own experiences in a particular area – intellectual, emotional or spiritual – but we can use to it to lead us on into the collective experience of mankind as a whole.

Each of the spheres upon the Tree has some basic attributions. So do the paths linking them. These are known as the Correspondences. One of Crowley's books was called *Liber 777*, and consisted of a series of correspondences for every sphere and path upon the Tree: Magical Images, Names, Letters, Tarot Trumps... he showed where we could place them all, and link one with the other. This is the book that the teenaged Bill copied when his mother's back was turned, without really understanding it. Although we can and indeed *must* learn to interpret the Tree in our own terms, using our own belief systems, the major and traditional Hebraic correspondences are given in the chart on page 78.

Sphere	Archangel	Divine Name	Colour	Magical Image
Kether	Metatron	Eheieh	Brilliance	Face of an old man, in profile
Chockmah	Ratziel	Jehovah	Brilliance	Masculine, bearded face, full-on
Binah	Tzaphkiel	Jehovah Elohim	Blackness	A mature woman
Chesed	Tsadkiel	El	Blue	A wise king, on his throne
Geburah	Khamael	Elohim Gibor	Red	A warrior king, on his chariot
Tiphereth	Michael	Jehovah Eloah va Daath	Rose-pink	A child, priest king, sacrificed god.
Netzach	Auriel	JHVH Tzavoos	Emerald	Beautiful naked woman
Hod	Raphael	Elohim Tzavoos	Orange	An hermaphrodite
Yesod	Gabriel	Shadai el Chai	Violet	Naked man, very strong
Malkuth	Sandalphon	Adonai ha Aretz	Olive	Mother Nature, on her throne

To understand how we can use each of these as keys into areas of consciousness, we need to look at each one in sequence.

KETHER The Crown. The Point within the Circle. Instead of visualising God as some omnipotent deity in human form, visualise him as an all pervasive radiance, underlying all and everything. Then go a stage further and imagine that light concentrating itself into an intense pinpoint which hangs within the absolute nothingness and complete blackness of the unmanifest universe, before The Beginning. This, then, is Kether: a pinpoint of pure white light which contains All. This is the universe before the Big Bang. This is the Essence.

CHOCKMAH Wisdom. When Kether became aware of itself it exploded outward in what we might describe as the first Cosmic Laugh. This is Chockmah, which represents the archetypal male and is the sphere of all the outrushing, thrusting and forceful energies as they emerge from the Source. One of its images is that of an upright pole, which should speak for itself in phallic terms. All phallic symbolism, therefore, can find an ultimate placement in this second sphere.

BINAH Understanding. If Chockmah is the sphere of pure and dynamic *force* on archetypal levels, then Binah balances it with the archetypal female qualities of pure and receptive *form*. It is the sphere associated with the black-robed Great Mother, the planet Saturn, and that revelation known as Sorrow, in its spiritual sense: 'All life is suffering' as Buddha said, but through that (through Binah) we can begin to understand the deepest parts of life's mystery.

These three spheres are known as the Supernal Triad. They represent the innermost essence of all that we find in denser levels of manifestation. All of us have qualities of positive and negative within us. How we use these qualities, as opposed to over-indulging in them, determines how much Wisdom (Chockmah) or Understanding (Binah) we have. It is nothing to do with what sex a person may be. Men can be Binah figures just as women can relate to Chockmah.

CHESED Mercy. The planet is Jupiter. It is the sphere of benevolence, generosity, philanthropy, and all those energies which go toward the creation of stable, peaceful civilisations.

GEBURAH Justice. Its planet being Mars, it is the natural balance to the sphere of Chesed. It is that energy which ensures that anything effete, corrupt and putrid (however this manifests) is regularly scoured, purified, or swept away completely. Although its traditional symbol is that of the pentagram, the modern image of a surgeon's knife is more indicative.

TIPHERETH Beauty. Both Chesed and Geburah resolve themselves within Tiphereth, the sphere of the Sun. It is the sphere of all those Sacrificed Gods who abound in major religions, and who bring harmony to the world by dying for our sakes. Harmony is, in fact, one of its titles. Not the placid and often pathetic harmony of, say, an English vicar, but the harmony achieved by the nuclear forces reacting with the Sun itself, with its power to heal or destroy depending upon where we are placed at the time.

This trinity of Chesed/Geburah/Tiphereth is known as the Ethical triad. They represent those qualities which lift us above mere self-absorption toward a consideration of life and humanity as a whole.

NETZACH Victory, or Achievement. This is the sphere of Venus, with all those quickening impulses which might loosely be termed 'romantic,' and find expression in the arts generally and in our emotional behaviour personally.

HOD Glory, or Splendour. This is the sphere of Mercury, whose qualities of pure intellect neatly balance the raw emotion of Netzach, and which find expression every time we act rationally and logically, or indulge ourselves in the sciences.

YESOD Foundation. The place of the Moon, and the unconscious mind, and what we might think of as the instincts upon which so much of our existence depends. It is also the realm of the astral plane, the 'treasure-house of images,' and because of the use made of this by magicians, this particular trinity of Netzach/Hod/Yesod is known as the Magical Triad.

MALKUTH Kingdom. The material world on which we all live and find expression. All of the above spheres "pour down" into it. Malkuth contains them just as our physical body contains our mind, soul and spirit. It is related to the four elements of Earth, Water, Air and Fire, which we might think of as Solids, Liquids, Gases and Radiations.

There is an eleventh sphere also, known as **DAATH**, or Knowledge where Malkuth used to be before the 'Fall', but that needn't concern us here.

As we can see from the diagram, the spheres of the Tree are joined by paths, which might be regarded as the blending points. Thus the path between Yesod and Netzach represents that area within our consciousness which rises from pure blind instinct and leads into the glow of more romantic considerations: where having sex turns into making love. Or else we can study that path connecting Hod and Netzach and make the careful balance that we must all strike sometimes between soulless intellect and brainless passion.

So we can begin to see how this unique filing system of the Tree of Life can work. Like a novice secretary, the neophyte will handle the system clumsily at first, often putting things into the wrong holes; but with rapidly increasing assurance the peculiar patterns and interrelationships between the spheres will begin to teach of their own accord.

For example, all those gods related to the intellectual 'Hermetic' arts would be equated with the sphere of Hod: Thoth, Hermes, Merlin, etc, while all those figures of romance and enchantment will go into Netzach: Nimue, Nephthys, Freya and so on.

There is no dogma attached to this (or there shouldn't be): militant feminists are quite welcome to reverse the polarities and adapt them to their own peculiar vision of the universe. As long as the neophyte makes his or her own efforts in determining the Correspondences for each sphere, that process known as 'Building the Tree in the Aura' will take place. It is when this happens that the filing system starts to become more akin to a super-computer of spiritual possibility.

In fact the magicians of the Golden Dawn and the Fraternity of the Inner Light would have done exactly that – building the Tree into the aura (i.e. fixing it in the unconscious) by visualising it as shown on page 75. They would ritualise it by touching the top of the head (the crown) and intoning the word *Eheieh*, while attempting to experience the qualities of Kether, or the 'pure white light,' within. Then to the right temple, and the left, and soon, down the body in the order of manifestation, doing all of the above while also visualising each sphere in its associated colour. In time – in a surprisingly short time – the magician will have a very marked sense of the reality of these spheres. It is as though the amorphous mass of his psyche has been moulded into a particular pattern, and highly specific areas of his consciousness begin to inter-react in the same way as the spheres upon the Tree. When he comes to work on his Correspondences (which involves no more than associating items of experience, symbols, impulses, etc., with the patterns of the spheres) then he will find links, parallels and suggestions springing into his mind which will be altogether surprising, and never less than illuminating.

A magician who feels that he has been unfairly dealt with might use Qabalistic magic to seek Justice. He would wear red clothes, light five red candles, intone the words *Elohim Gibor* in a fivefold rhythm, and even *think* red, before addressing his complaint to the Archangel Khamael, visualised as great, winged darkly red figure wielding a flaming sword and wearing a pentagram upon his chest.

This would not, however, be any kind of 'revenge magic'. Geburah (Mars) cannot be used for that. His plea would be: 'If these events are right and proper, if it is part of my karma to suffer this, then so be it. But if it is not, and I am being unfairly treated then please redress the balance, bring justice back into my life'.

The actual words are less important than the intention, of course, but the supplicant should be very strong in his belief that he is being wronged, for if such suffering *is* part of his karma, or nothing more than his own stupid fault, then the effect of such an invocation is to bring all the energies to a head, sooner than usual, with all the intensified suffering that might ensue. On the other hand, he may well find that balances *are* made in his favour, and ways made smooth, and burdens lifted.

The forces on the Tree are all perfectly balanced with one another. It is impossible to 'trick' these energies into giving something for nothing. There are always prices to be paid, harmonies which will be maintained. And when the Tree is built into the aura it becomes a device which enables us to connect our own limited consciousness with the unlimited consciousness of the universe. Whatever changes we affect within ourselves ultimately affect the whole of existence. We become part of the great cosmic balancing act and must accept a grave responsibility for an inward kind of decency and honesty.

But in purely magical terms it means that in time, the magician will be able to pick up one symbol – an *ankh* for example – and that single glyph will give him access not only to the huge store of his own ideas, but also to the infinite experience of the collective unconscious. By lifting this simple device from the altar of his conscious mind, with ritualistic intent, he is potentially in touch with the experience of every Egyptian worshipper of Isis, every latter-day hippie, every astrologer who has ever marvelled at Venus, and every Roman who has ever adored that goddess as she rose from the sea. It becomes simpler with practice: like driving a car, or handling complex machinery, it becomes almost automatic. In time, you can forget about it all with your conscious mind because it propels you inward from unconscious levels. And then, as so many other magicians have learned to do, you can sit down in some quiet place, summon up your gods, goddesses or guides, and start to perform real magic…

But the essential Jewish nature of the philosophy caused Bill many problems at first. This was certainly not racism, for he was never happier than when delving into the origins of obscure Hebraic words and concepts. But it just didn't quite gel with what he felt was necessary for the Western psyche. Years later, as he explained it, he had a sort of mild revelation:

"I had at last begun to make some sense of the Tree of Life problem which appeared to be a sort of hinge pin of our Western Inner Tradition. Following ENH's advice to become a living question mark I began to challenge its propositions and its dictums. Why, for instance, did all its exponents write about it from top to bottom only? Surely as humans we were supposed to climb a tree and not fall down it? Then again why did the language have to be Hebrew? We were not Jewish, nor was Hebrew our normal speech. Why the archaic language? Why did none of the

Tarot Trumps seem to fit in the right places? How did the thing originate? There were all these and many more queries which seem to have been very unsatisfactorily answered. It seemed to me that people in previous centuries had laid out their version of the Tree and no one else had ever dared to question it or attempt to extend the ideas any further. Why should this not be tackled, and why should not I be the one to do so?"

It wasn't quite like that. What actually happened was that his wife Bobbie looked at him labouring away over the Mysteries of the QBL one day and rasped: 'Why does it have to be bloody Hebrew? We're not Jewish! Why can't you use bloody English, eh?" That, by his own admission, was what got him thinking. That was what enabled him – ultimately – to find his own way into the understanding of a topic that he had found very elusive indeed.

His *Kabbalah Renovata*, however, was still some years ahead of this period when he lived amid the pyramids while serving King and Country, but at least we can be aware of the occult scheme that was bubbling away within his psyche at this time. In due course he left the Mysteries of Egypt behind him forever, and was about to explore an even stranger, crueller and more mysterious realm altogether: he was about to fall in love.

CHAPTER 6
Love, War, and the Concourse of Forces

So be very sure of yourself before seeking entry to the 'Inner Arenas', and don't say you weren't warned. Once in, there's no turning back. One **has** *to go on, and on, and on, to the bitter bloody end, because one has to. No matter how horrible, how frustrating, or more frequently how blatantly boring the Inner Path may seem, it has to be plodded to the very final and sometimes terrible end before it enters PERFECT PEACE PROFOUND wherein nothing can harm or hurt you ever again. You can't just 'take up Magic' like some hobby and abandon it when you feel inclined. You may, and periodically should, have resting periods during which nothing much appears on the surface while a good deal is developing underneath. Nevertheless, once you become part and parcel of the Magical Tradition, especially that of the West, expect difficulties from all directions...*

[letter to AR, 2nd March 1973]

After having been out of the country for five years, Bill was appalled by how much it seemed to have declined and become run down in the interim. He was stationed at Canterbury barracks, in what was clearly a depressed area, and spent some time touring local schools as a recruiting officer. He was deeply troubled by how puny and ill-fed the young boys were, and they had real problems in finding youngsters fit enough and developed enough to meet the minimum requirements.

Although to him Canterbury was largely a 'dead' place so far as esoteric experience went, he was greatly taken by the atmosphere of the famous cathedral, and he could almost feel the weight of history pressing down at every step. He also commented: "There is still a strange sort of feeling at the spot where the Archbishop Beckett was murdered at the whim of a King, and I could not help but thinking that the English made almost a habit of killing Archbishops of Canterbury since at least four of them have perished that way..."

Was this his intuition saying more here than his intellect realised? Or was he being unnecessarily coy? Later in life he would write about the Sacred King and the Willing Sacrifice at some length, and many scholars before and since have advanced the notion that Beckett was a 'Dark Twin', a holy surrogate who was ritually slain to enable the King to continue for another fixed period.

There is a brief Magical Diary which has survived from around this period. One particular entry is dated 10th June 1939, 10.30 pm. Saturday.

NATURE OF RITUAL	Ceremonial Prayers
OBJECTIVE	Knowledge of Holy Guardian
INSTRUMENTS	Wand, lamen and thurible bell
VESTMENTS	yellow silk goftan

REMARKS

I had intended to use the Ritual as given by Crowley in his '*Magick*' but had a strong feeling not to, and so used only Prayers and Invocations that came spontaneously. The substance of these was repeated many times, the bell being struck, the incense kindled, and the Lamen indicated.

The candles were extinguished and the prayers repeated in the dark between periods of waiting. Several times, for a fleeting instant, I became aware of a presence other than my own in the Oratory, but on attempting to examine the matter I was conscious of failure. No positive results were noted, but I am in no sense disappointed since the Divine Plan evidently does not intend that I may succeed in my design for the moment.

NB This attempt is not to be repeated for some time.

[from the archives of MC]

Then follows several other rituals, one or two with the aim: *Expansion of Cosmic Consciousness* – but most having the far more intense aim of *Peace throughout the world*. No sane individual at that time wanted anything else. He often summarised the rites as having felt unsatisfactory.

When his military service came to an end he went home to Southampton and found a job with the instrument maintenance section of the old Imperial Airways, at their Flying Boat depot at Hythe, where he worked with the Sunderland Short. After only a few months the German Army marched into Poland, war was declared, and life changed for everyone. Bill was troubled when his mentor ENH , being an Austrian, was immediately interned, but was relieved when some influential and presumably Masonic people campaigned in all the discreet corners and secured his release quite quickly. Meanwhile, all the military reservists such as he were immediately recalled, and sent off to the front.

"As a boy I had seen soldiers marching off to France with bands blaring, drums thumping, and crowds of cheering civilians lining the streets waving flags and singing patriotic songs. The contrast between that and our departure from Waterloo Station was amazing. The crowds were there, but absolutely silent and relatively still. Not a flag anywhere, or even a suspicion of a cheer. At one point some soldier climbed on top of something and yelled at them: 'For Christ's sake cheer up you miserable lot. We're not dead yet!'

After his arrival in France, where he was quartered in the little village of Bersée in the Pas de Calais area, he started keeping a diary. He found it a psychological help in adjusting to the stresses, and would make detailed pen-pictures of anything that struck him as poignant, ranging from the farm buildings they were billeted in, through the daily routine, the local cock-fights and cafés, and discussions with his French allies about 'La Guerre'. He had visions of inconsequential events that later came true, and he realised that "…what may be foreseen is often misinterpreted at the time". He tried to foretell the outcome of this 'Phoney War' through the use of divination and kept coming up with the answer of "Peace", though he seemed to put little faith in this. Despite his undoubted intuitive powers of prediction, traditional divination always eluded him, and towards the end of his life he was rather resigned to this:

> It sounds as if your politicians are as crooked as ours in a different way. Ours are getting ready to make war on Iraq any moment now, although my cards say there won't be any (which I don't believe).
> [letter to Brazilian Sangreal Sodality, October 1990]

But when the real war started, and he found himself involved in the harrowing but historically majestic retreat from Dunkirk, he had a magical experience which altered his life irrevocably, and which proved

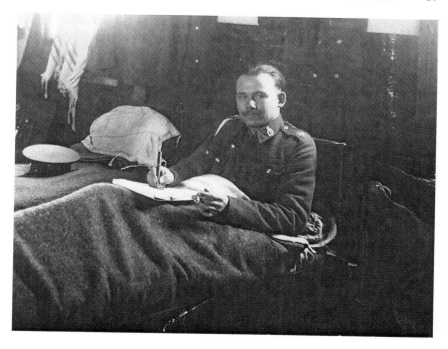

to be a soul-shattering and reconstructional experience. "In one sense I did die and another aspect of me was born..."

What happened was that they crossed the border into Belgium at 5.30am on Whit Sunday, 1940, with dull explosions being heard all around them, and an endless exodus of refugees heading in the opposite direction. He was appalled by their plight, the sheer despair on their faces. Their entire worldly goods were contained in single suitcases, sacks or bundles; the babies were clutched by their mothers and shushed and encouraged as if they were just out for a walk rather than fleeing for their lives, leaving everything behind. He got out his brandy flask with shaking hands.

"Yes, the women are the ones that suffer the most in a war. Loved men who die in battle can never be given back to them, nor will the gap in their lives ever be filled. The tragedy of it all appals me and... I find that what worries me most is this awful misery and anxiety of these women. They try not to show it, and their bravery is greater than anything I could ever manage..."

By the 19th, after various false alarms, forays and shelling incidents, they headed back into France, and started to come under regular and heavy bombing from the Luftwaffe. 11 days later after a forced march in which they abandoned anything heavy, they were at the beach, at dawn, where he saw thousands and thousands of troops scattered along the sands.

Jacobus Swart wrote how deeply moved he had been when Bill recalled that time:

If I recall correctly, he maintained that the troops were betrayed by their own officers who pulled out secretly while everybody was asleep. He depicted the slaughter of the troops the following day in such a vivid manner, that I was totally transfixed and literally experiencing what he was saying through the subconscious channel that existed between our souls. He said the noise was indescribable, there was the drone of airplanes, explosion of bombs, interspersed with the screaming and shouting of the soldiers. Bodies were being blown apart... hands, arms, legs, heads, bodies, blood all over the show! Boats – some of them quite small – were coming to the rescue, and many of them were bombed, or simply sank because they were pulled over by a number of soldiers trying to clamber aboard or being overloaded. Wherever you looked, on land, in the sea or sky, there was horror ... horror and more horror! He thought he was going to go mad, and he felt he was actually moving to the edge of insanity, which he reached and then crossed, thinking he would fall into a bottomless abyss. Instead of going insane, he found himself in an unbelievable silence. He described the silence as so total, so perfect, that the movement of this solitary little planet in space could not interrupt it. He had at that moment reached what he later described in his works as a state of Perfection, Peace and Profundity.

Bill said he turned to his friend who was with him practically throughout the war, and who appeared to have reached the same state he was in (I seem to remember Bill told me he was a Scot), and asked him if he had his chess set with him. His friend replied in the affirmative, commenting that some of the pieces may be missing, and Bill said something like: 'Oh, I thought we could have a game of chess.' I was awestruck! These two men had at that moment reached such a unique state of perfect peace in the midst of one of the worst battles of the era, that they were willing to play chess right there in that old bombshelter or whatever on the beach of Dunkirk... amidst all the fighting. He told me that from that moment on it was easy. He knew he would be fine, and you know the rest of the tale. I so badly wanted to ask him more questions at the time, but I could see that he was visibly shaken by the telling of that saga, with tears running down his cheeks, and he excused himself.

[letter to AR, 6th January 2003]

In the event, by June 1st, exhausted by the lack of food and water, constant shelling – not to mention the uncertainty caused by the complete lack of organisation – he led a foray which managed to find a dinghy floating offshore, by which means six of them rowed out to a small ship which had come as close to shore as it dared. Taken on board, and safe within the hold of the ship at last, he sank into oblivion until they reached Ramsgate.

This was, as Bill termed it, The Great Dunkirk Disaster.

But during it all, as might be imagined, there was that something else going on which he tried to explain to Jacobus nearly 50 years later. Great stress can often turn the most ordinary souls into involuntary mystics, and Bill's natural tendencies in that direction helped him plunge that little bit further into what magicians call the Greater Mysteries. His own words recalling that dreadful last night were:

"I did not understand it then, and even now it is only partly explicable. What it amounted to was a weird double-consciousness where I knew quite well what was happening on the material level, yet at the same time was experiencing something totally different in another dimension of existence. I was being told somehow that my earthly adventures were only an interlude in something greater than I was as a human person, and therefore I should not let them worry me unduly, but simply go on following the lines which would be shown me as I went along. I was not due to die here and now, but there would be a lot of work to do yet before this incarnation came to an end and another set of adventures laid out for me to experience…

"I seemed to be living two lives at once and each was diametrically opposed to the other, yet both were ME at the same time. One was an ordinary frightened human horrified at everything happening around him, and the other was a calm and almost disinterested observer watching everything that went on with mild interest so as to assess its proper value in proportion to its importance as an item of experience. It was almost as if one 'I' were looking at another and wondering why it was making such a fuss about being alive and having nasty things happen to it which were relatively unimportant when compared to this transcendent condition of consciousness…"

Although on the surface it sounds very similar to what S. described as 'interlockment' there seemed to be a clear distinction between the two states. In fact it is a common thing among mystics, this. Almost as if the Higher Self descends at crucial moments to experience first hand how things are getting on in one of its many manifestations. There really is the feel of two levels of existence which are actually one, and the discarnate portion of one's self saying: *This is what you have to learn. Now learn it.* Such Greater Mysteries are necessarily beyond intellect, beyond mere reason and logic and the abilities to describe them with mundane language. The best we can use hope for is to use simile and metaphor. The best he could manage was to add:

"In other words we have to experience hell in order to handle heaven. Humans have to be subjected to traumatic experiences which are sufficiently strong enough to alter their essential selves into entirely different types of being before they become able to deal with what might be called Divine conditions of consciousness…"

He went on to add that 'in olden days' mystics would be put through an arranged series of experiences calculated to cause such changes in normal souls, and culminate in enlightenment, "because the soul would live in a condition wherein everything seemed to consist of sheer light-energy."

For him, the nightmare of the retreat from Dunkirk was an initiation, his own personal Descent into Hell, which he felt altered his soul:

"I was altered neither for the better nor the worse, but for an entirely different direction. All that remained was to see where it would lead me…"

It led him to Cheltenham, actually. But not before he fell in love along the way.

After a brief interval at Leeds, his regiment regrouped and he finished up at a small village in Lincolnshire called Barkston. None of the men liked East Anglia, and they got the strange impression that the local population were hostile to British troops. Not fit for a return to combat, he was recruited into the Local Defence Volunteers – later renamed the Home Guard – intended as the last line of defence against invading troops.

Something happened then which affected him as deeply – almost – as the Dunkirk experience. In brief he met a woman whom he knew had meant much to him in a previous life yet who had caused him intense sorrow and been responsible for his death.

"I had many childhood memories of her and some of the circumstances as well. When I encountered her in this life she was standing in the village street bareheaded with her back to me, and yet at the very instant I saw her a profound shock seemed to hit me from head to feet. I knew beyond any doubt in my mind who it was, and acting entirely on an automatic impulse I went over and confronted her saying something like: 'You haven't changed much.' There hardly seemed any need to explain my outrageous conduct. Before long we were in close conversation explaining who we were and what we were doing..."

Bill in love, at last. This was the real thing, for which all the previous amours (not many, and not long lived or deeply felt) were just a preparation. Did it help the young man that he had started to glimpse the secrets of Time and Space, and was beginning to manipulate their energies?

Not a bit. Not one bit. When the heart leaps and the pulses race, even mighty magicians become as helpless and inept as the rest of us. He was learning to summon spirits from the vasty deep, but he hadn't a clue how best to handle this elusive little vicar's daughter from Barkston, named Alyce Thorold-Eller.

"Have you got a boyfriend?" he asked, straight out, ever the romantic.

"No," came her shy answer.

"Well you have now," he said, marvelling at what he felt inside.

Yet he confessed that although he was desperately attracted on physical levels he was also aggravated and annoyed to a corresponding degree on intellectual and mental ones. He found himself in a relationship with someone who would never answer a simple and straightforward question or deal directly with any problem arising. She made what he considered silly mysteries out of trivialities, and avoided coming to conclusions if she possibly could. "She also took a very long time to make verbal responses and was a remarkably silent person."

Poor Alyce. He must have been a difficult suitor. He knew that she had shared nothing of his interest in magic in a previous life, and was no better enthused in this one. Although he evokes her character more strongly than that of anyone except his mother, you can't help feeling sorry for her under the onslaught of this young bull. You might think the problem was that she was out of her depth, intellectually, but she could always thrash him at chess, and they even played by post just to add interest to their letters. Perhaps it is just the case that great inevitable loves which have their roots in a previous life are almost always doomed to grand and inevitable failure.

His mother, doing her chart, predicted that Alyce would make trouble all her life by surface deceits and silly subterfuges. She also chipped in with her own memories of Alyce from a previous incarnation:

"I do not think" she wrote, "that your sticky end had anything to do with Alyce or whatever her name was then. Her action spoiled your life and it spoiled mine. To be betrayed to the Inquisition was like being betrayed to the Gestapo, though it was not so bad in our country, and

I could have got you out of it. Your sticky end was caused by the fact that you would have become a black magician had you lived. In that ugly frame of mind and hating the Church as you did with all that force, it was just as well that you were bumped off. You tried to make another woman pay for her folly and so that ill-treated woman stabbed you to death." She, his mother, was the ill-treated woman in question.

Bill's own strongest past-life memories were of a terrific storm-scene between himself, Alyce, and a frightened priest who kept waving a crucifix. She had stupidly betrayed his connection with what were then known as the 'Forbidden Arts' to her confessor, who in turn had informed the Inquisition. Told that the agents were on their way to 'question' him, he naturally feared the very worst. Most of the dialogue took place between himself and the priest, while Alyce sat quietly to one side. He remembered raging and shouting about every accusation while she sat silently, twisting and twisting some soft material between her fingers. This simple action had enraged him for some idiotic reason, and in the end he managed to escape from his captors with only seconds to spare.

Forgiveness is a difficult art at the best of times, but given the fact that she betrayed him to an organisation like the Inquisition, which tortured and murdered for the love of God, then it would have needed a heart larger than Bill's to achieve it.

Of course memories of past lives are always problematic. The obvious objections are reasonable enough: (projections from the unconscious, wish-fulfilment, ancestral memories, etc etc) but the fact is that all real magicians learn to discriminate between those mere pictures in the head which are little better than the flotsam and jetsam of the unconscious, and those true memories of previous lives. Despite the snide but understandable comment that the occult world is filled with Cleopatras, the reality is quite different. The present authors have, over many years, known a great number of *real* magicians, and not one of them has ever claimed such a thing; not one of them has even regarded the question of past lives as being particularly important.

It didn't help Bill's uneasy courtship that his health had been steadily deteriorating. He lost weight rapidly, and with it his strength. His powers of concentration began to fail, and with that came all the symptoms of what he called a 'nervous breakdown', but we should probably call today 'Post Traumatic Stress Disorder'. Clearly, Dunkirk had taken a lot out of him. After being assessed by an army medical specialist he found himself rejected from further military service under the blanket clause of 'failing to fulfil requirements of physical fitness'.

He had mixed feelings about being discharged in such a manner, but a test pilot friend of ENH helped him find a job with a small firm engaged on aviation instrument maintenance work at Chester. It is worth detailing this because there has been a persistent rumour that Bill spent part of the War working for Military Intelligence. He said this quite specifically to several close friends. If he had been part of the Intelligence services, he would have had to take an oath not to speak of his activities that was legally binding for many decades, and morally so for a lifetime, in his eyes.

Even this might not be of particular note, but the fact is that a number of influential occultists at that time really were involved with that shadowy department: Cecil Williamson, who is regarded as one of the founders of the post-War Wiccan movement; Teddy Maltby, his superior, who was a senior adept within Dion Fortune's group; Charles Seymour, who had worked as Dion Fortune's priest, and who was himself a major influence on the Pagan Revival; Dennis Wheatley, who wrote many runaway best-sellers about Black and White Magic, some of which were turned into dreadful movies by Hammer Horror Films. ("Didn't you know that Dennis Wheatley was a little shit?" asked Bill rhetorically, more than once. "Couldn't stand the man!") And then there was Ellic Howe who wrote the first full history of the Golden Dawn, and who was involved in Black Propaganda – possibly aimed at concealing from the Nazis that the Allies had cracked the Enigma code, and were now reading all the German secrets as they were transmitted.

But certainly Seymour, Maltby and many others had been actively involved in magic of their own, aimed at counteracting the malign energies of the Nazi occultists. Just as the CIA had recruited psychics in the 1970s and 80s to practice 'Remote Viewing' on Soviet interests, and tried to find ways of using mind-power to influence enemy politicians, there was a hard core of British occultists during World War II (most of whom had Masonic backgrounds) who were involved in much the same thing against Himmler's own magicians. This is not fantasy; this really happened. The CIA's aim with the remote viewers of project 'Sun Streak', which operated from Fort Meade, was to: '…train individuals to transcend time and space, to view persons, places and things remote in time and space, and to gather intelligence information on them.' [*David Morehouse, Michael Joseph, 1996*] In a far less formal way, these were also the aims of the British occultists. Moreover Seymour spent some time in the Chester/Liverpool area advising a department there about the various occult and Masonic groups that German prisoners might have been involved in. He was almost certainly responsible for securing ENH's release.

Now it may be that Bill really did do nothing more than check instruments on aeroplanes, but… there is still an awful lot to find out about this very odd time.

Strangely enough Alyce found herself a job in that area also, and as they were almost engaged, they were able to spend a lot of time together. Or they might have done, if Alyce's father, the Vicar of Barkston, hadn't written to Christine Gray to ask some awkward and impertinent questions about her son – in particular, *why* had he left the Army? This provoked in Bill the sort of outrage that everyone who knew the man came to recognise. Bill once said that when he was a young boy in Canada he learned never to worry what others might think about him. This was true, but only to an extent. They could *think* whatever they liked, as long as they said nothing, for he could often construe simple disagreement as a direct personal attack, to which he would respond with all guns blazing. If he never managed to fire a shot in anger on the beaches of Dunkirk, he was to fire whole salvos against people in his personal wars of later years. Not surprisingly his prospective father-in-law's letter "enraged and provoked me beyond all belief. It was the underhandedness and the behind the back approaches which affected me so badly." He tackled Alyce about it, launching a terrible tirade. The concept of 'dishonourable conduct' reared its head, as it often did with Bill in later years. Two days later Alyce's mother appeared and hurled every accusation at him that she could think of, while her daughter sat completely silent… twisting a handkerchief in her hands. Twisting that damn same piece of cloth in the same way that she had done centuries ago. Twisting it so stupidly and maddeningly that it made him want to explode.

"The sight of that brought everything into the finest focus. All this had happened before… Once again I had the extraordinary sensation of living on two levels at once and not quite sure what to do on either."

What he did do the next day was dump her.

It was Crowley who wrote: 'The planes are separate'. That is, it is possible to achieve high spiritual wisdom without any of this filtering down and influencing the personality. Even the biggest fool or worst drunkard could still mediate divinity. So it is not surprising that a real magician should be as helpless when it comes to love as anyone else. After all, love is the most powerful of all the energies. It is also true, though, that when you start to knock on the gates of heaven, it is always – *always* – the gates of hell which open first. If Bill could be associated with any one sphere on the Tree of Life, then it is that of Geburah, or Mars. If he had to learn the positive qualities of this sphere, such as strength, courage, power, justice, then first he had to know what it was like to feel powerless, afraid, weak, and cursed with bad karma.

He certainly went through that then. As he had come to realise, it is life itself which provides the *real* initiations into real magic. Alyce cut him to pieces; it took a long time before, on very hurt and human levels, he got over the whole experience. He had many girlfriends after that – especially when he took up amateur dramatics – but his first real love meant failure and betrayal, and a young woman twisting a handkerchief while his life fell apart.

So he found himself at the end of the War emotionally bloodied and somewhat bowed, and in a temporary job with the Air Ministry in Gloucestershire. Although he was still painfully thin, he bought an old bicycle which he called 'Horace' and slowly, weakly, started to explore the surrounding countryside. It helped to strengthen and ultimately heal him.

"There was much to be said for cycling as a discipline of its own. It is after all only an extension of walking, and this has always been known to stimulate the thinking process. At any rate I am certain that my cycling customs led to strengthening my contacts with Nature at first hand, which taught me so many things I would otherwise never have learned or maybe even dreamed about."

He is being coy. What he meant was that he explored ancient sites – stone circles, hill forts, old churches, isolated standing stones, ponds and wells – and came to realise that the land itself is alive, and could teach him, that the countryside was brimming with magic. He no longer had quite such a yearning for grand temples filled with robed adepts who offered splendid ceremonies which could illuminate the humble neophyte. Instead, he could get on his bike, ride into the countryside and commune with orders of beings and near-forgotten energies that have always been there. Of course, to some degree, everyone in the New Age business realises that now. But in those days only a very few souls were privy to this secret knowledge of the Earth.

We owe that bicycle a great deal.

CHAPTER 7
Quit the Night, and Enter the Day!

"I shall [continue my Work] a lot better where I'm going. Don't worry about me, you've got yours to come yet and much more will depend on that than you could guess. You'll get no good out of it for yourself, but others will benefit more than you will ever know. This life is rather like a relay race where the next runner picks up the baton from the last one and carries on. Well you're the next one along the line, so take up the rod I'm passing you and bear it as far as you can go before you have to pass it along yourself, and hope it goes into good hands..."

ENH's last words to William Gray

When you start to work 'Earth Magic' – and Bill most assuredly did – you become aware that places seem to have powers and personalities of their own. We are often drawn to quite unlikely places and find that they become a crucial part of our existence in ways that have little or nothing to do with bricks and mortar, marriage and mortgage, or countryside idylls.

It is nothing to do with historic 'Power Centres' whose layers of myth can speak to the soul, but possibly something within us that is akin to a homing instinct. The most unlikely places can commune with us, or call us to them. Bill, on his long bicycle rides, freewheeled into Cheltenham one day and virtually never left it.

In his days the town had a reputation for housing retired Indian Army officers and Civil Servants, and for being a curious collection of people practising extreme snobbishness, gentility and social hypocrisy. Something of the atmosphere still remains. Here he:

- had several girlfriends who helped him over the Grand Passion with Alyce, though none of whom, alas, shared his passion for the esoteric;
- took up amateur dramatics, where he tackled several minor roles, and eventually that of pantomime Dame;

- worked at a couple of jobs (one as charge hand on a clock assembly line) and eventually qualified as a chiropodist, in which profession he worked for the rest of his life;
- learned to his astonishment that he had a natural talent for automatic writing, accurately channelling the thoughts of a dead priest who had had something of a reputation for spiritual healing;
- paid a final visit to ENH who was dying of cancer. Neither of them said goodbye, because both knew they would meet up again one day;
- bought the house on Bennington Street where he lived and worked, and in the basement of which he built his very first temple;
- got a cat named Selina with whom he had a telepathic bond...

Cheltenham, a phoney spa town in the heart of Gloucestershire, was the making of Bill. Whatever telluric energies flowed beneath the soil there flowed through him too. His psychism developed, sharpened, expanded. His inner life started to take fire. The war-battered figure of Bill Gray started to fill out into the persona of William G. Gray, the noted Qabalist, magician, and thoroughly awkward individual. Not quite an old sod as yet, but getting there.

He was in Cheltenham paying court to a young woman called Lavender when she excitedly told him about the atom bomb dropped on Hiroshima, thus forcing the Japanese to surrender and end the War. Instead of sharing her delight he went cold inside. The cold that all good seers get at such moments. "My god," he said, "you don't realise what you've just said. That could mean the beginning of our end. God help us all!"

Throughout his life he maintained that, on occult levels, the atom bombs created a crack between the Worlds which allowed energies and entities from other dimensions to access ours – not all of whom had our evolutionary interests at heart. He was greatly concerned at one point in the early 1970s by the books of Kenneth Grant, who seemed to describe a system of Magic that actively worked with these dark beings:

In point of fact the book [*The Magical Revival*] is one of the *nastiest* and most seriously spiritually damaging works printed in this century. And NOT on account of the sex-themes. Something far deeper and dirtier than any simplicity of sex could ever be. The sex is purely a 'lead-in' to the *really* vicious stuff, much as relatively harmless 'pot' may grease the slide to soul-destroying heroin and the like. Where the truly 'deep evil' comes in, lies with persuading people to abrogate or 'hand over' their own spiritual integrity

(and consequently every power and potential in them) into the grasping clutches of 'entities' whose interests are quite opposite to our best and highest possibilities as humans…
[letter to AR, 14th January 1973]

But these perceptions were some years ahead. At very least he was acutely aware, in the post-Hiroshima years, that the times they were a-changing.

"All that was once distant and frighteningly secret was coming out in the open and dancing around for us all to see if they wanted to, which relatively few did. Dion Fortune was dead at a much earlier age than might be expected [*she died in January 1946, aged 55*] and occultism per se was becoming a commonplace of conversation. The good old *Occult Review* had died also, and popular magazines plus a lot of amateur publications were trying to take its place not very successfully. The pre-Hippy period was upon us with a great deal of psychic disturbance. The effects of nuclear energy were responsible for a lot more than destruction of human lives and property on earth. Many changes had taken place on deep psychic levels of genetic inheritance which will take more than a few generations to estimate the results in terms of alterations to human intelligence and awareness, to say nothing of physical health and well-being."

At that time, too, his mother took to her death bed and amused herself in her last days by watching the others in the hospital ward taking their turns to die. When she received news that her husband had been found dead of natural causes she was not particularly upset, and even declined to go to the funeral. She was probably so close to the Otherside that she no longer needed mundane connections.

"When I visited Mother in hospital after [ENH's] death I did not need to tell her. She already knew and said she envied him his freedom and was looking forward to her own release. She told me she always knew who would be next in the ward to die because of a strange phenomenon she saw. About twenty four hours prior to death, clouds of luminous energy would appear to be emitted from that person almost like a large shower of sparks which rose above their beds and dissipated in the atmosphere. This would continue for several minutes, gradually becoming weaker and less visible until it disappeared altogether after dying down to a small expiring trickle. No one else could see this of course, but Mother took it for granted she was seeing the Life-force of that individual being withdrawn and reabsorbed into its natural sphere of origin. The person themselves would die within hours of that incident. Once, Mother swore she had seen the Angel of Death coming for someone in a bed opposite, and she had begged him to take her as well, but he had smiled sympathetically and explained that it was not time yet, though he promised she would not be forgotten. What impressed her most was his extremely kind and loveable face. She felt it was someone she could entirely trust."

What an extraordinary woman! Bill would never have understood that she came across as far more interesting than ENH. Certainly she seemed to have as much insight into *real* magic as the Austrian did, who is merely evoked through his ideas – which often seem quite thin. Often, reading about Christine Gray's own 'other' life, you can't help but wish that *she* had written her life story also. Bill evoked her as a living being, a larger-than-life individual who was proud, selfish, witty, non-judgemental, determined and strong. In the anecdotes, snippets and pen-pictures he used to describe her (only a few of which we have used here) he makes the readers wish that they had known her, and want to learn more.

He could do that for his own mother but never for himself. He tried so hard to keep his own personality out of his writing that in all the books he wrote the personal pronoun never appeared. Even when he described that extremely important bicycle trip to visit and commune with the Rollright Stones he never once evoked himself and said "*I* did this..." or "*I* felt that..." But perhaps that was an attitude common to his generation, which saw what had happened in Germany when the personality cult got out of hand, and a small man with a silly moustache was turned into a demi-god. In the multi-media world of today, however, it can often seem that personalities are more important than their message, and that is not always a bad thing. The personality can act like a vehicle, like the Egyptian ka, and can carry life far more effectively than mere words. He never seemed to realise that his heroine Dion Fortune had no such hesitation about hyping herself in all sorts of clever ways. She became the cult figure that she did more because of the strong personality which comes through her writing than her actual philosophies – excellent though these are. In fact, to use a magical term, she created a 'Telesmic Image' of herself that others used to link with the energies that lay behind her. Bill certainly used her image. But he never went any way toward creating one for himself.

When both parents die, the offspring (no matter how grey-haired), has the oddest feeling that he is not a child any more, and really must grow up. In Bill's case the Wonderchild now had to evolve into the Priest-King.

He was helped in no small degree by the purchase of 14 Bennington Street which, being centrally located and on ground level, would be ideal for his chiropodist surgery, and contained two bedrooms upstairs plus a basement of two rooms. One of these rooms would be his workshop, while the other – he knew beyond doubt – would be ideal for his temple. "And best of all the house felt 'right' somehow from the moment I stepped into it. Something inside of me said 'GO' and so I went."

In fact, apart from some later trips to America and South Africa, he never actually went anywhere. Outwardly there is a sense in which he never moved an inch for the rest of his life, yet inwardly he travelled very far indeed. If his business was never wildly prosperous, it at least provided an adequate living. It was having a basement temple which told him that he could now, without excuses, start practising the sort of Magic that had been brewing away for all his life. Even though he knew that the *real* temples are inside the soul, the actual fact of being able to earth his ideas and put his aptitude for ritual and ceremony into private expression gave his inner work an enormous boost.

It was at this period that he made his first visit to Glastonbury, in company with his girlfriend at that time who bore the odd name of Tim, who suffered from chronic intestinal ill-health. When he climbed the Tor he experienced: "…a considerable influx of psychic energy and a strange exhilaration which seemed to open me up inside myself as it were to much wider views than those I saw around myself from that elevated place. My first experience of the Tor in this life was another unforgettable one. When it was time to leave I knew I had been there before…"

When? How? This is when you want to grab him by the throat and shake him. His autobiography aimed to tell everything yet in many ways said nothing. At least nothing that is important to those of us who might want to soak up his magical persona. Although he went into great and unnecessary detail about Tim's physical problems, and how they were – truly – miraculously cured by drinking of the waters from Chalice Well, he said nothing about who he may have been in his past life in or around the Tor, although he was quite happy to tantalise. He went into great detail about the strange bond he enjoyed with his mind-reading, future-predicting cat at that time, named Selina, but gave nothing which might add accurate substance to his own personality, leaving us all to project things he probably would not have liked. And what about the time that his wife-to-be Bobbie later mentioned, when he exorcised a very malign entity that seemed to be clinging to the top of the Tor? That would have made a wonderful story in his own words.

Bill's home, 14 Bennington Street, Cheltenham

As it is, we have confirmation of this from The Druid Order itself who have retained a letter he wrote to them on 3rd July 1961:

> It would appear that he was interested in having The Druid Order perform its Summer Solstice Ceremony at Glastonbury Tor, as he was not happy with the 'rather unholy power' that he noted manifested there briefly at midsummer. 'It occurs to me that the Druid ceremony would most <u>adequately deal</u> with such influences which others than myself have observed independently.' Of the Druid Order Ceremony he writes 'It is obviously composed by some person or persons having a deep knowledge of Ritual working, and considerable

appreciation of sheer dramatic and poetic beauty. I note that it has been most carefully safeguarded so that it cannot possibly be used for even the slightest purpose of evil, which is a very valuable point indeed.'

That the Druid Order might perform a ceremony at midsummer at Glastonbury Tor was agreed in principle, though of course, not to be held on the exact date of the Stonehenge ceremonies which was the Summer Solstice, but this was dependent on William Gray organising local support at Glastonbury for the event. This idea did not mature however.

[letter from Jennifer Maughan of The Druid Order, 11th February 2003]

In the event, according to Bobbie, he did it himself.

Despite the minor miracle involving Tim he parted company with her shortly after, and during one Easter Bank Holiday period he went to a fancy dress party organised by the Science Fiction Group he had joined. Among the guests were an attractive young woman with strong occult interests who in later life wrote as E.A. St George, and her close friend Bobbie. The latter was wearing a costume vaguely resembling a Greek Warrior, while he was dressed as Richard the Third. The pair felt an immediate attraction, heightened by their joint belief that this King Richard had been one of the most misrepresented characters in British History.

Roberta F. Loach was a formidable woman, entirely self-educated, who had taught herself Latin and Greek before Bill appeared. She was a match for him in every way and every level. Toward the end of his life he once pointed out, with no trace of ire and lots of amused reflection, that Bobbie had never read a single book that he had written. She considered herself a real Celt, because of her Breton name and her parents' Scottish background, although she was actually born in Walthamstow at 10.56 am on the 25th June, 1921. A storm raged outside at the time. She was the seventh child in her family, and believed that she had 'come back' into the world very quickly, as throughout her childhood she had had dreams of having been an Army officer in World War I. Beyond that, historically, she also had a morbid fascination for the White Tower in London, and could never get over her irrational fear of spiral staircases.

Magically, she felt especially drawn to the mighty Celtic figure of Gwyn ap Nudd. On asking her about this once Bill interrupted in his usual way and explained that it meant, literally, *Light, son of Darkness,* adding: "It's just the old Celtic name for a Power of Eternal Alteration…" and went on to give a brief lecture on the derivation of many aspects of modern magic from ancient shamanism. However, his interpretations aside, the old Horned God of the West was a very potent figure for Bobbie and she too had the unconscious gift for teaching others in subliminal ways. 'Gwyn gives, but he also takes away in equal measure' she said, at different times to both of the present writers, and triggered off a major and memorable change in the psyche of each despite the apparently superficial nature of the actual words she used. One of her great friends after the war was the hereditary witch Paddy Slade, and both had served together in the Air Force without realising each other's esoteric interests. In many ways, acting below the surface, Gwyn ap Nudd helped draw the pair of them ever closer to the rebirth of Witchcraft in Britain.

"She too was interested in esoteric subjects and very concerned that the special mysticism of the West should attract the attention it deserved among Occidentals, in preference to all the imported occultism from the Orient. She had made a special study of Celtic mythology. ... Again there came the certainty that we had known each other in previous existences but probably as close comrades in something like the Mithraic or similar circles. There was a positive sense of deep bonding between us that went back a long way though definite details were missing."

In fact, as she confessed later in a letter to Alan Richardson: "My impression (shared by her) is that we were once in the 20th Legion together, but we feel there were other occasions as well." *[7 January 1986]*

There was none of this *I was a High Priest* nonsense. It is a sad fact that so many people in magic who can wave a stick often tend to call themselves 'High' Priest or Priestess, even though no-one has ever seen a 'Low' Priest. Quite apart from the fact that Bobbie in this life was a very down to earth woman, in any Mithraic past life she would certainly have been male, because it was a soldier's religion. In typical style Bill gave some insight into the world of those who followed Mithras in the Roman Army, taken in no small part from his own far memories:

It was rather a Masonic thing in a way, and strictly speaking a sort of Friendly Society with sick-benefits, burial fees and all kinds of social insurance available to members depending on rank, etc. It wasn't so much religious as plain humanitarian in nature, and had it been inclusive of women... it would have been the popular socio-religious cult of the West instead of Christianity. It didn't have what I would have called real priests. Above a certain grade about every officer took their turn at ceremonial duties, but in order to belong in the first place you had to be reliable and of proved honesty and integrity. The mythos behind the cult [was that of] the young warrior-hero who provided food for his kinsfolk at the cost of his own life, all linked with

Blood. One might call it the very essence of esotericism. Virtually our oldest form of Sacred Kin(g)ship. In Mithraism symbolised by the Blood-baptism of the tauroboleum. Can't you hear the controversy between the Mithraics and the Christians concerning what the former would call the *real* Baptism with genuine blood, while the latter were satisified with the weaker substitution of water... Mind you, that Blood-initiation with a whole bull was a hell of an expensive business, and God alone knows how long a Lodge had to save up in order to make one possible. The initiate was supposed to pay for a lot of it, and of course the whole Group had beefburgers for ages afterwards...
[letter to AR, 13th January 1988]

Apart from picking up traces of her past life, Bobbie also developed an unexpected interest in astrology, and although she had all of Bill's mother's books on the subject, she also began to acquire her own more modern ones and started a course of study with an accredited school. More, she was quite convinced that someone was instructing her during her sleeping hours, and strongly suspected Christine Gray of doing this.

Bill was clearly besotted. At last he had found someone to share what he still called his 'esoteric interests', and he snapped her up at once.

They were married in short order, and spent their honeymoon in Glastonbury.

Was it a match made in Heaven? Her best friend Elizabeth A. St George (the pen name of Sandra West) thought not. Her womanly senses twitched right from the start:

Bill and Bobbie did most of their courting at my flat in North End House. It was something of a whirlwind romance and in due course they held their wedding reception at my flat. I was a little uneasy when Bobby produced her 2nd-hand engagement and wedding ring but Bill insisted that these rings had the right 'vibes'. Personally I'd have thought that a new wedding ring would be more desirable...
[letter to MC, December 2002]

She also felt that Bill kept Bobbie short of money throughout their married life, and described her friend's dismay in the later years when she found out that her husband's bank was actually rather healthy. Bill had always told her that his books just didn't earn money and while Sandra felt this was nonsense, it was probably true. The plain fact is that books on magic just don't sell. It was more likely to have been inherited from his parents. Regardless of the source, however, he seems to have been less

Bill and Bobbie

than generous to his wife, and begrudging of what money she did spend on herself. It seems that even great magicians can be tight-arses with their money.

Even so, best friends though she was with Bobbie, Sandra came under Bill's spell in her own way. She makes the comment:

> He was a fascinating talker and I learned a lot from listening to him. He taught me Qabalistic ritual. He put me through a number of ceremonies. I acquired my cup, rod and sword from him although he had some reservations about a woman doing a sword degree but he seemed impressed by the result. …
>
> Bill and I worked closely together for a while. Although he did not drive, I could provide a car and on a number of occasions we dashed cross country

to bust up black magic groups. This led to some wildly exotic rumours about how a hundred bishops beat up black magicians with thuribles and croziers but there were only two of us – honest! And no, we didn't beat anyone up. We arrived quietly, did our pre-planned exorcism and drove off mysteriously. If someone wanted to call us the Hunting Lodge of the Solar Wallop – that was their name. They invented it! We were just a magician and one apprentice trying to thwart the powers of darkness. We happened to be pretty good at our work but each time we went out on that job, my heart was in my mouth in case something went wrong.

[letter to MC, 12th December 2002]

If anything was calculated to help create a legend, then that will do him no harm at all!

But Bill was married at last, with all the ups and downs that a normal married life contains. He was stable. His job was secure. He had a home. He had also learned that if you persist, and work at it right hard, then there comes a time in everyone's magical career when things start to take off and become realities, instead of a mass of exciting ideas which exist as potentials. The dream-magic becomes a waking magic; things happen. This was the time in Bill's life when his 'Clamour before the Gates' as he termed it, was finally heard. Quite apart from Bobbie and Sandra, all sorts of people appeared in his life.

"An extremely interesting character we met at Avalon was a once close friend of Dion Fortune called Mary Gilchrist. She had inherited from DF the army hut at the foot of the Tor which they had put up in a small piece of property named Chalice Orchard, and used for ceremonial purposes as well as accommodation. Mary was a Yorkshire woman who had been a professional medium, and while valuing her psychic abilities Fortune would not allow her to make a living with them if she joined the Inner Light Society which DF had founded as a vehicle for her own teachings. As a kind of compensation for abrogating her professional status and devoting her time to the Society's demands on her, DF had made her the Warden of this dwelling and its environs. Seeing that this was all the personal property which she possessed, Mary had made considerable sacrifices for her faith.

"There was nothing especially 'mystical' about Mary. She was a hard-headed woman of maybe sixty odd who dealt with everything in the most practical possible way. She was also an excellent cook, and would invite us for meals which we always enjoyed. We discussed esoteric matters at great depth, and it was she who really led to my eventual link-up with the

Society which she warned me had changed very greatly since Fortune's death, yet she still belonged with it although she attended the London meetings no more. She said DF had become more and more imperious as she aged, and had almost a persecution complex concerning a mysterious 'Black Lodge' she was convinced meant to prevent her from disseminating the vital esoteric secrets she guarded, even if they had to kill her. This is actually a not uncommon phenomenon among dedicated occultists who boost their beliefs in their own importance by imagining some Evil Entity is determined to destroy them because of the threat they constitute to its influence. I did not pay much attention to this however. Certainly Mary had no such illusions about herself. We would meet her again on several more occasions, and as soon as I returned to Cheltenham I sent away for the most recent Inner Light information."

He also met her cousin, Robbie, whom Bill rated as one of the best psychics he had ever met – which must be saying something. Shortly after they had been introduced the older man suddenly reached out and touched Bill's throat at the exact spot where he had been having a lot of quite serious trouble, health-wise. "Don't worry about that" he advised, apropos of nothing. 'It'll clear up by itself in the end.' This was the 'Uncle' Robbie who had examined the badly aching tooth of Dion Fortune and advised immediate medical attention. In fact, what he apparently said to the others in her group was: 'Christ! She's had it!' The ailing priestess died shortly afterward of leukaemia.

Meanwhile, he was greatly intrigued by the application form to join the Society of the Inner Light.

"When it arrived I was particularly struck by its impersonal and indifferent style which implied: *We don't care if you're interested in us or not, but if you are this is what we expect of you, and if you aren't prepared to do this then go to hell in your own handbasket.* A distinctly unfriendly approach with no attempt whatever to win your confidence and trust. The fees requested seemed exceptionally reasonable, and the preliminary course of training leading up to initiation appeared perfectly normal and rational, so I decided to take it and see what happened."

Well, this was just the sort of group that Bill had dreamed about: uncompromising, uncommercial, unglamorous, with an underlying ethic of self-responsibility and hard work. He would fall out with them of course, as he did with almost everyone, but not before sparks had flown in both directions.

And it was at Glastonbury that he met the old rascal-guru Wellesley Tudor-Pole, author of *The Silent Road* and *A Man Seen Afar* which purported to be 'far memories' of the life of Jesus. WTP, as he was universally known, was also responsible for the 'Silent Minute' during World War II: at the striking of Big Ben on the radio news at nine o' clock, millions sent up a prayer. For sixty seconds the entire nation was concentrated on a single purpose (peace through victory), synchronised by a radio time-signal. It was a very powerful weapon on both psychological and spiritual levels, as the Germans themselves realised. Bill and Bobbie first met him coming down the steep slope of the Tor waving his stick cheerfully and greeting them: 'Ah Good morning! Wonderful presence up there this morning.' He was over eighty then, Bill noted admiringly, for the Tor has frequently been too much even for relatively fit youngsters.

In his later years WTP also inaugurated what was called the Upper Room at his house St Michael's Lodge near the Well. This was simply but symbolically an upstairs room which was quite empty except for a long plain wooden table with twelve matching stools and a single upright chair at one end. There was nothing on the table but a loaf of common bread on a platter and an earthenware jug of wine. Hanging on the wall in a glass case was a millefiore decorated shallow bowl with a strange story.

"Apparently in pre-war days a local man had taken a holiday at a monastery in Italy, and purchased this as a souvenir without any special intention. When he returned he had a very distinct dream in which be was told to throw this dish which had no very great commercial value into St Bridget's Well at Beckery, say nothing of this to anyone, and that would bring him luck. He took no notice of this, but after he had had the same dream three nights running he thought there might be something in it and obeyed the impulse. Beckery Well with its Saint Bridget associations was only some four or five feet deep at the time, and has since been filled in. Some time after this incident, a Mrs Sandeman (of Sandeman's Port) who was keenly interested in the esoteric side of Avalon had a very distinct dream to search St Bridget's Well for the Holy Grail. She too had the same dream on several occasions, and eventually she confided this to a friend, and they both went to the Well wearing their bathing costumes and grubbed around in the muddy bottom. Presently with an equivalent shriek of Eureka! Mrs S emerged bearing the Holy Dish in her hands and started a sensational rumour that at last the Grail had been brought back to the world.

"The moment it was seen by any reasonable person however, the impossibility of a relatively modern artefact being the genuine Grail was too painfully obvious. In any case the story soon reached the local papers and the original owner came to acknowledge his part of the proceedings.

Yet the dreams themselves were quite authentic and there was certainly no collusion between Mrs Sandeman and anyone else. No one ever explained that away. There was always a legend that Joseph of Arimathea had brought the cup of the Last Supper to Britain with him and concealed it in a well at Avalon. Beyond that there is no indication of exactly where such a priceless relic might rest if indeed it still exists as a literal object..."

That is an accurate account of the well-known story. It would have been wonderful to have Bill psychometrise the ersatz Grail but the plain fact is that he saw through it at once, and made no judgement about the genuinely odd circumstances around its concealment and discovery. One thing it did get him thinking about, however, was the true nature of that Holy Grail which occupies so much of esoteric lore in the West. To him, it was really a message for Mankind: *Strive for the impossible as long as you live, and that will make Life meaningful for you!* "It is the questing itself which is important," he added. "The constant search for something just beyond immediate reach... Constantly achieving the idea, yet never the actuality it indicates... So for Western European people the Holy Grail might be termed the X factor of our lives, or a suitable symbol of whatever we are looking for to justify ourselves. We might almost call this a Selfsearch for one's own individual identity."

He did eventually find his own Grail, but that was a few years later, in South Africa.

And as he continued to selfsearch for his own identity, he came upon the Druids. In fact he joined the 'Friends of the Druid Order' in Feb/March 1962, which was an organisation which The Druid Order ran for a few years for those interested in attending public ceremonies and meetings, but who did not wish to become initiated members. His membership lapsed, but was renewed again in 1967.

"Meanwhile I had got [the Seasonal Rituals] going in London with a small circle of people who offered the use of their houses for this purpose. Some of them became known in occult circles. We certainly enjoyed ourselves celebrating the Seasons in our own fashion according to the scripts I had authored. We eventually congregated mostly at the home of a leading Druid official whom we knew as Dezzie, or familiarly as Dizzy Dezzie because of the many foolish things he would do."

This was Desmond Bourke, archivist at the British Museum, whom Bill felt belonged to just about everything it was possible to join in the open occult market. Apart from being a a member of the Ancient Druid Order he was Grand Secretary for the Societas Rosicruciana in Anglia (known invariably as the Soc Ros), a 'Sar' in the Church of the Holy Redeemer, a Knight Templar, Martinist, and belonged to various Witch covens. The difficulty was actually *not* to know him, if you were involved in the esoteric in any way.

One of the 'foolish things' he often did was invite unexpected guests to their gatherings, without anyone's previous knowledge or consent:

"Once he did this with Hans Holzer the American journalist who wrote it all up afterwards quite inaccurately in a section of his book entitled *British Witchcraft*. Subsequently a facetious friend put on an entirely phoney 'Witch-Rite' for his benefit in which they wore Halloween costumes to enact an absolutely inaccurate mish-mash which they solemnly claimed all sorts of spurious authenticity for. Holzer fell for the performance hook line and sinker and duly included the experience in his next book, since when I have doubted many accounts of professional hack writers. Yet had someone suggested introducing curious non-members into his Masonic meetings, Dezzie would have been horrified.

"Dezzie's Druid movement had been split between two leaders, one of which was keen on Oriental philosophy and esotericism, while the other section which he supported was under the direction of a Scot known as Dr Maughan who was sometimes referred to as 'Hail Smiling Morn' or just 'Smilin' because of his dry Scottish wit and outgoing nature. No one quite knew what he was supposed to be a doctor of, but homeopathy was the general guess. He was then approaching seventy and living with a very much younger mistress who had an incredible gift for cooking and producing the most appetising eatables for the innumerable people who visited them. He also had a collection of the weirdest drinks he freely dispensed on every occasion. He had various Winchester jars in different cupboards around the house into which he would pour haphazardly all the spare drinks left over from his latest party. Drink left in any glass or bottle would go into the nearest jar regardless of what it was. Sometimes he would have a casual sip himself and then decide what might improve the flavour. He would lick his lips thoughtfully and say quietly 'I fancy yon could do wi' a wee drop of brandy.' Then in would go about half a bottle of the stuff. It could be anything from the best brandy to the cheapest plonk. When he had a whole jar full of drink he would offer it to casual guests who had not been warned in advance. Those who knew watched those who didn't with interest and amusement."

Maughan, who was head of the Order from 1964-76, does indeed seem to have been one of the great characters of the occult movement, a Trickster figure who seemed incapable of telling the truth about anything:

Philip Carr-Gomm kindly sent us the following from his biography of Ross Nichols:

Although he referred to himself as Dr Maughan, the origin of his doctorate is uncertain: Bryce Bond in his tribute to Maughan, *A Touch of Alchemy*, says he obtained it from the Sorbonne in France, but he also says that Maughan was 'one of the teachers of Helena Blavatsky, the founder of Theosophy, and Aleister Crowley before the latter embarked on the left hand path.' Blavatsky died in 1891 – before Maughan was born. Peter Morrell, in his internet essay on Maughan , says '[regarding] his alleged Doctor of Science in Biochemistry: Some people say it was from London University's School of Hygiene and Tropical Medicine, others say he got it in Mexico. On my request, London University have checked all their postgraduate records from 1925-1976 and there is no record of any doctorate for a Thomas Lackenby Maughan'.

In talking about Maughan's past, Morrell says: 'He is reputed to have had six brothers and sisters, though I can find no trace of them in Births Registers. He [joined] the Royal Navy in c1917 ... It is said that he went to fight in the Spanish Civil War c1936 and 'spent several years there fighting fascism' ... He was in Naval Intelligence during WW2 and was also a tank commander at some point in WW2 in Glasgow ... He met John Da Monte in N. Africa in WW2, who was also working for British Intelligence and keen to learn homoeopathy ... It should come as no surprise, therefore, for us to learn that Maughan is rumoured to have spent many years travelling, both in the Near East and in the Orient. He had studied with gurus in India and the Himalayas, with Sufi Dervishes in Turkey and Afghanistan and he had been highly instrumental – reputedly – in getting the Dalai Lama safely out of Tibet and down into India in 1959, following the Chinese invasion. He also travelled in Central America and Australia, where some of his relatives live. Maybe some of his students believed these stories. They were certainly meant to. They added to his credibility, authority and mystique. Are they True? No-one seems to know; the facts always seem very vague and shrouded in mystery of some kind' .

Who could fail to enjoy the company of someone like this? Despite Bill's later tendency to detest a wide variety people for what he felt was their 'pathological lying', he actually had a lot of time and respect for at least a couple of individuals (Robert Cochrane is the other) who seemed incapable of telling the truth!

"I attended several Druid festivals whereat Maughan presided, once as the 'Distinguished Stranger' at Stonehenge, which is part of their symbolism. Although the present Druids go back no further than a couple of centuries and Stonehenge itself was nothing to do with our original Druids at all, the good Doctor discussed many of his ideas about earlier fertility customs with me. With a wicked twinkle in his eye he opined that in previous times it had been the solemn duty of well-born men to copulate with complacent females as often as they could on ceremonial occasions. In that way only might the finest genetic strains prevail among the people. Queues of willing women would wait for the privilege of being served by the priapic priests of the Druid faith. 'Ye had tae spread the seed, d'ye see? Ye had tae spread the seed among the lassies.' He was a rather delightful old Druid…"

Distinguished Stranger. That was nice. The druids knew he was different. They knew that here was a real magician. And it was quite clear that, at last, Bill was having fun. Normal, healthy, extrovert, party-going fun, meeting fascinating people who in their own ways were as committed to the 'Quest', as he had started to think of it, as he had always been. In some ways, thanks to Bobbie, he had become a real party animal; you get the sense of someone being lured in from the cold to join a happy gathering, and him learning to thaw out aspects of his personality that he had long been frozen stiff. Plus he was getting all the magic he could handle and was mixing with folk who could understand exactly what sort of things were going on inside him. Many people who only knew him through his correspondence or his books, never realised the extent to which Bobbie was the making of him – in more ways than one.

Bill was always modest about his own psychic talents, yet, as we will see, it was often the first thing that struck people about him. His impressions of people and places were often gut-reactions deriving from his inner perceptions, and it was always interesting to hear his comments on any topic from that angle. On one of his jaunts around the countryside in company with his new friends, he visited the little church at the Somerset village of Mark, where it was rumoured that furtive Black Magical practices had recently been worked.

"Although it was a glorious summer afternoon when we arrived, there was an atmosphere of gloom around that church which nothing would dispel. It gave the immediate impression of a Hammer horror-film set. The churchyard was hopelessly overgrown and neglected, one of the crosses on the church roof broken, and the flagstones to the door uneven and cracked. When we pushed the door open it creaked in traditional ghost-story style. Inside was a terrible smell of decay and a feeling of damp darkness which was probably due to the dirty closed windows.

Despite the warm sun outside there was a sense of cold and desolation to an almost palpable degree. Ken's wife who had entered with us left in a few moments followed by Bobbie, and not long afterwards I felt so awful that I joined them. We had all been overcome by the atmosphere. Maybe my oncoming illness had made me especially sensitive to it, but until then I had never encountered anything so subtly oppressive and elusively evil in a so-called House of God. While we were comparing notes Ken reappeared. He would say very little about his impressions beyond his feelings that the church felt unusually sad and forlorn. A somewhat strange thing was that although we did not see one single human being in the whole of that village, we all had the feeling of being closely watched during our visit. It was an uncanny experience..."

And if he encountered the feeling of pure evil at the village of Mark, he was stunned by the exact opposite in Keinton Mandeville, when he paid a visit to the man known as Zadok, at a time when he was feeling particularly unwell with chronic glandular problems.

Zadok's real name was Ronald Heaver, who was widely seen as something of a Fisher King character, a guardian of the Holy Grail itself. He was born on 10th February 1900 and died on 10th February 1980. In some strange sense he seems to have been closely in touch with the Folksoul of Britain. In 1919, when crossing Westminster Bridge, he had an extraordinary experience. Suddenly the scales fell from his eyes and he was able with the gift of inner sight to see directly into the spiritual worlds, and know their reality. Prior to that, as a young man he trained in the Royal Naval Air Service and became a crack pilot which operated in a group to meet the daily reconnaissance raids of the great German air-ace von Richthofen. In fact Heaver's squadron came to be known as the Anti-Richthofen Circus. Shot down behind enemy lines, with a badly damaged back, he still made frequent attempts to escape from the prison camp. In 1926, perhaps as a result of this damage, he became crippled.

One of the contemporary legends surrounding him was that he was so closely identified with the Folksoul of Britain that when the General Strike was called he actually became paralysed from the waist down, like the Fisher King himself. It was not something that Zadok himself claimed, and he may even have been unaware of the story. His cousin Polly Wood, who looked after him for years, simply said that he had been crippled by poliomyelitis which had resulted from a swim in the river Somme.

When the Second World War began he approached the highest authorities in Britain and persuaded them to launch the National Day of Prayer. As someone said at the time: 'Heaver is not a man but a force'. Or as Polly insisted: "He was an Adept. A great mystic and Astrologer." *[letter to AR, 20th April 1986]*

His centre in the small village near Glastonbury was known as the Sanctuary of Avalon. The inscription at the door read:

> Enter this door as if the floor were shining gold and every wall alive with glowing gems of wealth untold. Enter as if an unseen choir in robes of fire were ever praising the Shekinah glory here. Abandon Earthly fears, be free from care, for in this Sanctuary, enshrined with the illimitable power of all encompassing Eternal Love Divine, the emanations of Divinity draw near.

He told one visitor, E. Marion Griffith, that buried deep beneath the building was a vial containing a mysterious substance that put one in direct contact with the Otherworld, and had links with the Ark of the Covenant.

Many people fell under Zadok's spell, and Bill was one of them:

"[Zadok] had been a First World War Air Force pilot who had flown many sorties over enemy lines before being crippled. He was now confined to a wheelchair and cared for by his cousin Polly. From his farmhouse home he ran an esoteric link-up on quite extended lines and he had converted an old dairy shed at the back into their chapel. On hearing of my present condition he suggested I sit there a while and ask for healing. It was about the emptiest place physically and the fullest one spiritually I have ever encountered. Although its dimensions were not large from a physical viewpoint, my immediate impression was that I had entered a vast Cathedral which pressurised me from every remote point. There was considerable light since he had installed large frosted glass windows. The walls were pale cream and perfectly plain like the ceiling. The flagstones of the floor had rush mats on them, and there were several plain rush-bottomed chairs. The altar was at one end of the room against the wall. It was of the elongated Christian type draped with an unembroidered white linen cloth whereon were only three symbols. A handsome brass Celtic Cross with a large topaz or similar stone in its Centre, an ordinary Anglican prayer book, and a Tibetan *dorje*.

"Almost nothing to look at from the material angle, but the spiritual structure of the location was overwhelming. It seemed to reach into the deepest recesses of one's soul and clean every trace of corruption out of them. Precisely the opposite was happening as with the church at Mark. There, the atmosphere seemed to be pushing slime at you, and here it appeared to be cleansing and filling human souls with light and hope. The strong sensation of vastness and Inner Space was quite unique and I could scarcely credit that my body was factually sitting in a small back room of a Somerset house. I am not even certain how long we stayed there. The topaz in the altar cross seemed to glow with a pulsing golden light That suffused me with a brilliance bringing an increase of confidence at every impulse. I felt a lot happier leaving the Temple than I had on entering. Zadok and I had a longish talk on esoteric topics and I expressed my thanks for the solace his Temple had brought to my mind. We kept in touch sporadically until the day of his death about fifteen years later."

Clearly, the Glastonbury area was the land of his heart's content, his power centre, and he had stumbled upon it before – in a very real sense – it became global. It had strong associations with Dion Fortune, who became his main Guide or 'inner contact' in later years; it was soaked with the mythology of the Holy Grail, which was central to his own developing magic. So did he perform any actual magic at the Tor? Yes he did. With the help of Bobbie and E.A. St George he started some experimental ritual workings of what he described as a not very serious nature.

"We were mostly trying to put together a set of seasonal ceremonies which would celebrate and accord with the four main seasons of the year. When these were eventually finished, they were published as my *Seasonal Occult Rituals*.

"It is probably our human attempts to harmonise ourselves with the changes of Nature taking place around us which resulted in our first real rituals. We desperately needed favourable climatic conditions in order to grow the vegetable food supplies which we and our animals depended on for survival and prosperity. There had to be the right proportions of wind, sun, rain and soil if we seriously wanted to make anything of our civilisation and fulfil the promise in our own genetics. Our primitive hunting days had taught us the necessity of ritual skills in order to obtain flesh foods. Imitation of animal appearance and movement which included wearing skins and horned head-dresses. Anointment with animal fats so that hunters would smell right to grazing beasts. Copying their noises so as to lull them into a false sense of security. When hunting became superseded by herding and arable farming, all those old skills had to be transferred into agricultural areas of action.

"This time we had to try and influence the elements themselves. Whistle and sing in imitation of wind, light fires to suggest sunshine, scatter water or urinate to hint at rain, mould artefacts from clay or defecate to demonstrate earth. Centuries of usage [made these evolve into] sophisticated acts, until today they have become the religious practices of singing hymns, lighting candles, offering holy water, and making solid artefacts. All we have really done is to develop and civilise our primitive customs into acceptable modern forms. Our ancient animal skin clothing has become our modern Lodge aprons. Our once smelly grease has changed into pleasantly perfumed oil. Our animal grunts and squeaks into choral chants. Our historical links with religious rituals go back as far as homo erectus himself and maybe beyond that. We have only to observe the elaborate mating procedures of animals to realise where our most modern dances are derived from. Some of the movements and rhythms are almost identical also.

"What I was trying to do at this period was create a complete set of four distinct Rites which would incorporate a meaningful majority of spiritual symbolism in keeping with the main modes of the year. They had to be practical and purposeful, entirely suitable for modern people of all ages and temperaments, yet with sufficient content to be considered esoteric in character and derivation. Then they had to be cyclic enough to embrace the complete progress of human life itself. Thus youth would be aligned with the freshness of Spring, adulthood with Summer, maturity with Autumn, and old age with Winter. The 'whole psychodrama of an entire existence would thus be ceremonially covered over the course of a single year. It was all a question of gearing up the correct symbology and pattern of procedure. This actually took several years of study and experiment during which time I was also engaged in other activities such as my Mass-Rite, which was then developing nicely but far from finished, and needing a lot more work yet."

One person who experienced the efficacy of these rituals first hand was the witch Pat Crowther, who wrote in *One Witch's World*:

The first time we performed the Rite of Autumn, I officiated as Officer of the West: the principal role for that season. Arnold took the North, and Bill and Bobbie were South and East, respectively. During the meditation period it was customary to sit in one of the four elegant chairs provided, listening to a tape of sea sounds. Very soon I began to feel a surge of energy coming from the West, behind me. It grew stronger and stronger until it enveloped me entirely. I knew it for the great tidal force of Birthing and Becoming, and at that moment I was the vehicle for that power. I needed, quite desperately, to give birth to it through my physical body; it was taking me over. I realized that I must control this manifestation – transmute it into its higher expression of Compassion and allow it to flow to the other Companions in the Circle. I quickly shifted gear, from the sexual to the emotional, and accomplished my intent.

Once, while celebrating Autumn with my friends, I observed a bright flash of light. It occurred so quickly that I wondered whether I had indeed seen it, but after the Rite, Bill said he had also observed it, and we agreed that our eyes had not deceived us. That it manifested from realms other than the material, there was no doubt. I think Bill was pleased with our work, as he announced, 'Do you know, I prefer to perform the Seasonal with you two than with anyone else.'

She agreed with Gray's comments about the flexibility of the rites, and noted: "When this book was first published, in 1970, it was said that the rites were too pagan for the Christians, and too Christian for the pagans. In fact, the rituals are universal, and one has only to adapt a word here and there to satisfy the pedant."

Things were clearly taking off for him, on all sorts of levels, and it seems that when he worked with the witches, he worked exceedingly well.

"On our next holiday at Avalon (as I came to call Glastonbury) I took the necessary equipment with me and, collecting a friend we had made there, the three of us ascended the Tor just before dawn, and facing the solar point I set up a temporary altar and commenced celebrating what I called from that time forth the Rite of Light. That moment marked a major pivot of what could be called my magical career. To this day I am not clearly conscious of exactly what happened in myself at that particular time, but I can remember my sense of wonder and surprise at the experience I underwent. The strange sensation of past present and future all being compressed as it were into an intensity of consciousness that threatened to burst my entire being into as many fragments as there were other humans alive on earth. If they all shared one atom of me apiece I would still remain intact as every one of them. There were literally no words which would properly describe what I underwent. Some very minor part of me was speaking the words of the ceremony and making the appropriate movements while the real ME was existing in this parallel state of perception inclusive of everything. Somehow I seemed to be working my physical body by remote control while simultaneously enjoying an independent and much more meaningful existence on another level of life altogether.

"Eventually of course the ceremony came to a close, and as I began to collect its symbolic equipment together we noticed a somewhat odd little occurrence. A single red rosebud I had included in the symbolism had opened out into a full-blown rose. It was not placed in any kind of a vase but simply laid flat on the ground. No one had noticed it opening.

When we started it had been a rather tight bud, but when we left it was an entire red rose. Perhaps that was symbolic of what had happened to me on that occasion. Previously I had been a bud packed with potential and now influenced by the Inner Light similarly to the sun which had become brilliant, I was opened and altered into a full flower ready to offer itself wherever required. I seemed to float down the Tor filled with living sunshine…"

Now that was *real* magic. What might be termed the art of causing changes to occur in consciousness. Changes which will, eventually, effect us all. And although the intellectual approach and the insights are standard to our understanding these days, and can be found in any of the dismal *How-to* tomes which make the bookshelves groan, they were developed in such a clear and effective way by William Gray a generation or so before the current Inepti were born. Simply by being the pedagogue he was, and talking about his craft brilliantly, the techniques he had developed in his own magical practices were already being passed on to other would-be magicians and witches long before he ever started writing his books. An awful lot of 'names' owe their own direct and earthy approach to magic to the very presence and perfectionism of Bill Gray. Quite simply, no-one before had thought of it in quite the way he did. When Aleister Crowley wrote 'Magick for All' he merely showed how abstruse, obtuse and elitist the whole thing could be. Suddenly there was a supremely natural and effective magician from modest Cheltenham telling the world that you didn't need to know Greek, Latin or have huge libraries, but that they could work with their own senses, linking with the natural elements of earth, air, fire and water.

There is a curious little item from his private papers which details some of his early researches at that time into the precise nature of ritual.

Experiments are being carried out with a Mirror Galvo to determine some aspects of the electrical phenomena connected with ritual practice. One evening's work has established that:

- A state of positive charge exists between the Operator and the ground as negative. All the metal Ritual equipment handled by the operator thus takes on a positive charge in relation to the ground.
- By rhythmic contact between the operator and the Instrument or floor, a frequency pattern of electrical energy is established. Amplitude is increased by harmonising the frequency so that contacts co-incide with Zero of pitch, on the pendulum principle.

- It is important to have good ground contact via the feet. If bare feet are impractical, then a sole with metallised connectors of some description will be necessary.
- The Circle-dance produces a distinct flow of current in the dancers. The step which produces maximum effect is the deliberate shuffle, or the LAME STEP! The Stamp produces a momentary current only.
- A major source of this electricity is the earth's magnetic field. The Circle Dance induces a low frequency rise and fall of current in the dancers' bodies, there being, of course, one complete cycle to each circumambulation. The faster the dance, the greater the current. Since it is alternating, it makes no difference whatever whether the direction is deosil or widdershins.
- An interesting effect was produced by connecting the galvo to a simple field coil and then making ritual gestures with magnetised instruments such as the Sword. Even at a little distance the galvo indicated the induced currents from this magnetic motion. This alone would show that every ritual is productive of an electromotive pattern. The action of whirling the Sword round and round the head would most certainly generate an etheric current, and the Witches of old must have felt this instinctively when they took to ladle whirling.

This is a wonderful piece of research! No-one had thought of doing this before. No-one. Quite apart from the symbolism and psychodrama involved in treading the circle, he showed that rituals of this nature were actually causing things to happen. Things that could be measured and assessed in purely objective ways. This was not just playing at magic, this was a question of pushing magic in new directions.

In many ways his general approach was so simple and earthy that it was appropriated and developed by many of those who were busy at that time creating the simple and earthy 'new' religion of Witchcraft. And of course, in ways which he would have loathed, you can't talk about William Gray these days without mentioning the Witches.

He taught them an awful lot…

William G. Gray in full kit

CHAPTER 8
Drawing Down the Moon ...

"I'm afraid I've seen and heard so much bloody rubbish masquerading as Sex Magic, that I'm just about disenchanted with the topic. I think of the great Aleister Crowley sitting up in bed casting I Ching sticks to decide whether or not he wakes Leah up to poke her or not. I think of skinny old Gerald Gardner, King(?) of the Witches prancing around with elk-horns from a coat-rack tied on his head while the girls tickle his tool with a pink feather-duster. I think of all these so-called Master Magicians and High Priests of Witch Covens living on National Assistance and trying to convince themselves they are Adepts and God knows what of Sex magic when they couldn't even raise a good fart between the lot – let alone anything more dangerously fertile. All because of a pathetic puerility and a lack of genuine love anywhere. Poor, poor little people. God grant them love in their next life-rounds. They need it desperately."

[letter to AR, 1st November 1972]

"I've metaphorically booted more would-be occultists out of my doors than I can remember. Witches, bitches, twitches, and all their odd little itches I couldn't care less about. (Though I've met most of the self-styled 'witches', and actually kept on more or less friendly terms with rare examples.)" So he wrote in an undated letter to Alan Richardson in 1969.

Of all the different kinds of occultist that he met, he really did seem to be able to relate to the witches better than anyone. Although he had a reputation in his later life for falling out with absolutely everyone, he never had a bad word to say about Doreen Valiente, E.A. St George, or Pat and Arnold Crowther – all of whom were heavily involved in what has been seen as the rebirth of the Craft. He also knew and worked with Robert Cochrane and became slightly bewildered by the cult status that the younger man rapidly started to achieve after his untimely death. All of them worked differing kinds of magic together. Things passed between them on magical levels. If, in a formal way, the druids had once made him their 'Distinguished Stranger', then the completely informal witches used him – unconsciously – in exactly the same way as he attended the rebirth of their own religion.

Perhaps he got on so well with them because these pioneers of post-war witchcraft were as busy evolving their systems as he was, and he saw them as kindred spirits. Or perhaps because the witches related to him on less cerebral and more affectionate levels, and were not seen as threats.

However Bill detested the actual word 'witch', despite getting on very well with the witches themselves. You had only to drop the 'W' word into the conversation and he would rise to the bait every time, launching into a fiery and exasperated monologue about the sheer *wrongness* of the term. There was something of the amateur etymologist about the man; in fact he once argued that an etymological dictionary should be a compulsory item for anyone essaying the magical path.

One of the witches with whom he argued word meanings was the legendary Doreen Valiente, who might be regarded as the Founding Mother of the modern Craft, as they came to call it. She had been initiated by Gerald Gardner in 1953, and used her own very real talent for poetry to write and shape the so-called 'Book of Shadows'. She left Gardner's coven in 1957 and formed a daughter coven of her own. In 1964 she was initiated by Robert Cochrane into what the latter termed a traditional, hereditary branch of witchcraft. After her death in 1999 she left behind a series of excellent books on the topic, and a large number of devoted followers.

"We grew fond of Doreen from the start although we had endless arguments on the topic of the word 'Witch'. She would persist in calling herself such despite all we could do to persuade her otherwise. In the end it was she herself who mentioned that the American folklorist Leland had first claimed this meant a 'Wise person', and everyone since had simply taken his word for it. In fact Leland had made a sad little mistake in confusing the Anglo-Saxon term 'wicce' (wicked one) with 'witega' (wise one) and assumed that the modern spelling of our word 'witch' must mean a wise person, whereas it means a wicked person in the sense of being a weak one. Any good Anglo-Saxon dictionary should clear this point in moments. Increasing numbers are beginning to realise this and drop the 'witch' description of themselves in favour of the word 'Pagan', which is perfectly permissible though etymologically incorrect."

Fortunately Bill died before he saw the upsurge in those Witch movements which he in no small part influenced – directly or otherwise, wittingly or no – or had to endure the myriad books with that dreaded word writ large upon the covers.

Ronald Hutton, the Professor of History at the University of Bristol, did the first full-scale and scholarly study of what has been described as the only religion England has ever given to the world: modern pagan witchcraft. The resulting book *The Triumph of the Moon* might be regarded as the first real history of this new-born revelation, and although coolly objective throughout, it still manages to be sympathetic. On reading the book, despite all the squabbles and disagreements between the personalities, the outrageous claims and outright lies, it is hard not to come away impressed by the witch movement he so lucidly describes, with its underlying ethic of 'An it harm none, do what thou wilt...' Gray's assessment of the new religion was typical:

"What the whole cult really amounts to is a socio-religious protest against the so-called 'Establishment' of Church and State which seeks to impose a set of conventions on human society in expectation of conformity. There have always been sections of that society which resent and disagree with such impositions because they object to interference with their purely personal opinions. So they usually organise something which symbolically opposes the overall rule of the prevailing majority. Almost anything to distinguish themselves from the mass of mankind forming the bulk of human beings. What they become depends on the degree and inclination they decide to follow. Those calling themselves Witches nowadays would have called themselves something quite different in former times. In my mother's day they would have been 'Bohemians', in earlier times Adamites, and all down the ages they have called themselves whatever seemed appropriate for their era. The Church called them heretics, the Law knew them as malefactors, Politics described them as revolutionaries or reformers. However they termed themselves, they were just humans who determined to be different and the way in which they tried this provided a name for their methodology."

He went on to give some more unique insights into this delightful woman with whom he often crossed swords:

"Doreen was a very genuine scholar with one of the best private libraries on occult topics which I have encountered. She was a very tall woman of just over six feet, who married a very small Spaniard who worked as a chef, and had been a rebel in the Spanish Civil War. This was Cassie, short for Casimir. Although he understood English perfectly, his pronounced accent was so strong and fast that I could never understand him. He took no part in Doreen's 'witchcraft', but made no attempt to interfere with it, being of atheistical persuasion. She sometimes called him her dear little gnome, lifted him by both elbows to kiss him and then sat him in his favourite chair to watch TV while we would follow her into their bedroom, to talk without its interference. His great passion was watching all-in wrestling, and his pet budgerigar would fly out of its cage to join him on his shoulder, and the sight of the small man and his tiny bird bouncing up and down with excitement together while horrendous howls came from the box was highly amusing."

And then there was Pat Crowther (née Dawson), who had the traditionally fey Breton forebears. She too had been initiated by Gardner, in 1960, and was seen by many as his spiritual heir. And in turn Pat initiated her husband, Arnold. During the rite she had a powerful trance experience in which she saw herself as being reborn into the Moon Mysteries, passed gauntlet-style through the spread legs of a line of howling, naked women. Apart from the teachings she received from Gardner, an old witch from Inverness (whom she called simply Jean) passed on what she said was a 300-year-old secret inner tradition. Her husband Arnold (1909-1974), so often overshadowed by his famous wife, was a remarkable man in his own right. In a previous age he might have been termed a Cunning Man, and in this one showed a passion for stage magic, ventriloquism, sleight-of-hand, puppeteering and illusions generally. He also had very clear memories of his past lives and was keenly aware that beneath the legerdemain there was another kind of magic, and other worlds. He introduced Gerald Gardner to Aleister Crowley in 1946, thus creating the speculations about the latter's involvement with the former which have endured to this day. Delightfully, he died on the ancient feast of Beltane (May 1st), and was given rites appropriate to a member of the Old Religion.

"Pat Crowther had a magnificent singing voice, and had at one time been one of 'Mr Cochrane's Young Ladies' but had quitted that company to marry Arnold, a much older man who practiced ventriloquism and conjuring at which he was highly talented. Pat still took Principle Boy's parts in pantomime, and they sometimes together worked to run holiday camps in British summer resorts. They were seldom without an engagement somewhere, and from time to time would visit us in Cheltenham celebrating Seasonal Rites there."

Both Pat and Bill did a lot of work in respect to the sonic aspects of magic – the so-called 'Words of Power' – and in particular the use of the vowels to link with elemental forces. It is hard to read Pat's analyses without imagining Bill; when you study Bill's work you cannot fail to visualise Pat.

And *then* there was an extremely charismatic young man who called himself Robert Cochrane.

Roy Bowers was his real name. He was born in 1931, and had spent some time as a blacksmith, hence the coven was called *The Clan of Tubal Cain*, after the smith of Hebrew legend. This alone tends to make the purists bristle: if the coven was part of an ancient 'Native British' tradition then one might reasonably expect an ancient Native British name, rather than something plucked from the dreadful Old Testament – or as Bill pointed out, simply lifted from Robert Graves' *The White Goddess*. However, this merely shows the scholarly innocence of the early pioneers in Wicca who had not yet begun to weave their mythologies into a cohesive pattern. Like many before and since, he claimed to have had his knowledge passed down to him through his family, after his initiation at the age of five. Doreen believed this at first, then changed her mind. Bill was never taken in for one second.

In November 1963, the *Psychic News* saw Cochrane defending witchcraft as the last survivor of the ancient mystery religions of Europe, and touting it as having a complex and sophisticated philosophy. According to Valiente his people worked in black robes instead of nude, and preferred to hold their rituals out of doors whenever possible. He was the coven's Magister, who mediated the Lord of Death, and the ceremonial tools consisted of a knife, a cord, a cup, a stone, and a forked staff known as a 'stang'. They worked on hilltops, clearings or caves. They sought the goddess or the horned god.

He was one the great rascal-gurus of the Wiccan Movement – and there were many. One of his coven members, Evan John Jones, described how Cochrane always tried to baffle, bewilder and mystify everyone he met, in order to prevent them forming a clear opinion of him, therefore making them easier to control. Cochrane also knew that things became real if people believed in them fervently enough, and that acts which began as mere trickery could be turned into genuine magic.

He was right, even if he had never heard of the psycho-spiritual techniques used by the Trickster archetype common to many mythologies. Sometimes, to get a kind of lift-off, you need to act 'as if' something was real. And then it becomes real. Jones went on to say:

As I was told it, 99% of our form of working was nothing more than an illusion created by word, actions and atmosphere. At a certain point in time, the illusion stopped and reality took over. From that point on, things used to happen, of course. We all knew from the start that what we were doing was an illusion in the sense that we employed all the usual tricks and trappings. Sometimes you'd get through a whole ritual without anything happening. Then one time you'd be working and the whole rite would be taken over and you would start doing things that you'd never intended doing. On more than one occasion we'd had a physical manifestation that was more than just the usual nebulous figure seen by one or two of the group. Far more concrete than that, we all saw it and recognised it, the horned God/King of the May Eve rites. This didn't happen every time, far from it, in most cases, the only thing we saw and felt is what I described in my book as the 'Hidden Company'. …These are the shadowy beings that gather round the outside of the circle while we're working as though drawn to us through what we are doing more than anything else. The strange thing is, I also noted that just before Roy Bowers died and we all split up, the hidden company gradually faded away and for the few times we worked together after, they just weren't there.
[letter to AR, undated, c.1991]

Cochrane might have been manifesting Tricksters such as Loki or Gwydion through what seemed to some his irritating games, but on the personal level Bobbie Gray commented (affectionately) years later: "I saw through him *right* away." So did Bill. So did all of the coven. But there was the added fascination that Cochrane had real power, and in the eyes of the others became transformed during the rituals – 'transfigured by supernatural energy' as one them described it. And there was no doubt in Bill's mind that Cochrane had given him more genuine healing than any of the other miracle-workers had done…

"Someone showed me a personal advertisement in the Daily Telegraph [*others remember it as being The Guardian, in 1962*] which I thought advisable to answer. It was obviously inserted by someone with deep esoteric interests appealing for contacts with other souls who understood its encoded message. Though my reply was brief, it brought a response signed 'Robert Cochrane' consisting of a very guarded feeler to ascertain my authenticity. It was plainly a pseudonym, and yet the nature of its phraseology indicated someone very much aware of an Inner Tradition albeit not of my particular brand. I replied appropriately, and after several exchanges of letters we formed a strong enough bond for the writer to reveal his real name – Roy Bowers. He was claiming connections with a very ancient pre-Christian faith which he said had run in his family and genetics since very early days. His letters were quite fascinating and revealed a great deal of instinctive familiarity with esoteric philosophy from a Pagan point of view. He claimed to have an operative Group in working order which took part in ceremonial practices which he outlined for me and invited me to attend one some time. All his type of ceremonies had to be performed in the open air, and he would notify me of the next opportunity. In fact if possible he would collect me, but first it would be as well to have a personal meeting. I told him of my health difficulties and the problems arising therefrom. Subsequently he rang me up at my home.

"After saying who he was, he went on casually: 'We're going to have a healing for you tonight if that's OK with you.' I replied that I would be only too pleased, and was there anything special he wanted me to do? He went on; 'No, nothing in particular, just go to bed as usual but don't be surprised at any dreams you have. We'll need you asleep so that we can work on that level. Try and be asleep before midnight if you can. Oh, and don't take any sleeping pills whatever you do.' I asked if my mild analgesics would hurt, and he said; 'No, those'll be all right but don't take anything stronger. Good night.' and hung up. I was duly in bed before the specified time, and eventually dozed off. At some unknown hour I had the distinct feeling of being tossed from one person to another in a peculiar pattern as they chanted or sang amongst themselves. I seemed to be something like a ball or small parcel which they handled quite freely and easily between them. Suddenly I became conscious of lying in bed on my stomach with a piercing point of agony somewhere under my lower right ribs. Slowly it moved to my left side, then back again, after which it went in a downward direction and finally faded out entirely leaving me exhausted but entirely free from any pain. I felt so utterly relieved at this I straightway slipped back into sleep with intense gratitude..."

From that time on, the worst of his illness was behind him.

Who would not be interested in a person like this, with such power? Whatever masks he may have worn for whatever reasons, Robert Cochrane was a *real* witch who left an indelible mark upon his co-workers. In fact Evan John Jones, who is part of that select and very small band of people whom Bill never fell out with, defined the witch in this way:

If one who claims to be a Witch can perform the tasks of Witchcraft, i.e. summon the spirits and they come, can divine with rod, fingers and birds. If they can also claim the right to the omens and have them; have the power to call, heal and curse and above all, can tell the maze and cross the Lethe, then you have a witch.

Let us make it clear; let us make it *very* clear: few of the self-styled witches today can do any of that. Cochrane could. In differing ways, so could Bill Gray.

And you could tell that he liked the younger man:

"Eventually Roy did visit me with his wife Jane, and young son Adrian who was not permitted to take part in ceremonial observances. Roy was several years younger than I, tall and slim built with slightly wavy brown hair. He had a good sense of humour and a very pleasing personality. He was working as a draughtsman for some firm at Slough. We somehow knew each other from old times though we were now working quite different branches of the Western Inner Way. Mine was the Hermetic indoor Temple and cultural type, whereas his was the wilder outdoor Orphic and animistic variety. We might learn a few things from each other. His ideal of a Supreme Spirit was definitely feminine, stemming back to the Great Mother concept, while mine, if anything, was more on the masculine side, although common sense alone told me that if the Life Spirit had indeed created its creatures in its own image and likeness, It would necessarily be a unified bisexual being."

Histories of modern witchcraft are being written so fast and furiously now that the comments of someone like Bill who was in it but not of it are invaluable. Ronald Hutton's only reference to him is when he comments: 'Cochrane collaborated closely with one of Britain's most famous ritual magicians, William G. Gray, an expert on the Cabbala and tarot; he moved among a sophisticated circle of occultists.' [*Triumph of the Moon*, p.315, OUP 1999] It is worth giving Bill's account of these early witches in full, because of the sidelights he can offer in respect to their personalities and magic…

"At that time a younger son of the Earl of Gainsborough named Gerard Noel was evincing a lot of interest in what was known as Witchcraft, and attempting to meet as many people as he could in connection with it. He was a Masonic friend of Dezzie's and was running a small magazine of his own called *Pentagram*. He liked attending my quarterly Rites in London, but insisted that he was only an observer. Gerard had been one of the so-called 'Cockleshell Heroes' during the war, and always appeared and acted as if he were an MI5 operative. Immaculately dressed, suave and sophisticated, impeccably mannered, he was every inch the ideal stage English Gentlemen. Height, hair, figure, costume and colouring, he could never be mistaken for anything else. Learning of my connection with Doreen and Roy, he conceived the idea of holding an official Witch Banquet at some London Hotel and inviting all the known 'Witch' figures who might be willing to attend. Doreen was to be guest of honour and make traditional speeches as a star attraction. Poor old Gerald Gardner had recently died during a pleasure cruise quite happily of a heart attack at breakfast, or he would have been welcomed also.

"Gerard did eventually hold the 'Pentagram Dinner' as it officially became called at a not unknown London hotel with all the 'Gardnerian' witches along one big table, and the independent or 'opposition lot' including Roy's group seated at another. We were at the top table with Gerard, Doreen, and some other notables. I had written a special little 'Grace' in verse to open the proceedings with. It greatly amused me very many years later to see it printed in a book of 'Witch' rituals as a genuine 10th century 'Banquet Blessing'. Though the occasion was a fascinating one from a purely personal viewpoint, it was memorable for being one of the worst meals I ever ate in my life. It was so bad I can remember every item. A thin soup made probably from Oxo cubes, a small lump of suspicious substance which might be meat from some unknown animal, flanked by two scoops of reconstituted potato powder and a single heap of boiled dried peas. This was completed by a thin wedge of cardboard tasting tart, part drowned by watery custard. Better meals are served in prisons every day.

"Among those present was Justine Glass the writer who had been commissioned by some publisher to write a book on witchcraft about which she knew rather less than nothing and had come on a copy-gathering mission. She was a very gushing woman slightly past middle age who oozed up to me saying , 'Oh I'm so glad to meet you, do tell me all about your wonderful Witchcraft', laying a hand on my arm at the same time. Gushy women repel me, and I hate being handled, so I was quite rude to her and told her to get someone else to write a money-making book for her. She promptly tried the same trick on Roy who amiably obliged on later occasions, quite deliberately misleading her and subsequent readers for several chapters, also supplying her with a few very phoney photographs of alleged authentic implements which were factually nothing of the sort. By the time Doreen and her little friend Leslie had made their contributions, Justine had got an almost ready written book for herself with a waiting readership who were presented with professionally produced fiction for their entertainment.

"One interesting thing which did develop from that disappointing dinner was Roy's promise to conduct a Samhain ceremony for us at some suitable site. Doreen suggested this was available at Newtimber Hill a few miles outside Brighton which seemed a reasonable project to all concerned so we agreed to congregate at that point on the 31st of October. Gerard would pick some of us up in his Land Rover, and others would make their own arrangements. Roy would travel with his personal friends, and we were all to meet at a prearranged place and time. Since it was Doreen's area, she would have to show us the actual spot she had in mind. Each of us would have to bring their own equipment which in my case consisted of a six foot forked stang, a hempen cord around my neck, and a dark warm woollen cloak with a hood. Otherwise we were normally dressed for the season, and for good measure I had brought a small oil lantern.

"It was dark when we assembled in a field at the foot of the hill, but one of Roy's disciples was wearing a miner's helmet with a lamp and he proposed to lead the way on the upward steep and difficult track. This in itself was supposed to be symbolic of life as an uphill climb with an eventual levelling out representing the relief of rest at the end of everything. You were supposed to pick up stones as you went to signify the burdens of responsibility gathered during a lifetime. These would be shed at the top of the hill to show how these might be laid down after death. They could either constitute a memorial cairn, or become the surrounds of a fire that cooked the communal food. Everyone brought something for the feast at the end which symbolised the individual contributions we all had to make to make toward human society and its consciousness. Seeing that this celebration was especially to honour the dead, we were to carry a photograph of, or something that had belonged to some departed relative or close family friend. I carried a small snapshot of my mother. In more or less single file we trudged to the top of the hill by what I thought a somewhat perilous path, the one with the miner's lamp and a sack of charcoal leading [Evan John Jones]. When we finally reached the top of the hill I was only too glad to shed my few stones and sit down on the soft grass. I had read the requirements of this Rite, and knew what must be done. Roy was busily organising the placement of everything, and would give the signal when we should commence. Some were getting a fire going with the charcoal and setting a cauldron on it which was partly filled with some dark fluid. Presently Roy began binding the component parts of his stang together. A leafy wreath, two crossed arrows, and lastly a reaping hook, sometimes called a sickle. The sickle stood for death, the arrows for transformation, and the garland for eternal life. This symbol was set up and fidelity sworn to the Faith it represented. Then the blessing of the Leaf-Mask was undergone individually.

"Presently the men began to pace around the fire plunging our knives into the pot and chanting as we did this. When we finished the women came forward, elevated a platter on which something was bound with red and blue twine, then tipped it into the pot and retired to the outer perimeter. It was now the turn of the men who advanced and a sword being produced this was plunged into the pot and its fluid scattered to the Quarters. Lastly the sword came under the control of an officer, called the Summoner, who laid it with the besom as a bridge between the main circle and another adjacent one of smaller size which was to be used for the Mill. Then the Maid of the ceremony who happened to be Doreen came forward and brandishing a ladle whirled it rapidly as she danced around the fire widdershins. After pouring a ladleful on the ground as a libation, she next filled a cup with the concoction and it was passed around those present in a deosil direction, all partaking of the contents. The Summoner then kicked the cauldron over with his left heel so that it extinguished the fire and only the light from my lamp supplied any illumination.

"Next came the Mill practice or the 'Grinding of Fate'. Everyone entered the smaller circle across the Sword-Bridge, males and females alternating. The Summoner led, and Roy as the 'Devil' of the group brought up the rear. His title as 'Devil' actually derived from the Sanskrit 'Dev', meaning a God-being. The Romany word for God to this day is 'Duval'. He said that in old days the group leader would frequently try and get his people going by lashing at them with his ceremonial cord and hence the phrase 'Devil take the hindmost' because the slowest dancer usually got most of the blows. We scurried around the little circle widdershins almost on top of each other stamping and chanting as we went. Sooner or later someone fell flat and Roy halted the rest of us with a sharp call. It was Doreen on the ground and Roy commanded her by various Deities to tell us what was being revealed to her. She began to giggle, and then said in an elderly and quavering voice quite unlike her normal tones; 'Snow! Snow! Its going to be a long, hard winter.' When we finally got her to her feet again we abandoned the Mill practice by common consent. The subsequent winter was one of the mildest in the century.

"From the Mill we went into the Summoning of the Spirit. Roy remained in the small circle while the rest of us grouped closely in the large one with our left arms around the shoulders of our neighbour, right hand clutching our individual stangs. The Summoner took charge and began to recite an invocation in Anglo-Saxon which said in translation: 'Blessed Goddess of the Horn, beyond and above all, who made and fashioned the gentle Earth, Thou art Love most merciful, blessed and formed by wonderous Fate. O Love. Pour forth! Love Pour forth. Greatest of all is Love.' During this we kept up an undertone chant of *Ah. Aha. Eu. Eu, Ah.* at the end of which we uttered a sharp cry as we raised our stangs and brought their ends down on earth as hard as we could. This procedure was repeated several times and then we fell silent and waited, all of us as we had been instructed, sending out power in the direction of Roy now crouching in his circle facing us. There seemed to be a strange sort of luminosity around him.

"It was difficult to see very clearly, but we all felt the intensification of the atmosphere and heard the curiously increased sighing of what was probably a wind in the nearby trees. Somewhere an owl gave three distinct hoots and everything was enveloped by the type of silence which always seems a lot louder than any sound. Whatever happened then occurred entirely inside ourselves. Afterwards, everyone described it differently though all agreed it was a sharp psychic shock. Roy was on his feet with outflung arms in our direction, when he suddenly raised them above his head and swept them downwards and sideways with a convulsive movement at the same time emitting an indescribable sound. It was piercingly penetrating, not very prolonged, and I would not have thought an ordinary human male could have uttered it. It was far more like the heartcry of a woman attempting to convey in a single second all the agony and pent-up passion of many millennia. There was something desperate in it as if everything in creation depended on the comprehension of its hearers and their ability to understand its urgency. Later, one or two claimed to have seen a lightning-flash image of their Goddess appear over Roy's indistinct form, and others thought they heard intimately whispered words of care within their ears. I neither saw nor heard anything like that, but I was very well aware of a most potently powerful Presence which was unmistakably a feminine force of a most compelling character.

"For a few moments we remained rooted to the ground, and then Roy rejoined us by the bridge into our central circle saying in a perfectly natural tone: 'Come my children, let us cheer ourselves with wit and wine.' We stirred ourselves and followed him out into the area we had previously chosen as a sheltered social gathering place. Some lit another fire, others fussed with food, and one or two of us endeavoured to record immediate impressions and thoughts. Presently the whole circle was in animated conversation, mostly with comparisons of individual experiences. All had some story to tell which was worth listening to. Our new friend John had fresh false teeth which hurt so much he took them out and lost them somewhere. Everyone searched frantically for a while until a strangled screech announced that he had found them himself – by sitting on them. The absurdity of a situation which enabled a man to bite his own bottom had us in helpless laughter for a long time. We broke up before dawn, most of us returning to Doreen's place for a short sleep prior to seeking our proper homes. Bobbie was the last one coming down the hill and she could have sworn she heard footsteps behind her all the way until at the end she realised they were phantom ones. It had all been an experience I would not willingly have missed."

That was real magic too. It was powerful; it touched upon something deep within the land and the psyche (if there is a difference); it was congenial, moving, bonding – and fun! He could not fail to be reminded of the vision he had had when he was ten, when he learned that God could be worshipped as effectively by laughter as by anything else. By this time Bill and Bobbie both clearly knew how to party, and also – judging from his comments about what must surely be seen as the witches' First Supper at the London hotel – he knew how *not* to party also.

Yet Bill was by no means a member of the Clan of Tubal Cain. He was never initiated by Cochrane. Yet again he was a sort of Distinguished Stranger, or an honoured outsider. As Evan John Jones commented, in his attempt to clear up developing rumours: "I can state without any fear of contradiction, it was Roy who admired Bill rather than the other way around. As for Bill working with Roy, he did, but not as a member of the group, rather as someone who was invited along." *[letter to AR, undated, c.1991]* As Bill himself was acutely aware, they came from very different Traditions: he from the Hermetic, and Cochrane from the Orphic. Or in qabalistic terms, Gray was *Hod* and Cochrane *Netzach*. They seemed to balance rather well.

However, as Bowers became increasingly unstable he started to pick fights with the older man, who sent him a long letter saying:

If I cannot accept your Rite, why should we argue? According to you my whole beliefs are wrong, up the creek, deluded and so forth. I am nothing but a pretentious upstart who knows nothing and has even less to offer. I stand humiliated. I pour dust upon my despised head and retire in confusion. Shame be upon me!

and then later in the same letter:

> Before you start loosing off the forces of Death and Destruction on me,
> cursing me out of countenance, releasing the Hounds of Hecate, and generally
> blasting me into fragments for the justification of your principles, perhaps
> you might ask yourself – 'is this really what I want???' If it is, then I can't very
> well stop you can I? I doubt very much however if you would do this without
> paying the price yourself. I should not curse you. I don't believe in cursing for
> its own sake. But I would request that you received *exactly* what you intended
> for me. Neither more nor less by one iota…
> *[private archives of MC]*

Meanwhile on the domestic front also, the Cochrane/Bowers household
was becoming stormy:

"Roy was having marital and family problems, besides experiencing
the usual troubles with his group which was engaged in breaking itself
with disagreements and dissentions among its members. The conventional
'Other woman' amongst them was making the customary claims on his
virility, and everything grew more confused with each day that passed.
As I was told at a much later date, Roy seemed to be falling into a fantasy
world which claimed his attention with increasing insistence. He was
being overtaken by what I had been warned about so often, occupation by
an alternative and alien life-energy. He had failed to learn how to control
consciousness so as to keep the various states separate from each other,
entering any of them only at will and closing the door carefully behind
him when altering areas. Consequently he was trying to live on several
levels at once and making a mess on all of them. Every student of the
esoteric should be made aware of this danger at the very outset of their
studies and taught the simple techniques of entering and leaving each
separate condition of consciousness through its proper doors which are
opened and closed very much like those of an ordinary room.

"At any rate Roy's condition deteriorated until he began to knock his
wife around and frighten her to the extent that she fled to her sister's
home and took her son Adrian, who was ten years old, with her. For a
little while Roy carried on by himself taking many tranquillizers and
growing more morose as Midsummer approached. Then he sat down
and wrote some farewell letters, mailed a few of them, and ate as much
belladonna from his garden as he could, finishing up with a whole bottle
of librium tablets, so by the time he was found he was unconscious and
going into coma. Gerard Noel notified us of his condition in hospital the

next day, and I rang them to enquire. He had only emerged uncertainly from coma and had relapsed again almost immediately. They held out no hope at all..."

Roy Bowers *aka* Robert Cochrane, the Man in Black, and Magister of the Clan of Tubal Cain, died on the early morning of July 3rd, 1966. It was his earnest desire that after death his head should be cut off and placed between his knees, but his widow was having none of that. With the kind of revenge that only a long-suffering wife can devise, she had him buried very privately in an unmarked grave in Slough, with a funeral service conducted by an Anglican cleric.

"I have never believed that Roy entirely meant to completely kill himself, but intended to take a supreme risk with his life and be dragged back from death at the absolute edge of extinction with greatly increased knowledge of what lay on that other side of life. He would term this 'gambling with the Goddess'. There were too many inconsistencies. Why did he mail those letters in time to give warning of what he had done? Knowing Roy's character, I am still convinced that he was determined to 'fling himself in the face of the Gods' so to speak, when in his view they would have had to return him to the world with the knowledge he sought, or accept him into their own company. He had thrown them a challenge of *Take me – or else*. His Gods did not seem very interested, and so he lost his bet."

However, that was not the end of it. The best thing about magicians, from the story-tellers' point of view, is that they tend to hang on after death, taking up completely new duties, and often exercising those who were left behind in odd ways.

"For a while [Roy] seemed to hover between the worlds, a common fate of suicides, and he haunted us for several months. Bobbie was very conscious of his presence urging her to commit suicide as well and join him. She distinctly had the impression of him saying shortly after his death; 'I've got a group going here already.' When she queried this he remarked airily; 'Oh quite a nice young couple killed in a car crash yesterday.' She told him where to go in no uncertain terms, and he faded, although she could feel him hanging around for a long while. So could I, and he became so persistent that in the end Basil and I arranged an exorcism together and Roy almost materialised for a brief moment, then faded out again for a while, though we felt him in the background for quite a long period after that."

Now that is a good story, casually told. It shows how commonplace contact with other worlds had become in Bill's life by that time. The person who helped him with the exorcism was Basil Wilby (Gareth Knight), an extremely important figure in the Old Sod's life even if he couldn't bring himself to admit it. Basil's own memories of this event are as follows:

> The story was that Roy had recently committed suicide, by accident was Bill's opinion, as an attention getter aimed at his wife. He (and again all this is as I heard it and understood it at the time) had somewhat frightened his wife into thinking that he might be going to sacrifice their child so that she had deserted him. Be this as it may, Bill's avowed purpose was to set Roy Bowers' soul at rest by combining a Requiem Mass with an exorcism, which included undoing the knots in the cord, and at a particularly dramatic point breaking the broom stick (a disguised phallic symbol under the birch twigs) – no mean feat of strength on Bill's part. I just acted as a kind of junior acolyte in all of this but had a vague feeling that this was not going down too well on the inner, and in Bill's version of events Roy had not liked it at all, and at one point was suggesting that we turn the athame on ourselves and join him! Anyway that was the end of that more of less, although it taught me one lesson afterwards about the need to "keep silence" about such events, as I did recount it to my wife who suffered some quite strong psychic disturbance as a result. I later, fairly recently, recounted the story to Bob Stewart when he was preparing to leave for America, and he found Bill's account of events somewhat incredible and not at all in accordance with what he knew of Roy Bowers. So what the truth of it all is I have no idea, not being very close to anyone in the wiccan world. Bill at that time, however, was quite taken with the movement, which was just beginning to 'come out' at that time, and indeed *New Dimensions* carried articles from Patricia & Arnold Crowther, Gerald Gardner and the like, as being all players on the contemporary occult scene. I remember Bill being quite excited about discovering the nature and purpose of 'flying ointment' but whether he ever used it or took part in wicca ceremonies I have no idea.
> *[letter to AR, November 2002]*

Even that was not quite the end of Robert Cochrane. Some time later Bill was performing a group ritual which included a young pregnant woman. At one point in the ritual Cochrane – or his spirit – walked through the door and straight into the room, large as life, and headed toward the mother-to-be. Bill interposed his formidable self in protection but the wraith sort of 'dissolved' into the young woman's stomach. In due course, after the baby was born, Bill approached it with a pointed index finger and said: 'If you really are Roy, then let me know'. The baby grasped his finger, as if he had known him for years...

Now that is a *wonderful* tale. Whatever the 'truth' of Roy Bowers really was, it is certainly less important than the myth. Myths have power; they can link us with things that are greater than mere historic truth. Myths were drawn to the image of Robert Cochrane like moths to the flame. And when that flame was extinguished? As Evan John Jones pointed out, after Roy's death the Clan of Tubal Cain was never quite the same. The 'hidden company' gradually faded away. The last manifestation the group ever had was a life sized head, rather fat in the face with puffed out cheeks and very very wild and tangled hair. The impression that he got from all this was that they were all being blown away and scattered by the wind, or perhaps to the winds. Within a month of this happening, they were finished as a working group.

They *were* blown away: they were seeds.

CHAPTER 9
Gray Meets His Inner Light

Don't bother with the 'Inner Light' lot either...
Few genuine initiates stay with them for long.
True they serve a purpose, but surely you can do
better than that dismal and depressing crew of
self-righteous and semi-sanctimonious souls...
Dion Fortune dead has more vitality and energy
than all the I.L. lot have while still in this world.

[letter to AR, August 1969]

During this time, honoured though he was among druids and witches, and a sort of Prince of the Apple Lands, as Avalon was called, he was still earnestly (and it almost seems effortlessly) plugging away at the lessons sent by the Society of the Inner Light. He had also made a powerful 'inner contact' with his heroine Dion Fortune, founder of the SIL, whom he felt was a much warmer, nicer presence dead than she had been when alive. As we had noted in a previous chapter, he had liked the tone of the initial correspondence from that society, and rather hoped that by joining something from the mainstream of the Magical Tradition, it might ratify and develop the work he had been doing by himself over many long years. It is possible, also, that with the shade of DF behind him, the apparently austere and utterly genuine group would welcome him with open arms as her heir apparent. A conceit, perhaps, but not a particularly unreasonable one given his formidable background and achievement. He wanted a genuine initiation into the Hermetic Tradition by people who really knew what they were doing. He wanted to be surrounded by real adepti, in an atmosphere of incense and chanting, overlooked by august and enlightened beings from the Otherworld, where the power was so great within the temple that you could hardly walk. He wanted to be touched by the magic at the very deepest levels of the soul, and transformed by new energies, and find himself – at the last – in a lodge where he truly belonged.

In the event, it was disastrous.

The lessons, which were sent by the Society of the Inner Light on a regular basis, dealt with the Qabalah, the Paths on the Tree of Life, the Archetypes, Group Minds and God Forms, Artificial Elementals, Initiates and Initiations, Character Training... and more, much more. As might be expected the information provided a thorough grounding in the ideas of the Western Mysteries as interpreted by Dion Fortune, and with a lot of emphasis on her obscure and difficult treatise *The Cosmic Doctrine*. After each lesson came a series of meditations or questions. For example:

> Compress into 15 lines the main features of Esoteric Anatomy.
> Explain the term 'Astral Consciousness'.
> Discuss the conception of Life, Death and Evolution as set forth in this lesson.
> What are the gods of a race?

And so on. Bill's answers were detailed, pertinent, and in depth. They often showed a quite unique level of insight that must have made his examiner's head spin, although in each case they were returned with the simple comment: 'Adequate +. Thank you.' And you can't help but get the feeling at times that he was – just a bit – showing off. His own system of attributing the Tarot to the paths on the Tree of Life is unique. It is brilliant. It also highlights the fact that two generations of magicians before him had been using a system of Correspondences which simply didn't correspond. "There may be copyright on this," he added.

Slipped in among the surviving papers were fragments of the work that he was doing at that time, such as the following table which outlines an approach to ritual work within a Circle:

Move on and stop	EAST	SOUTH	WEST	NORTH
Breathe in and out	INHALE	HOLD	EXHALE	EXCLUDE
Call Name	OOOOAY	EEEOOO	HOOOAH	HAYEEEE
See the	SUNRISE	NOON	SUNSET	MIDNIGHT
Think of Moon at	NEW	FULL	OLD	DARK
Feel the	SPRING	SUMMER	AUTUMN	WINTER
Greet Archangel	RAPHAEL	MIKAEL	GABRIEL	AURIEL
Experience the Element	AIR	FIRE	WATER	EARTH
Feel	PURE	RADIANT	FLOWING	FERTILE
Feel as if	FLYING	BURNING	SWIMMING	WALKING
Take and use the	SWORD	ROD	CUP	SHIELD
Emote	SORROW	EXCITEMENT	JOY	CONTENTMENT
Use Magnetism to	REPEL	CONTROL	ATTRACT	HOLD
Decide to	WILL	WORK	WANT	WAIT
Have	PERCEPTION	POWER	PURPOSE	PATIENCE
Dedicate	MIND	SPIRIT	SOUL	BODY

This list can be added to indefinitely. It is recited and acted upon while circumambulating...

This was the sort of scheme that he had been working through for years, and honed during his time with the witches, who generally don't have much time for the Qabalah, and prefer the simple circle-cross with Pagan attributions. Nevertheless, it was probably light years ahead of anything being done by the initiates within the group he was trying to join.

His examiner wrote: 'Adequate +. Thank you.'

At the end of the course, asked to add his own comments, he wrote:

> From a personal viewpoint the objective part of the Course taught me nothing whatsoever, since I was previously acquainted with every single word and idea in it, but the interesting thing is that subjectively from the Inner Planes, a very great deal came through, and quite new vistas opened up. ... The course acted as a catalyst which projected existing knowledge and experience into fresh combinations. Again I must re-iterate that this did NOT come through the printed matter of the Course at all, but from contacts at subjective levels which were associated with the consciousness expressed throughout the Course. The subject matter of the Course simply acted as foci through which these Intelligences operated...

What he was trying to say, is that by this time he was well and truly connected with the spirit of Dion Fortune herself, and he damn well hoped that they realised this. Although he got a nice letter from the Director of Studies, dated 15th December 1963, saying he was quite sure that Bill 'had what it takes', and looked forward to the interview and likely initiation, it all went downhill from then.

"About this time I had completed my Inner Light studies and was invited to London for the preliminary interview they always had with prospective candidates for initiation, so I duly attended at Steeles Road. There were several people present, some of which came and went after brief introductions, but the main part of the proceedings was played by Arthur Chichester who sat with the tips of his fingers pressed together steeple-fashion in the traditional pose of a stage lawyer. His style was extremely frosty and unwelcoming in complete contrast to an ex-Army officer type who was apt to be genial. I realised they were trying the hoary old 'friend and foe' trick on me, and later learned that Chichester had been an Intelligence officer in the Air Force who was accustomed to interrogating enemy prisoners. I had a psychic impression of him as an inquisitor present at an *auto da fe* clad in spotless white robes and black scapular watching the wretched victims burn in agony with complete indifference until a large smut settled near the end of his left sleeve. At that he becomes seriously concerned with how to get rid of the smut without leaving a dirty smudge on his clothing. He tries removing it by blowing at it, and finally succeeds with a combination of this and a flick from a finger and thumb of his right hand. After that he folded his hands and returned to his impassive contemplation of the well-deserved suffering of sinners. This momentary vision was so clear and intense, I am sure it must have been a distant memory of an actuality.

"I must confess that Chichester had such an off-putting effect that I was in more than two minds whether to accept initiation into the fraternity or not, but I came to the conclusion it would be best to do so after all the work I had done up till that date. So I fixed a future date for my initiation and determined to attend. There were very simple requirements since they had rather sensibly cut out a great deal of their previous superfluities which were incongruous to this century. The robes and hoods had been replaced by standard black cassocks with white cord girdles and black slippers. The elaborate degree system had been superseded by the modern Outer Court, Initiate, and Inner Circle formation. I had already passed through my Outer Court procedures, and was now prepared to enter the Initiate stage. The only other requirement was that I must choose and adopt a special 'Magical Name' or motto by which I would be known as its initials throughout the fraternity from thenceforth. This was to be written by me on a card which would be kept in a silver box in their altar, and returned to me if I ever quitted their companionship or was expelled from it. I was naturally disinclined to impart my real 'Magical Name' which has to remain unknown by anyone except the owner, and so I chose a substitute sobriquet which entitled me to be known as Frater 0. From another angle Zero – Nothing. Armed with these items I attended on the date at a somewhat earlier hour than specified, and was shown into the library to await my call.

"This was normally the sort of common room for the Fraternity, and prominently displayed were notice boards of a very familiar type such as used in the Army to promulgate Regimental and Company Orders. I was highly amused to observe how similar in style the detailed notices read: 'It has come to the attention of the Warden that some members are using highly scented hair oil which is of a distracting nature. In future this will not be permitted during meetings.' I almost expected the Service phraseology of 'This practice will cease forthwith' to be used but it was not. There were further comments of an admonitive nature forbidding somnolent members to snore during the inspired speeches of 'The C' (who was their Spirit Guide and believed to be either Thomas More or Lord Erskine) and advising adjacent members to awake the delinquent with timely prods. Maybe the best one was a complaint about someone's smelly feet which had threatened to overpower the incense and '…entirely nullify the solemnity' of some ceremony. I began to wonder seriously just what sort of a society I would shortly be joining. They appeared to be an odorous and inattentive lot of layabouts to judge by the caustic comments of their controllers. Just then a robed attendant came in to call me, and I followed her whispered instructions down to the basement where their Temple was located.

"It was roughly square with mainly Masonic furnishings and a double ashlar central altar bearing a votive lamp. I did not see this at first of course, being blindfolded. I was given only two responses to make, the first being a request for light, and the second an assurance that I sought enlightenment in order to serve. I was directed from one point to another where I was briefly lectured at by presiding officers and stood between the Pillars in the centre of a painted Zodiac circle while a short hymn was sung, and finally directed to the darkest point of the circle where I sat on a plain kitchen chair with its back sawn off while I was subjected to an incredibly boring address from an elderly trance-medium, packed with the usual platitudes and outworn oracular utterances. No wonder people in previous audiences had dozed off. I discovered later that the circle of kitchen chairs had had their backs all removed quite deliberately to prevent occupants from leaning back against them and lapsing into slumber. Only the officers' chairs were intact.

"The Temple was dimly lit with candles, but as I glanced around the circle of some twelve to fifteen members I was suddenly shocked to discover that about a quarter of them were Nigerians. Dion Fortune had made it absolutely plain that her organisation was intended for Western Europeans only. She was totally against mixing the ethnical spiritual cultures, insisting that each had its own to follow as outlined by its particular Avatars. This especially was why she had fallen out with Theosophy which insisted on Oriental 'Masters' and their reputed teaching. She had seen Jesus as the special Avatar of the West and although I had not totally agreed with her there, I have always seen the Western Inner Tradition as something to be preserved intact for Occidentals only. I had nothing against Nigerians as such, my feelings would have been the same if they had been Koreans or Chinese. I saw them as no more than aliens in an ambiance to which they were unentitled by birth or blood. I called to mind the Temple at Jerusalem which had a special 'Court' or location where Gentiles or non-Jews were allowed, yet precluded from all other parts. I regarded this invasion of a Western Traditional esoteric Temple as absolute sacrilege, and as they were obviously here by invitation and with full permission from European officials, as a deliberate betrayal of all I believed in. I continued to sit there amid the dreary drone of supposed spirits considering my best course of action.

"In due course the ceremony came to its conclusion, and if this was a typical example of Inner Light ritualism, I was not deeply impressed. My instructions were to remain in the Temple until called for and then I would be at liberty to leave. Presently my female cicerone came to collect me and handed me a large envelope full of papers which she said was information I should study carefully. I asked to see the Warden or anyone in authority, but was told they had all left the premises. She could not answer any of my questions beyond telling me that allowing Nigerians or other non-Europeans to join the Fraternity had been a recent decision which had not been popular with all members but was a majority decision by a small fraction. Now would I please have this tea she had brought. She left me alone to eat a pleasant little collection of cakes and saw me out of the house afterwards with a barely polite parting. I studied the mass of papers in the bus going home and found them of very small importance.

"There followed quite a mass of correspondence between Chichester and myself. As I anticipated, his letters were brief, icily cold, and as remote as possible. Mine were quite deliberately friendly, informal, and gently quizzical. I did my damnedest to obtain one single sign of normal humanity or admission of ordinary feelings from the man but was totally unsuccessful. All he was concerned about was that I should return the precious papers with which I had been entrusted and was obviously unfit to retain. I was careful to specifically point out that he could have them at any time that he saw fit to write to me in a friendly and fraternal manner as befitted brethren in the Holy Mysteries, but to such a suggestion he only replied in a more remote third person style. We were getting nowhere fast. In the end the problem of the papers was solved very simply when Basil Wilby, who was a locally living member of the Fraternity, and also connected with what I was beginning to call 'my Group' asked me to hand them over to him as an act of friendship. I did so forthwith and bothered no more about them..."

It is hard to imagine two human beings less likely to get on than William Gray and Arthur Chichester. Both of them were great magicians in their own way; both of them were awkward, formidable individuals. If Gray had a vision of Chichester as an Inquisitor, then what visions might Chichester himself have had of Gray? In some ways, they had many similarities.

To counterbalance the above portrait of that former Warden of the Inner Light, Basil Wilby chipped in with a pen picture:

"'CC' as we called him has come in for a lot of stick from people who felt that he had deviated from the original DF line of the SIL. Gerald Gough, one time librarian, was very bitter and used to refer to him as 'Stainless Arthur'. There was some truth in this as in all jibes, but it was a gross distortion of the character of the man. Gerald Gough could never forgive him for decimating the library stocks... This was all part of the 'de-occultising' of the group's work in favour of a Christian mystical bias. I thought this trend went too far and so, with a number of others, eventually resigned ... in my view the SIL was becoming not a Christian oriented occult group but a religious sect. Some people went so far as to speculate whether CC was an undercover Jesuit! I am sure this is not so, but his manner could give grounds for thinking so. He was a very conservative minded person and, of Anglo-Irish stock, had been educated at Stoneyhurst, which had left its mark very evidently. He confided to me once that he had not really intellectually awakened until he was about 23 when a colleague said in some exasperation 'Why don't you ever think for yourself?' In my experience he was well able to think for himself, and he could penetrate with devastating accuracy and keenness through any sloppiness of thought or lack of definition. He could however be very pedantic and even morally prissy. ... He had an admitted high regard for Roman Catholicism and was very knowledgeable about RC spirituality and mysticism. This is in fact was a great help in evaluating psychic experience of one kind or another. He could not have been all that conservative, however, for he led the Society into some varied pathways – Scientology, Subud, Alexander technique for example... Also he introduced weekly meetings of readings and hit upon Tolkien before he became popular, also Teilhard de Chardin. And also the later books of Alice Bailey. He... had a strong feeling that the Earth was neglected by occult students and that the etheric web of the Earth ought to be as, or more important than, working up to Cloud 9 or speculating on Root Races, etc. Here he was on to ecological responsibility of man to the planet, years before it became a fashionable concern. I would accord very high respect for him as a wise, spiritual and humane man who taught by example as well as precept. His pettiness and conservatism could at the same time be infuriating – but it was a minor blemish. I also thought him politically naïve and shortsightedly right wing... He did not have a particularly polished ritual technique or vibrant voice but in practical magical work he had a spiritual presence that made workings conducted by him eagerly awaited and long remembered. ... He was once described by an inner plane contact as an 'examplar of service'. I would agree with that... He was on a different line from DF and the way the SIL should or might have gone, I think. But it remains to be seen whether he set in the seeds of its destruction, or transformation to a higher level."

It is hard not to get the impression that Bill had already decided against getting involved with the SIL, even before his interview. Basil himself had become disenchanted with the way the group had altered, and he must have said something about this to Bill. Plus in reading the sheer depth and originality of Gray's answers to the SIL study topics, and the often floundering comments of his tutor, you cannot help but feel that the latter was never in the same league.

With Bill however, the negative attitude tended to come first, and the justification followed: in part he affected to be rattled because the candidate was expected to say: 'I Desire to Know, in order to Serve'. *Serve What or Who?!* thought Bill at the time, his defences up, although if he had read any of DF's books he would have known they would expect this attitude and declaration.

And also, there was this question of the 'Nigerians'.

In point of fact, he was perfectly correct in saying that multi-racial magical work was inimical to Dion Fortune herself. As she wrote in *Sane Occultism*, some 30 years earlier:

The pagan faiths of the West developed the nature contacts. Modern Western occultism, rising from this basis, seems to be taking for its field the little-known powers of the mind. The Eastern tradition has a very highly developed metaphysics. ... Nevertheless, when it comes to the practical application of those principles and especially the processes of occult training and initiation, it is best for a man to follow the line of his own racial evolution. ... The reason for the inadvisability of an alien initiation does not lie in racial antagonism, nor in any failure to appreciate the beauty and profundity of the Eastern systems, but for the same reason that Eastern methods of agriculture are inapplicable to the West – because conditions are different.

We must make the distinction here between the woman known as 'Dion Fortune' who wrote some of the most poignant, humane and evocative prose in the genre, who was larger than life and one step ahead on the evolutionary road, and the little known V.M. Steele who was just a narrow minded bigot with very little literary skill, and whose novels deserve to be trashed. They are one and the same, of course. *Beloved of Ishmael*, written under the pen-name V.M. Steele, is an embarrassing tale that is filled with every sad and insulting racial stereotype: wops, chinks, and niggers abound, and if a man ain't a Freemason then he's only half a man.

V.M. Steele was a pen name of Violet M. Firth, and she expressed the prejudices and ignorance of her class at that time, no more, or less.

Dion Fortune was the pen-name of Violet M. Firth also, but *she* expressed the insight and power of a Priestess of Isis – and a very great one.

Unfortunately, although Bill Gray never read any of V.M Steele's novels, he would have liked them very much. But that's Cheltenham for you.

Let us be blunt: Bill didn't like niggers. His term. He didn't think they should be in this country. He didn't think they should be involved in our magic. He argued once (but not unreasonably) that no-one would criticise Australian aborigines if they refused to let a white man take part in their inner ceremonies: why should we criticise white people if they felt a black man was not appropriate in the 'Native British' rites? As we will see later, Bill eventually modified his opinions to the extent that he used the term 'racialist' to describe his ideas, rather than racist, and fiercely objected to any suggestions that he was Nazi in spirit.

Basil Wilby saw it from both sides. He described how Bill went through the entire initiation in a state of what might be termed 'psychic self-defence', and commented:

> In some ways I have felt that maybe Bill's experience at the SIL was a classic example of meeting the Dweller on the Threshold in a more than usually concrete and dramatic way. Bill felt that the SIL was betraying the British heritage by admitting blacks and had two lines of argument in justifying his position. One was that he had a natural aversion to them, much as some people are said to have with cats, and could not abide being in the presence of one. The other position was more philosophically oriented, along the lines that the black races, and particularly immigrants to Britain, were part of an evil plot to undermine the fundamental principles and purity of the British nation. Jazz and popular music was one part of this (so I took good care to keep quiet about my own longstanding interest and participation in jazz music) and at about this time "Amazing Grace" played upon the bagpipes

somewhat bizarrely featured in the top ten of the pop charts, much to Bill's satisfaction – to the point of him advocating listening to the playing of the bagpipes as a kind of psychic cure-all in times of difficulty.

But quite apart from the colour aspect, it really did seem to even the most easy-going of mystics and magicians at that time that the Western Tradition was under threat. Most young people with a burgeoning passion for the occult didn't know that there was such a thing as a Native Tradition, deriving from mythology, legend, folk-lore, earth energies, stone circles and surviving esoteric practices. They knew nothing about the Old Gods and Goddesses, and the secret places and the powers in the Land. Everything spiritual was seen as Eastern, and everything Eastern was necessarily spiritual. The Western world was swamped by gurus in their Cadillacs who spouted their sub-Yogic philosophies to adoring Western *chelas* who had more money than sense, and hoped that what they had found was Essence. Even Christine Hartley, a true adept of the Golden Dawn and political Liberal of the grand old kind, often despaired. To her, Westerners trying to use Eastern systems was akin to left-handed people being forced to use their right: it could be done, but it wasn't necessarily healthy. Once, in the early 1970s when one of the present authors tried to get someone to illustrate a tarot pack using Arthurian imagery, the young lady artist criticised him for wanting to make Arthur look like 'a bloody Englishman', and couldn't understand why the Krishna-fication of the Once and Future King didn't appeal to him. *But King Arthur probably didn't have a bindi and play a flute!* he said weakly, but the point was lost on this lost representative of a nearly-lost generation who insisted that the secret behind Glastonbury could *only* be found in India. *Only!* she insisted, pointing a long finger at his Third Eye. The first time he actually saw Bill Gray the latter was furiously scrubbing away at a poster of the teenage Guru Maharaj-ji (*Why peep through the keyhole when you can open the door?*) which had been stuck on a wall in Bennington Street, muttering to the image *Clear off you little bastard…*

In a previous century the poet Yeats and a few companions founded a cultural and occult gathering which had the avowed intention of awakening the Irish Group Soul, using the ancient archetypes of the land to vivify the national struggle for independence. Bill and Bobbie had a similar idea, though it was, like its forbear, to founder in the politics of personality. With a few acquaintances, including the writer Marian Green, they attempted to found an Order, based within, and fighting for, the very

identity of the British Mysteries. The genuine fear that an ancient heritage
was in danger of being engulfed and lost is evident in the papers of the
day. Ambitiously, they planned a written course, magazine and meetings
at sacred spots. A call to arms was issued in the form of a pamphlet. How
far it was distributed is impossible to say now, but it is worth reproducing
in full because it goes to the heart of the motivations of Bill and Bobbie
Gray, their attitudes to identity and race, and underlying life aims:

The British Mysteries

What are the British Mysteries? In effect they are the natural activities and
developments of the British soul as a complete entity throughout the history
of these Islands. They are the rightful spiritual heritage of all who truly belong
to Britain, whether such people actually live physically in this country or not.
These mysteries hold the keys to British character and individuality, and they
are, as it were, the bedrock on which stands the Mystical Castle symbolising
the true Inner Home of every Briton.

Britons do not stand their spiritual treasures on display for all to see. They
are so deeply hidden that most Britons are not greatly aware of them with
normal consciousness. Nevertheless they are an unfailing source of Inner
strength which Britons use instinctively when sheer necessity arises. It was
this unique spirit which carried the British through the desperate days of the
last war. Unhappily we do not seem to establish such close contact with our
own Soul during these uncertain days of artificial peace.

To be truly healthy, an individual or group needs to be in right alignment
with their fundamental souls. Everyone should maintain contact with their
own roots, so to speak, and what may be called the British Mysteries are the
true spiritual roots indigenous to both the soil and soul of Britain.

The British Mysteries are as old as these Isles themselves, and have come
down through all the centuries and various types of inhabitant in one form
or another. No matter who came, the mysterious Spirit of these Western Isles
took them in, absorbed them, and made them British so that they eventually
differed from everyone else. Naturally this process took time in terms of
many generations. If we look back at history we find that British druids were
just that much different from Continental ones, the early Celtic Church
had its own complete character, and British Paganism evolved as a special
type. Ultimately, Britain broke away from foreign dominated Churches, and
produced its own brand of official Christianity in various forms. Behind

the scenes, the British Mysteries still flourished Inwardly, and continued to influence all spiritual imports. Eventually the time came when the British spirit moved out into the world openly enough, and altered the course of human history in a great many ways.

Who and what keeps these Mysteries alive? The answer lies in the souls of Britons and their allies, whether these are attached to physical bodies or not. By devotion, faith, and inspiration, through almost insurmountable adversities, the soul of Britain, as such, remains intact today, though in what condition is a matter of concern by all who belong to it. Unless sufficient people are prepared to help regenerate the Soul of Britain and keep its Mysteries intact, there is a grave danger that these will deteriorate until they are eventually absorbed by alien Ethnoi. This is because of serious weakness due to wars and other recent causes, and also because of alien invasions on spiritual levels, which are increasing at a greater rate than the British Soul is able to transmute them into its own terms. "Eat or be eaten" is a universal law extending into spiritual dimensions, and if the British Soul and its Mysteries are to survive, then it must be equal to its present task or lose its identity entirely. The matter is as serious as that.

Up till now, the British Mysteries kept going in their traditionally diffused way. Legends and Fairy tales held some of their secrets, country customs contained others, contacts infiltrated into the Churches, Lodges and through Court and military circles. There were pieces to be found almost everywhere, while the entirety remained hidden in the depth of the Group Soul. As matters stand at the present time, these lodgements are becoming inadequate and insecure, being sorely in need of support or extension through new dimensions.

If the British Mysteries are to continue their existence in Earth and be preserved for posterity, then concerted action is essential as soon as possible. Men and women of ability within the British Ethos must link up with each other and establish a practical corpus through which the British Soul and its Mysteries can not only survive, but also re-new itself. Unless British and allied occultists are prepared to transcend personal or doctrinal differences, and work their various systems through the common Mythos of their own Group Soul, there is little hope for the future of the British Spirit as such.

There is no question of creating new systems or groups except those which may form spontaneously. Any system adaptable to the Western Tradition functions through the British Mysteries as a whole framework. Nevertheless there is a definite need for a practical working body in earth using essential British Mystery formulae and methods, yet inclusive of all allied systems in their own functional ways. This would serve as a kind of Earth-based contact point through which the British Mysteries would maintain touch with individual members. In addition it would act as a type of reservoir or container for everything connected with the British Spirit at its very best. The actual formation of such a corpus seems an almost impossible task, but genuine Britons love accomplishing the impossible.

At this point there is nothing more to say for the time being. Obviously a great deal has not been said, and if even some of this comes to mind, it will establish a link through the Inner World leading to the Mysteries. If the underlying message reaches the right people they will act accordingly, providing they value their identity as a British soul enough. The final questions might well be:

"Who feels the British Soul as a Reality?"
"Who is willing to defend the fortress of the British Faith?"
"Who will safeguard the survival of the British Mysteries?"
"Who understands the message of the Past sent to the Future?"

There could be a single answer to these difficult questions:

YOU

As the echoes of this *cri de coeur* died away, so did the enterprise in this form. Bill makes no mention of it in his autobiographical papers, though it is known that he and Marian Green had a rancorous fall-out. His ireful descriptions of this in later years evoke memories of the youthful Nimue attempting to beguile and steal away the secrets of a naïve Merlin, yet nothing was ever that simple with Bill. All we are left with of this first attempt to set up a society based on the Western Way are a few letters, notes and constitutional aims. Not even a name for the Order remains, yet their work may well have stirred some deep inner currents of the Western Psyche.

Now, of course, you can't enter a shop without getting strangled by Celtic knotwork, pentagrams, or runes; glass cases are filled with witches' daggers and chalices; while the various Arthurian, Merlin, Druid, Wiccan and Wildwood tarot packs dazzle the eye like stars, and it is obvious that the Western Magical Tradition is not just alive but rampant, and that the ancient deities are being invoked and worked with right hard every day by a new generation that has rediscovered them, and brought them back into the light. And all because a few bloody minded if often misguided and bigoted souls like Bill Gray stuck to their rites fifty years before and wouldn't compromise.

William G. Gray's real and supposed racism is a complex issue, and we will discuss it more later, but in the meantime he could be every bit as antagonistic toward people of his own creed and colour.

CHAPTER 10

The Years of Speaking Angrily

*"Do I know who [my] 'Inners' are? No, not by
any names which might be familiar. And do I
trust them? Not by one single inch…"*

[letter to AR, 19th December 1987]

There is a true story about a man in a Hollywood restaurant who, quite inadvertently, offended one of the other customers, who happened to be the legendary star Bette Davis. The old woman berated him with all the power and venom that alcohol, a sharp tongue, and 60 years in movies could provide, and then stormed out. In the deadly hush which followed, her victim was heard to gasp: 'Bette Davis – *the* Bette Davis – insulted and abused me! *Me*! Gosh, that's the greatest thing I've ever known…'

Similarly, at the time of writing, there are many ageing souls in occultism who can look up with some retrospective pride and say: *I've been bollocked by Bill Gray…*

Put it down to the male menopause, paranoia, or impossibly high principles, but this was the period when Bill seemed to fall out with and/or end up insulting almost everyone: R.J. Stewart, Marian Green, John Hall, Robert Turner, Jacobus Swart, Dolores Ashcroft-Nowicki, Marcia Pickands, Alan Richardson… the list is long, very long. And if by this time the actual word *Witch* had developed powers to make him bristle and fume, then this paled beside the dread words *Gareth Knight*.

Gareth Knight is actually the pen-name of Basil Wilby, a prolific writer on magical topics whose books have ranged from the two volume *Practical Guide to Qabalistic Symbolism*, the *History of White Magic*, up to the definitive *Dion Fortune and the Inner Light* and *Pythoness –* a biography of the truly extraordinary and completely unsung priestess Margaret Lumley Brown. He has run excellent magazines on a shoestring, published writers who would otherwise never have got published at all (WGG included), lectured on and practised magic with every bit as much fervour as Bill himself, for just as long, and with as little outer reward. Although the old sod would have chewed wasps rather than admit it,

Gareth Knight was a very important figure in the life of William G. Gray. Yet anyone who came in contact with Bill in the last three decades of his life was led to believe that Knight had committed some unspeakable crime, some dark deed that could scarcely be mentioned. In fact, Gray spent so much time assassinating Basil that in the interests of truth, justice, and the British Way, it is now only fair to let the man himself have his say at last...

"I first came across Bill Gray when I was editing an occult magazine called *New Dimensions*. He wrote in to me in the first instance with some appreciative comments, and some not so appreciative, but quite justified, and in the course of time he began to contribute the occasional article. As he lived in Cheltenham, some ten miles from my business partners John and Mary Hall (we had recently started up Helios Book Service at Toddington, Glos), I mentioned the correspondence favourably to them, but John was not slow in warning me off him as being not an entirely pleasant character.

"I was to meet Bill within a year as I moved from London down to Tewkesbury to help with the business in August 1964, and after meeting Bill I could see what John meant. Bill had a very strong personality, in fact almost a charismatic one, except that those who tended to be sensitive to such things felt put off by what was generally described as what he was generally trailing about him psychically, something which seemed a bit grimy and vaguely unpleasant. (I often used to think of him as 'Gray by name, and grey by nature' – perhaps unfairly.) He had not endeared himself to John Hall, who had been undergoing a hard time businesswise and was just recovering from what had come close to a nervous breakdown, by clasping John's hand very firmly in a strange masonic handshake whilst fixing him intently in the eye. I experienced this myself, as did most I imagine of his new acquaintances, and it was not an entirely pleasant experience, but had felt quite devastating to John in his depleted state.

"However, I felt that there was more on the plus than the negative side with Bill and continued his acquaintance. This included attending an 'at home' he used to hold on one Wednesday every month at which he would usually lead the conversation. John Hall initially came to some of these, so relations were not all that strained, although being a well brought up gentlemanly type of the old school used to bring a bunch of flowers each time for Bobbie, Bill's wife, which she accepted with reasonable grace although I do not think she liked flowers very much. Any others around the house were invariably plastic. Bobbie used to butt in with astrological comment at these evenings from time to time, and she did indeed seem to be a dedicated and knowledgeable astrologer. She was also very interested in science fiction and used to attend the occasional convention. Apart from that her esoteric contributions tended to make references to 'Merlin', an occasional inner contact who was apparently notorious with her for his irascibility.

"Apart from myself and John Hall (in the beginning) others who attended were generally a couple of more or less beginner enquirers from Pershore, but on occasion there were visits from the likes of Gerard Noel, a very dapper gentleman who ran a shortlived magazine called *Pentagram*, and Marian Green and a couple of pagan friends, also a lady who called herself Elizabeth St George, who helped to found the still running *Quest* magazine, and on one occasion Doreen Valiente, whom I rather offended I fear by saying that I would not cross the road to get any more witchcraft articles – perhaps not very felicitously put, but there were rather a lot of them being bandied about at that particular time (1965).

"After a while Bill began to use these occasions to read out some communications which he said he was 'getting through' and which, somewhat to his surprise, seemed to emanate from the late Dion Fortune – for whom he had a grudging respect as far as he respected anybody on the esoteric scene. I had at this time very recently resigned from the Society of the Inner Light on the grounds that they seemed to have abandoned the old DF lines of work, but I felt, somewhat against my better judgement, that Bill might have been right in his assumptions about this contact. Credence was added to this when he felt impelled to take the Study Course of the Society of the Inner Light, much against his will, for he had little but contempt for it (and to be fair it did have its limitations). Yet he persisted to the point of going for interview and being accepted for initiation. This event turned out to be a disaster for all concerned. Bill had markedly racially biased views, and it so happened that on the day he presented himself for initiation the door was opened by a West African member of the SIL (there were quite a number of Nigerians and Ghanaians in London in those days as students of one kind or another and the SIL had a handful as members).

"This immediately antagonised Bill who then went through the entire ceremony in an attitude, as he explained to me afterwards, of psychic self defence. The practice immediately after the ceremony in those days was for the candidate to be closeted alone, given a cup of tea and a biscuit, and a great raft of knowledge papers, and then sent on his or her way. Bill immediately said that he was not interested in the papers and did not want them. The poor junior member assigned with the task of giving them to him, felt obliged to gently insist that he take them with him, study them and think things over. He took them away with some bad grace – sent in a letter of resignation as soon as he got home and then in high delight, because the SIL had a very protective attitude towards their knowledge papers, refused to return them. ... In the end I was able to act as a mediator between both sides and relieve him of the papers, and at the request of the then Warden/Director of the SIL, Arthur Chichester, duly burn them (to save the trouble and cost of postage)...

"However, I was much impressed by what Bill was 'getting through' whatever or whoever its inner source might be, and having just opened up a publishing side to Helios Book Service, I published it in volume form as *The Ladder of Lights* and I think I am right in thinking that the title, after much deliberation, was my idea. Anyhow, it was I who put Bill on the occult book publishing scene. He then got stuck into another manuscript, which ran out to considerable length, and which I also published as *Magical Ritual Methods*. The genesis of this publication is an interesting story for I had nothing like the capital available to publish such a large book. Bill then suggested that perhaps we try doing a ritual to evoke the money. After a lot of heart searching I agreed to take part in such a venture, and this we proceeded to do, composing a ritual based upon the Sephiroth of Binah and Hod so far as I can recall.

"We duly did this in Bill's ingenious temple downstairs at 14 Bennington Street. It was an odd narrow house with the basement leading out into a yard area. This basement could be walked through without anyone suspecting it to be anything other than a normal kind of scullery type room, but there was a trellis-work arrangement up in one corner that could be opened out to reveal an altar and with the addition of some curtains and a floor cloth a temple immediately appeared. Bill had robes for the occasion and had himself fitted out with a kind of Qabalistic biretta as a hat – having four blades instead of the conventional three. Anyway having done the ritual I was somewhat surprised to receive a letter from Israel Regardie, some of whose essays I had published as little books, who said that a very wealthy American, Carr Collins, was about to pass through London who was keen on splashing his money about on what he thought esoteric good causes, and Regardie felt that he would rather see me in receipt of some of this cash than many less worthy recipients. Accordingly, as instructed, the following week I telephoned Carr at the Dorchester Hotel and charming and generous man that he was (he could well afford to be – being 'Texas rich') he doled out £1000 – a sizeable sum in those days, equivalent to about £20,000+ now. (In my first job as a publisher's rep soon afterwards I felt lucky to have a salary of £1000 p.a.).

"And so *Magical Ritual Methods* was duly published, which contained, at some length, some very important magical principles, in my view, that served to train and instruct a whole generation. I published in 1969 a short version of the general principles, under the title of *The Practice of Ritual Magic* under my own name, for I felt that they were too important to be left embedded within Bill's somewhat weighty tome. I don't know if Bill ever objected to my doing this, but if so he never said as much directly to me at any rate. With my withdrawal from the SIL Bill more or less took me magically under his wing, seeking to train me in his methods, although this had a down side as I was later to discover. John Hall and my wife Roma were not too happy about this development, and threatened to cease working with me (something of the lines of work I was engaged upon with them can be found in the last chapter of *Experience of the Inner Worlds*).

"However, I felt I was right to stick to my guns, and things continued to run in tandem for a while until I constructed an 8 ft square concrete hut at the bottom of my garden and furnished it as a small temple according to the Bill Gray principles. In this I did some work with three local students, David and Silvia Hicks and their friend Patrick, of the *Helios Course in Practical Qabalah* which I had started up in 1964 in concert with Ernest Butler (and which later in 1973 became the SOL, with Dolores and Mike Nowicki installed to run it in conjunction with Ernest – but that's another story). At this point John Hall and Roma backed off for they did not go for the whole ritual magical scene. Any work with Bill was done at his place though, which could be quite exciting, as he was very liberal with the incense, which in a confined space could be like a London fog, and he was quite imaginative with other aids as well, including naphtha flares on occasion. He did rather like the sound of his own voice chanting Qabalistic mantra of his own composing, which could go on a bit at times – a sample of this I later recorded on a couple of cassettes for general sale.

"He did have a strong feel for the outdoors, and used to bicycle for miles. Out to Toddington from Cheltenham for example, and on one occasion to the Rollright Stones by night, only to arrive at dawn and find the place occupied by a man with a caravan having a shave to the accompaniment of his radio… Bill also decided that he would like to initiate me to follow in his footsteps, which I agreed to with some reservation, as I felt, rightly or wrongly, that I had already received far more important initiation into the Greater Mystery grades at the SIL. However, I went along with it, as

I felt that Bill knew his stuff and as an editor/publisher to the bone felt it almost a duty to learn all I could from the old boy.

"Bill was no slouch when it came to writing rituals, or to making ritual equipment; he was quite skilled at metalwork and could make, for example, standing brass or copper crosses, inset with gemstones and engraved with sigils. In this he was an exemplar to most tyro magicians – and, as may be read in his books – the budding magus should have four principal symbolic weapons, a wand representing his will which he should fashion himself, a cup representing his ability to give and receive love which should be given to him, a sword which must be earned – although purchasing one was allowable, and a pantacle which should be inscribed with his own symbolic understanding of the universe. He also had quite good prophetic powers on occasion. At the time when I realised that Helios could not support me any more and I found a job as a publisher's representative, he said at the time: this will not be your final employment destination, that will come later – and sure enough after 18 months I did move to another company with whom I worked and progressed until retirement.

"However, having passed through most of the initiation process I happened to be on the road in south west Wales and put up at a small hotel for the night. The next morning I had ordered *The Guardian* with my early morning tea, but for some reason *The Times* was delivered instead. Somewhat to my amazement it contained an article about ultra right wing publications and gave quotations from some of them including readers' letters – amongst which I discovered quoted 'W.G.G. Cheltenham'. I felt now that he had gone too far. Although somewhat soft left of centre myself, I have no great concern with the political opinions of those with whom I work, and some of those at the SIL could be naïvely quite right wing, but being actively engaged with the neo-fascist press was a step too far. I accordingly told Bill I felt I could no longer work with him. His reaction was furious, and I realised the truth of Dion Fortune's remark somewhere in *Psychic Self-Defence* about teachers who cannot bear to let go of their students. Nonetheless I was adamant in my decision, although Bill insisted that this was just a 'test' to be expected by all who had received initiation, and it was important that I should not fail it. That however cut no ice with me – as I considered my more valid initiation had been with the SIL anyway.

"He then insisted that I attend a ritual in which I took upon myself all the bad karma resulting from our association. This I naturally declined to do. And anyway, he went on to say, the initiation he had given me was not valid because the "lock word" had not been pronounced (whatever that is). Too bad, I thought, but was a little apprehensive in that I owed him a cheque for a small amount of royalties and I knew that he might be very likely to use my signature upon it as a link for some kind of magical riposte. I heard no more until a year later when a slim unexpected package arrived through the post. It contained a replica of my magical wand, broken in two. End of story more or less, except that I was somewhat amused by his cheek in writing to me soon afterwards for a duplicate cheque, as the other one had expired without having been cashed! Of course, good guy that I am, I provided it. It was at this time that having sold out my editions of Bill's books, and being strapped for cash to print new ones, I was very happy to find Aquarian Press willing to take over Bill's titles – and I felt they could most probably find a wider market for them. I was quite happy for Helios to find talent, bring it on and pass it on to 'proper' publishers. Aquarian Press, which originally had been a one man and his dog kind of business, rather like Helios, under Frank Clive-Ross, had at that time been taken over by a young man and his father who were in process of doing the same with a number of other small companies, until eventually they were in turn gobbled up by HarperCollins.

"It must have been in the early 1970s that I had a new approach from Bill. Apparently Aquarian had become so fed up with his attitude as an author that they had arbitrarily put all his books out of print overnight and wanted nothing more to do with him – bugger the expense. Bill said that he had meditated hard and long but his inner plane contacts seemed to insist that his only way forward was to approach me again. I must know, he wrote, obviously through grated teeth, how much this must be costing him! Nonetheless, being a naïve and idealistic cove I took on his next two books, *The Tree of Evil* and *The Rollright Ritual*. With the latter was a tape, as at much the same time Bill introduced me to Bob Stewart, and I took on the experiment of issuing a set of four tapes, two by Bill and two by Bob Stewart. (As a sign of the times I remember agonising long as to whether we should issue them as long accepted 'open reel' or as new-fangled and little tried 'cassettes' – the market was about split 50/50 between).

"In the course of time it became apparent that Helios should be run down, having more or less served its purpose. Bill by this time had made closer acquaintance with Carr Collins, and was beginning to receive wider recognition as a result of his books. He thus began to be invited over to the States and made a big impression, particularly in the South – as also in South Africa (surprise, surprise, although Bob Stewart tells the story of meeting a Zulu who said he had been helped no end by Bill when out there. So Bill it seems, was prepared, as he claimed, to tolerate black people as long as they were 'in their own place'). It was from a close friend of Carr's, the Jungian psychologist Dr James Hall, that I heard that Bill had not a good word to say for me and was spreading malicious tales about me to Carr and his circle. I imagine much the same was occurring with the Weisers, with whom he also struck up a fairly close relationship. However, as none of this affected me materially, and it was all in another country anyway, I did not worry too much about this. However, I drew consolation from James Hall's opinion of Bill, which he summed up in one word: 'Paranoid'.

"In the meantime I never exchanged any correspondence with Bill. We did once nearly meet by accident in Cheltenham one day but he diplomatically crossed the street before we came face to face. The last I saw of him was at one of the big party receptions that Carr Collins flung in London. I forget the exact date but it cannot have been a great while before Bill became incapacitated. He was leaning heavily on a stick and I happened to come across him in the gents toilet where he turned upon me savagely, banging his stick on the floor, and shouting about some grievance that I could not make head nor tail of. I assumed that he must think I was somehow engaged in publishing still, or had given advice that was against his interests. God only knows. I simply left him to it. And that was the last time we met.

"Bob Stewart has since told me that he went through much the same performance with Bill, who it seems was part of a tradition that believed that each magician should, before he died, pass on his knowledge (and also his karma!) to a chosen successor. This had obviously been on the cards with me, hence Bill's considerable chagrin at being thwarted at the last moment. He had, after that, settled on Bob Stewart apparently. But you will obviously have to approach Bob for the detail of that, if he is willing to talk about it. I had always assumed Bill to be a loner, apart from going off to Brighton each quarter for what I imagined to be a masonic meeting, but Bob reckons him to have been part of a larger group. I'm not sure about that.

"As far as Bill Gray is concerned, I count it as an important contribution of mine to the common weal that I first 'discovered' him and set him on his way as a published author. Pity it all had to end in recriminations on his part, but I think I can be hardly alone on the receiving end of that kind of thing. I quite liked and admired the old bugger – warts and all. He was extremely knowledgeable and could be highly entertaining as a mimic, his taking off the local spiritualists was a great hoot, and I regret that I never saw him playing the Dame at the local pantomime as I am sure he would have done it marvellously. My main reaction being one of happily waving farewell to him from a distance and then retiring, singing to myself a Shakespearean song that begins with the couplet: 'Blow blow thou winter wind...' But he is hardly the only one to fit that bill. Simply the most prominent."

Now look at Bill's version:

"I have always been interested in racial Traditions and their importance in esoteric practice. I believe ethnic identity is of great spiritual significance and has its very valuable part to play in human history. At that particular period I was very concerned at the huge immigration problems which I believe threatened our country in many ways from many angles. Everyone is entitled to their own views on miscegenation and mine are definitely against the practice. At all events I wrote to an association calling itself the Race Preservation Society and expressed my views privately. Some of my comments were published out of context in an article written for the *Times* newspaper but the only signature given was 'W. G. Cheltenham.' I did not even know about this, and had certainly authorised no permission to print from private letters in a public paper.

"My first intimation of this was a letter from Basil saying that he wanted no more to do with me personally because of my racialistic views which he felt were 'deeply evil' in origin, but he was prepared to continue our association on a purely business and commercial footing."

The irony is that Bill goes on to tell the tale of Basil's dissociation in almost exactly the same words. There is no spin, no twist, no undue emphasis. Yet in Bill's mind the listeners are clearly expected to gasp in astonishment, to ooze empathy in one direction (his) and send waves of scorn in the other (toward Basil). Perhaps the older generation did. Perhaps their standards are different, higher or more precise, because the fact is that most people today – regardless of their personal attitudes on race – can't really see that Basil did much wrong at all. Certainly not enough to justify years of spleen from 'W. G. of Cheltenham'. Without going into deep psychological analyses, perhaps it is simply the case that Bill really didn't like to be criticised. He could give it out, but he couldn't take it.

Sandra West also drew swords with him over this very same issue, and at the same time:

The more Bill got interested in his race hatred, the more I found myself forced to disagree with him. Negros, white men, redskins, Chinese and so on – we are all the same species. Genetic drift and different climates have given rise to different racial characteristics but we're all Homo Sapiens...

The more Bill became involved in his ideas, the more we began to diverge. Bill was still inclined to come up to London for the various 'psychic fairs' which were becoming popular but his behaviour was making a lot of people uncomfortable. I was building up my own firm of *Spook Enterprises*, selling candles, incenses, scented oils and so on at these psychic fairs. Bill would come and look at my stall and then be rude to my customers.

On one occasion, he was incredibly insulting to a black student of mine. He then turned to me and said that he hoped to be born in South Africa next time. To quote his exact words, 'At least a nigger knows his place in South Africa!'

It seemed to me that at that moment something – some alien spirit/ entity/recording angel – passed and heard Bill's words. Somewhere on some other plane, something emitted a very sinister laugh. It reminded me of the legend of the Flying Dutchman. Satan overheard the man's rash words and condemned the Dutchman to sail the seas forever, never to return home. I believe that Something overheard Bill's rash words and his next Incarnation may indeed be South African. I wonder what colour his skin will be...
[letter to MC, December 2002]

Much as we both loved the man, in differing ways, we cannot – will not – skirt this unpleasant side of the very mundane Bill Gray from Cheltenham. He was a racist: a typical product of his time and class. And while he was certainly not alone in his attitude, he was more than usually forthright when it came to expressing it. However, his comment about South Africa was oddly prophetic in more than one way because Jacobus Swart, a native of that country, invited him over many times and saw for himself how Bill modified his viewpoint, and indeed became both extremely comfortable in Black company and extremely angry on their behalf over the way the Whites had crushed native traditions. So over the years he mellowed into what he termed a 'racialist', and we will look at that a little more in the next chapter, on the Sangreal. Anyone who wishes to excuse him, or look for the higher side of William G. Gray, must look within that rather esoteric term and find what they need therein. They might get a surprise.

And to forestall a current slur that Bill was also anti-Semitic, it should be noted that this was a man who, as a young soldier was present during the birth throes of the modern state of Israel and was intensely sympathetic to the tribulations of Jewish settlers. He worked harmoniously with Jewish magical systems and, let us not forget, chose a Jew, Jacobus Swart, as his magical son. Nor did he ever show any antagonism toward Alan Richardson's first wife, who is Chinese. Perhaps now we can hope that in Bill's next life the Lord of Justice will make whatever balances are deemed appropriate.

Another man who was deeply affected by Bill at this period was R.J. 'Bob' Stewart, whose own books and work have had a great impact on the development and expansion of the Magical Tradition. His memoir provides important insights into Bill as a man and as a magician…

"So this was my life in the late 1960s: I wanted to find a teacher, but was aware mainly of Eastern (actually neo-Eastern) traditions, highly popularised by the hippy era. How I discovered W. G. Gray is a story not of diligent research or failed attempts at contact with obscure teachers, but something quite different. I found Bill Gray through inner contacts. Inner contacts is a term widely used nowadays to mean conscious psycho-spiritual connection with actual coherent and identifiable spiritual entities in other dimensions. As this concept is central to all practical magic, it seems hardly surprising, in retrospect, that inner contacts played a major role in my relationship with Bill. Here is what happened:

"Around 1968 or '69 I was meditating, in my garret, much like any other impoverished musician in his late teens or early twenties, but without the drugs. To my surprise someone appeared to me in my meditations, each day at exactly 4 pm: this appearance was what, today, we call an inner contact. He was an old oriental man, radiating an intense blue, which had a calming and inspiring effect. When I became practiced at Qabalah, I later discovered that this was an inner contact mediating the spiritual forces of the 4th Emanation, that of Mercy and Compassion.

"This inner plane master taught me the basics of meditation and work with the subtle forces of the body: not so much in words, as in sensation and (usually) wordless intimations. Indeed, much was somehow stored in my consciousness by this contact, information and dormant abilities that opened out over a number of years. This process is known to adepts (though I did not know about it at the time) as an interaction whereby concentrated "seeds" of development are transmitted to the student instantly, but flourish and grow over time. Providing, of course, the student chooses consciously to work with them. Otherwise they stay quiet, perhaps to flourish in a future life.

"So what, I hear you ask, has all this got to do with W. G. Gray? Well, in 1969 Helios Book Service, run at that time by Gareth Knight and John Hall, published Bill's book *Magical Ritual Methods*, which became a revolutionary classic of 20th century magical literature. I found this book, in hardback, newly printed, in the staid conservative Reference Library of Bristol city, in the west of England, where I was living. There must have been a librarian with active esoteric interests there in those days: when I visited this same library, nostalgically, in the early 1990s there was not a magical or esoteric book to be seen.

"So I found this curious book, *Magical Ritual Methods*, and began to study it at one of the library reading desks. While reading, someone looked over my shoulder, and asked me repeatedly and persistently about the book, though reference libraries are supposed to be Temples of Silence. Was this mystery person W. G. Gray, as you might suspect? No, it was someone who probably stole the book from the library that very day, and it was never replaced. I had to order a copy from Helios, thus buying my first W. G. Gray book. In those days they were mailed 'in a plain paper cover' to ensure anonymity and the safety of the recipient. My first tarot deck, the Waite/Coleman Smith deck came the same way, much as if it were seditious literature. Which of course, it always has been.

"When I returned to the garret for my 4 o'clock meditation, little knowing that Gray's book would not be in the library the following morning, my inner plane teacher appeared very strongly to me. Something unusual happened: he drew close, as if making a powerful effort to reach into the human world, and said very clearly in my mind 'Good. You have found the book. You will not see me again for a long time. Goodbye'. And from that day to this, I have not encountered him again.

"So, when my discreet mail-ordered copy of Bill's book finally arrived, I began the practices described therein, and knew immediately that I had done this before, and that it was central to my life. I wrote to W. G. Gray care of the publishers, and received a reply. We corresponded for a while, and I was invited to visit the Grays, William and Roberta, in Cheltenham. So began our relationship, which lasted for about 7 years, until Bill and I fell out.

"Fell out is perhaps a modest understatement: in truth, Bill cursed me ritually for failing to live up to his expectations. This was a pattern with him, though I knew it not at the time.

"To the gentle modern magician or pagan it may come as a shock, but the old school occultists were able and willing to utter powerful curses if they were displeased. Bill Gray had very trenchant opinions about everything, and backed them up with magical actions. I do not think this is appropriate today, but for a wartime generation who had seen many hardships, many broken promises, many deaths of loved ones; this attitude may be understood, though not condoned. Also, Bill and Bobbie were of that strong-minded generation of English military and air force officers with powerful nationalistic and racist opinions. *Tut tut*, say we all, as politically correct magicians of the 21st century, but that is the way it was.

"So Bill Gray cursed me ritually, after 6 years or so of my work as a student or apprentice. The details of the falling out are less important than the event, but we argued over some music I had composed and recorded for his major work 'The Rite of Light', and I was not to be forgiven.

"Here is the strange truth of this incident: it was good for me. At the time it was painful and difficult, and the effect of a curse from W. G. was not to be taken lightly. It was good for me: I learned a great deal from it, on the inner levels, and discovered that the dark side of a spiritual teacher is as valuable to the student as the light side. In short, W. G. Gray was the best teacher I could have had, was the teacher that had been lined up for me by the inner contacts, and I remember him with affection and respect today. Spiritual forces are not as simple as we like to think, and the inner temples always bring us into contact with those who will best serve.

"Of course there was much that happened in those five or so years: I had the good fortune to take part in rituals with Bill and Bobbie Gray, Patricia Crowther (a high priestess of Gardnerian witchcraft, and very powerful) and Pat's first husband Arnold, who was no slouch at magic himself. Arnold used to poke fun at Bill continuously, and call him 'the Pope', as Bill liked to dress in a rather Roman Church style for ritual. Arnold also, playfully, mocked Bill's habit of doggerel rhyme, such as Bill's signing a book to me *To Bob from Bill / Be What You Will*. Arnold once said, in aside to me, 'What's in the ritual tonight, is it Air and Fire, Earth and Water / Doing what we think we oughter?'

"I lost many photographs from the 60s and 70s, but a photograph of Pat, Bill, and my youthful self, taken at the Rollright Stones in Oxfordshire, appears in Pat's autobiography, *One Witch's World*.

"Roberta (Bobbie) Gray was an astrologer, a science fiction writer, and she knew a lot about Celtic mythology long before it became fashionable. In retrospect I realise that I learned much from her, though I thought Bill was the sole teacher. There were late nights drinking whiskey and listening to outrageously right wing opinions from Bill, who would revert to Russian after several glasses of whiskey, a language that he could not speak when sober. The Grays were cat people, and I even took my cat to visit their cats. One of the few photographs I have of that time shows my cat and one of their cats, peering at one another through the kitchen window.

"I learned the foundations of Qabalah during those years, the basics of ritual, and, most important of all, I was initiated by Bill into the inner priesthood. This is done by laying on of hands, in a ceremony that must reach back for thousands of years, no matter what current form it takes. So I received the sacred touch, handed down through the ages, just as Bill had received it from his initiator and mentor. By this time Bill had argued with all his old friends, and he had to make a plea to Norman Gills to take part in the initiation ceremony, as it must always be witnessed and mediated by at least one other initiate. That was the only time I met Norman, and I have no idea where he is today, or if he is still alive.

"There was one remarkable event, other than the curse, that stands out for me, and which gave rise to the core of some my own magical work. Once again it is about inner contacts, not outer teaching or learning.

"One day Bill gave me a rather crumpled and stained scrap of paper with a magical square drawn on it, a square of just four numbers, 1-4, in a particular order. *[See below]* I kept the original for years, but mislaid it somewhere along the way to the 21st century. Magical squares were a big deal for Renaissance magicians, but 19th century occultists and their heirs had lost the understanding of them ... if you do not believe me, just read any of the many books published that repeat the squares but give no insight into how they work.

1	4	2	3
4	3	1	2
2	1	3	4
3	2	4	1

"Bill handed me the paper and said, 'This is a magic square. I think it is about music, but as I am tone deaf I do not understand it. I think it is for you. Let me know what you make of it'. Thus began the system of Elemental Chant and associated magic that I later published as two books, and which I use in my own magical work, and which has now been taken up by many people worldwide.

"Bill had received the square from his inner contacts, and handed it to me. I had to figure it out, work with it, and transmit its effects, knowledge, and power, to the world. No small task. And, surprisingly, as soon as I meditated upon that simple number square, many remarkable results followed. So I have Bill to thank as mediator, and the inner temples to thank as originators, for opening out this powerful path of magic, which has played a strong role in my life.

"In the early 1990s I had one last sequence of inner contact involving Bill Gray. One day I had a deep urge to go to Glastonbury, and I convinced my wife (now a former wife) and a lady friend of hers who was visiting that we absolutely had to go there immediately. It was raining some of the time, and we trudged around the Abbey, the Tor, and the sentimental touristy New Age stores. Somewhat of an anticlimax, I thought. But I was told a few days later that this had been the day when Bill's ashes were scattered on the Tor.

"Around the time of Bill's death, I wrote to Bobbie, saying briefly that they had both been a powerful influence on me, and that my feelings were of respect and deep affection. A reply came from Bobbie's sister, who told me that Bobbie had died more or less as I was writing my letter. I always felt that she had somehow received it.

"Finally, I have no sense of W. G. Gray in the spirit world, though I can sense other mentors such as Ronald Heaver, one of the Glastonbury adepts, in the Inner Convocation.

"So, to summarise, I might say this: if you consider living the magical life be aware that books will always be stolen, curses uttered, mysterious scraps of paper circulated. But there is also inspiration, power, love and mystery. W. G. Gray combined deep spiritual impetus and mysticism with rabid eccentricity, neo-fascism and complex occultism, but he was as influential as Dion Fortune before him in moving the Western magical tradition forward. In Bill's case it was the old British Army method of three steps forward and two steps back. But that one step is still being measured today, and I am grateful for it.

"He used to joke that he wanted the rude two-fingered V sign, a very British way of giving offence, carved upon his grave: indeed, he had a wooden model hand carved with its first two fingers extended and an offensive motto on the stand. Was this trivial? Maybe, but when the rude V sign, given with the back of the hand turned outwards, is turned the other way, palm outwards, it is the V for Victory sign, which had deep meaning and emotional association for the British generation who lived through, and survived, the Second World War.

"From an esoteric perspective Victory is the 7th Emanation of the Tree of Life, that of sensuality, exaltation, the goddess Venus, and the Archangel of Wisdom. This Archangel is Auriel, keeper of the Sacred Book of Wisdom, mediator of Grace to humanity, and guardian of the deepest Mysteries of Earth. Such a seemingly paradoxical mixture of wild feelings, deep emotions, and hidden wisdom, all of the 7th Emanation, summarises, for me, the drama of W. G. Gray's long and influential life. Victory, Bill..."

It is surely a measure of Bill's impact and innate status that people who have been ritually cursed, or lambasted, or assassinated on all sorts of levels can still look back upon the man with an admiration and respect bordering on fondness.

The fact is that this period marked the time when the chiropodist of Bennington Street took on the rather impressive persona of William G. Gray, the learned writer. The books he poured out at that time really did have an enormous if indirect impact upon a whole generation of magicians. Basil and Bob are right: *Magical Ritual Methods* alone really did contain some important magical principles 'that served to train and instruct a whole generation'. A whole generation then later stole them, used them, developed them, and passed the knowledge on – often with the pretence that these were part of an ancient tradition to which they belonged.

The techniques were the end result of years of hard work, starting with that time he made a temple out of a tent in his childhood home in Southampton, carrying unremittingly through to that modest basement temple in Cheltenham, but increasingly sparked by what was 'coming through' to him from the inner planes. In typical Gravian style, he writes:

"By that time I had my 'contacts' as connections with inner intelligence are known in occult circles. These really amount to no more than a kind of telecommunicative link with deeper classifications of consciousness than those usually available to an average human mind. I would see what could be done with them."

No more than a telepathic link with deep inner intelligences! Bill really wasn't boasting here. He took that sort of thing as a matter of course, and almost assumed that everyone could do what he did.

There was DF of course. He insisted – and Bobbie agreed – that she was the major influence behind much of his technical work, and in particular the associations of the Tarot with the Paths on the Tree of Life. Bobbie once said that when she was helping type up *The Talking Tree*, which dealt with this in vast detail, that she couldn't tell where Bill's prose ended and DF's began.

There were hints that Merlin came through in typically brusque and uncompromising fashion.

But mostly there was a cluster of inner Intelligences which didn't really respond to names, as such, or link with any historicity:

> Are they often wrong? Frankly I don't know, but I am often wrong in interpreting their communications. How do I 'get in touch'? Again I don't know. Sometimes I am conscious of a sort of 'presence' more or less just behind me, somewhat to my left (the receptive side), or of course it could be my left brain activating itself. ... Do I know who these 'Inners' are? No, not by any names which might be familiar. And do I trust them? Not by one single inch... They aren't interested in doing anything for me, but with me if you get the difference, so you might say we have a love-hate relationship.
> *[letter to AR, 19th December 1987]*

Jacobus Swart, who probably got closer to Bill than anyone, contributed a long letter [6th January 2003] which said a great deal about the older man's own attitude:

"You know, he actually never mentioned to me his 'inner' contact with Dion Fortune at all. We did talk about our respective 'Inners,' and like him I did not find them very forthcoming in the least. I recently listened to an old cassette recording I made of a discussion between Bill and myself on this very subject, and we both agreed that our respective relationships with 'spirits,' or 'Inners' as we liked to call them, were shaky ones. My particular 'Inners' are not a very forthcoming lot, however admirable they may be in other ways. They do their job, but they do not give any prizes so to speak. They are such a cryptic lot, and I do not believe they treat anyone else better than they treat me. As in my own case, Bill also felt that he certainly has never had a hot line to God or lesser authorities. About all we could say about our relationships with these 'inner entities' during that discussion, was that we were told to shut up and get on with the job. Personally I find these 'Higher Orders of Life' very hard to deal with, not particularly co-operative so far as human affairs are concerned, and not very exciting to work with. You will naturally wonder why I bother at all. The reason is simply because it was in me before I was born, just as others have it in themselves for the same purpose. Call it 'Fate' if you like. We came here to do specific jobs, and until we do them we shall be bound to human bodies. That sums up what Bill and I discussed as far as 'inner guides' are concerned.

"Now, that may not be as revealing as one might want for a biography of William Gray, but there is one point that he made that I find rather interesting. On questioning him as to where he thought his 'inners' could be positioned on the Tree of Life, he replied that they are forces of Judgement expressed on the 'path' between *Binah* and *Chockmah*. I told him how I recalled him writing that Initiates have to answer three vital questions, these being:

What is my right Judgement in this course?
Am I entirely justified?
Is opportunity favourable?

"He replied something like: 'Yes, and I am not a good example of that.' On querying why he said that, he replied that his 'Inners' were often hitting his own back with his Rod, and that he was physically suffering the consequences of impatience and rash judgements, but that he would rather have it out that way, than having to wait for a future life to deal with the consequences of his actions, perhaps in a worse manner..."

The old mage's advice to anyone who might want to argue with the wisdom or otherwise of their own Inners echoed what ENH had told him years earlier: The best protection is to become a 'living Question Mark' . Query everything all the time, and in the end, let the ultimate decision be your own.

In a letter to Alan Richardson dated 1st October 1989 Gray wrote:

A long time ago they used to be called the 'Watchers' because that's about all they did. Watched Humanity to see how we were developing, but didn't actually *do* anything one way or another. Neither helped nor harmed. They might pass an opinion or possibly offer some advice IF they took all that much interest in you (which was seldom) but because they had a clear perception of what was going on in this world and the most likely outcome of what would result, it was advantageous to *try* and persuade them to communicate – if they would. They were usually quite indifferent to the casual fate of humans, much as we might be about insects or even microbes, but *sometimes* they *might* be manoeuvred into extending a 'hand' in our direction if we showed signs of particular ability or interest... In other words they aren't sweet and loving critturs any more than laboratory technicians are 'caring' specialists for their bench-animals. They are there to see that a particular process takes place, and that is that. I don't have any illusions about the nature of the 'Spirit Guides' we're dealing with…

A cold, cold lot were dealing with him on the inside. And they were 'hitting his back with his Rod'. Or in colloquial terms, they were giving him some stick.

They certainly weren't infallible with their predictions. He had told a number of people that the cassette recordings of his rituals were going to sell hugely, that they would really take off on both sides of the Atlantic. In the event, only a handful of people ever heard them. ENH was certainly right about becoming a living Question Mark: Use your own judgement. Take full responsibility for your decisions. Don't trust *Them* an inch.

Not all magicians take such view of their own inner contacts, it must be said, and that's a story for them to tell. But the austere nature of the entities who lay behind the Sangreal Sodality is in marked contrast to those who lay behind the Rollright Stones. In a letter to Pat Crowther, published in *One Witch's World*, he wrote:

> I have pointed out that although the Rite 'came through' me, it is not my personal or exclusive property and the Inners at the Stones seem keen to get those in sympathy with Them to start something regular there. They said they would do it in the end, (but I did not really think they could do it, to be quite truthful) …
>
> It's the Pattern which is of more importance than the words I got through to translate the old intentions behind things. Of course it is like an initiation, for it is the Initiation of Life-Death-Life, etc, in the Cosmic Circle we all go through. The idea is to get the Pattern sufficiently deep into the basic consciousness, and the rest should take care of itself like an autopilot.
>
> Oh yes, the Words teach too, because they link on very deep levels of awareness indeed. Whatever 'They' are behind the Rollright Stones, 'They' are certainly a very kindly and beneficent lot, for some reason still very concerned with this land and their living descendants and spiritual dependents in it.

If there is any wisdom in hindsight, it can seem as if the unexpected diversion he took via the megaliths was an opportunity for him to move his life into a completely different direction. The quality of work he did at these ancient British sites is so high, so unusual, so in touch with the about-to-explode Pagan Revival that you can wish he had stayed in that

William G. Gray in action at the King Stone, Rollright

area of Earth Magic, and not been sucked back into the cerebral mysteries of the Qabalah. Who knows how that might have affected his own personality in the years which followed.

This was the period of his most intense writing, beginning with the *Ladder of Lights* rapidly followed by *Magical Ritual Methods*, both originally published by Helios Books in the manner already described by Basil Wilby.

The *Ladder of Lights* looked at the Qabalah afresh. It started at the bottom of the Tree, and worked its way to the top – and beyond. It is apparent in every line that this is not the work of someone rehashing Dion Fortune's work on the topic (which in itself has often been accused of being a rehash of Crowley's), but that the writer has experienced every stage, and is talking from long and exquisite insight. Obscure concepts are made clear. Occult secrets are revealed. It is rather as if Crick and Watson were to say: *Look, we've discovered something that we're calling DNA. Look at this diagram of the double helix. How DNA relates to us is as follows...* The book is as good as that. It takes such a radical approach, and is written clearly despite his almost Victorian tendency to capitalise.

Magical Ritual Methods is exactly that: an exposition of all the techniques he had been developing – by himself – over many years. At one stroke he wipes out hundred years of verbiage and gives deceptively simple techniques that will enable everyone to make deep inner links by means of basic outward symbols. He looks at the use of the Elements, Weapons, and Tarot in a completely new way, and does so with such variety, originality and depth that you have to sit back and gasp. He gives clever diagrams that will help create Words of Power, and talks about the overwhelming importance of Nothingness, and how to return to it. The ponderous 'Lesser Banishing Ritual of the Pentagram' which was used by the Golden Dawn and regarded by the unimaginative as the *ne plus ultra* of basic magic, is made to look archaic next to his own banishing ritual which uses the vowels IAO and the concepts of Time, Space and Events. In the context of the time, he is almost akin to the present day Chaos Magicians, who likewise reject the traditional workings, not realising that Bill was there 50 years before them. And his chapter on 'Ritual Sonics and Invocations' alone is still light years ahead of most things being done at the moment.

If his inners were giving him inspiration to write, then not all his books were brilliant, despite the insistence of these contacts. Some are rather dated now, such as *Seasonal Occult Rituals*, although it has to be pointed out that when this was published many of the new witches had no notion of linking their rites with the seasons, and the actual rites themselves as practiced by Bill attracted a wide range of influential occultists.

To the pagan British psyche, which is not well interested in the images and energies that are symbolised by Raphael, Michael, Gabriel, and Auriel, *The Inner Traditions of Magic* can seem uncomfortably Judaeo-Christian in tone. Even so, there are some superb visions of the Native British past, such as his description of the techniques and rites involved for the incarnation of a Sacred King. Basically, when the time came twelve active and potent males were chosen, one for each Sign, and each was required to have some outstanding quality which would make him a worthy father. One male might be chosen for his wealth, another for his skill at hunting, another for intelligence, and so on. Together they formed the circle of seed-donors, or 'God-fathers' as he termed it. The eventual object of their attentions, the Virgin-Bride, was specially selected for her moral and personal attributes as a fit mother of the god-to-be.

> The men formed the perimeter of the circle, the Maid the centre, and the Old Woman had her peculiar dance-pattern between the two. Procedure varied considerably according to local custom. Sometimes the Maid danced spirally between the men and came to a central rest position embodying the waiting Earth-Womb, or sometimes she was scarcely conscious of the operation at all, being in a state of semi-drugged ecstasy. Elaborations such as music, etc., depended on resources and beliefs. The men might be as still as their staffs, but mostly they evolved a species of on-the-spot sort of jigging movement, possibly accompanied by chanting and drumming.

> Each male taking part in the Rite had to work themselves into a condition of consciousness where they were convinced they had successfully embodied their particular God-Aspect. This of course was done by characteristic miming and invocations for as long as might be necessary to obtain the effect needed. Sometimes hours were passed this way before conditions were right.

The focus of it all lay within the Old Woman, who went from one to another with suggestions and commands, weaving the spell, bringing the whole rite to its climax. Whatever ecstatic or trance state the others might work themselves into this Old Woman had to remain in full control, no matter what. She brought with her a particularly sacred object: '…a fairly small phallic shaped horn from some suitable animal with a pierced point normally kept closed by the Old Woman's own hand.'

When the time was judged right, the Old Woman of the Cup went deosil around the circle from one male to another collecting their seed into the horn cup as quickly as possible. They donated this not as their human selves, but in the character and on behalf of the God-Aspect they represented.

When the critical moment came, the Old Woman injected this accumulation of seed into the Maid by means of the horn which she blew into from the broad end, thus applying the necessary pressure. This was the 'breath of life' needed for the insemination process.

These are genuine glimpses of megalithic magic. They are *superb*. Why couldn't we have seen more, much more, of this sort of thing, and less about the Hebraic YHVH that lay at the core of his magic! In fact he obliged, and right handsomely, with a small book called *The Rollright Ritual*. In talking about it, even he seemed bewildered at times by the fact that it was a complete departure from his normal sort of work:

"[This] was in the nature of an experimental encounter with the esoteric side of the Rollright Stones, a very ancient Circle monument in nearby Oxfordshire. This was totally different from my usual class of writing, being virtually Pagan in construction. The ritual in question was directly inspired by the stones themselves during a series of visits I made by solitary bicycle rides when weekend weather was favourable. It was the only one of its kind I have ever attempted, and it was most probably influenced by remembrance of Roy.

"Since I had been asked for photographs with the Rollright Ritual, these were duly done by two members of my personal circle, Lee and Janet James, who were both musical entertainers working a circuit of clubs as a cabaret turn, he with a trumpet and comedy commentary, and she with a Moog Synthesiser and deadpan act. They lived in the North of England and only visited when their circuit was close to us, but this was enough to establish a good rapport and a working relationship. Janet and I were the models while Lee (or Jim as I called him) took the pictures. We were careful not to reveal our faces and selected only the best pictures from a whole stack of them."

In the opinion of many – the out and out pagans – the *Rollright Ritual* was one of his most influential books, and one in which Bill actually allows himself to appear even if he does avoid the personal pronoun. Quite simply Bill would take his old bicycle 'Horace', put on his clips, fortify himself with a few sandwiches and a flask of whisky, and – despite his increasing arthritis – would cycle the fourteen miles or so to the

The Rollright Ritual

Rollright Stones in Oxfordshire. He evokes the journey superbly. His insights are quite moving. And it was through his work with this cluster of standing stones that he learned something of the true purpose of such circles throughout the world.

> To each individual member of a Circle, the "family Stone" or "Old One" had a depth of spiritual significance very hard for us to understand now. That particular Stone stood for all they ever were or would be... The Stone... not only offered status in this world, *but was the gateway to the spirit world also [authors' emphasis]*. In it lived every ancestor. If an ear was pressed closely to the stone when the countryside was fairly silent, those Otherworlders might be heard whispering good counsel or warnings to their living descendants. No use listening at someone else's Stone to learn his secrets. Only family spirits spoke to blood-links with Life. That was the Law. Of course, there were special Stones which spoke to the people periodically, but only those "in the know", or Wise Old Ones could make those talk.

He knew this because the stones themselves told him over a long period of time. By psychometry, or sometimes just a simple empathic leaning back against them, Gray learned how the circle was as much a binding, social focus for the tribal folk who built it, as anything more esoteric. Each stone stood for definite people living in that particular area, together with their relatives alive or dead, and indicated how those people fitted into the community from a social standpoint. He insisted that any intelligent man of those times could take one look round a stone circle and more or less guess what sort of folk had set it up. Though they had no alphabets to read, they did have symbols in the shapes and sorts of stones which stood for certain types of people. This Stone, for instance, showed the wealthiest and most influential people in the place. That one stood for a small family whose speciality was basket making.

But there was blood and gore too. Just after sunrise at a full moon, when the orbs of the luminaries came level and represented 'both Eyes of Heaven', he saw the victim brought before the King-Stone, where he stood with his arms spread out something like a crucified man, and was then swiftly speared from the front up into the rib-cage, straight into the heart. 'Sometimes his body was cooked and shared out as a sacred meal, but often his flesh was eaten raw in small morsels, his blood being drunk by the chosen few, and the remainder sprinkled over the assembly 'as a token of a spirit shared among everyone,' he added.

This is William G. Gray at his best: when he is 'looking back' through the stones and at the ancestors, gleaning lessons for ourselves to carry into the future. How many of his contemporaries were doing similar work? How many of them would bother to get up in the middle of the night and cycle up hill and down dale to commune with a cluster of obscure stones? Not many.

In a way, it is almost as if he helped to awaken the stones. A few years after his work was done with the Rollrights some orthodox researchers whose primary concern was in trying to record the ultrasonics of bats, found that the Rollrights were emitting sounds of their own – that they were singing. Thus began the multi-disciplinary Dragon Project which carried on for some time afterward, and in its own way was responsible for the next generation becoming aware of the forgotten landscapes through which we move.

He then took another radical look at the Qabalah:

"An earlier work of mine *The Tree of Evil* had been published, and it dealt with opposing qualities of the Spheres on the Tree of Life. If those were all beneficial aspects of Life, there had to be malignant ones to oppose them, and no author appeared to have identified or dealt with them as they deserved. So I tackled the job and tried to expound the problem as well as I could. So many people have accepted that positive aligns with good and negative is purely evil that I have done my best to correct this false impression. There are both positive and negative aspects to Good and Evil alike, and I have attempted to clarify this in my exposition.

"By this time I had several books to my name and plans for offering more. *Seasonal Occult Rituals* and *Inner Traditions of Magic* by Aquarian Press. Helios produced *Ladder of Lights*, *Magical Ritual Methods*, *The Tree of Evil*, and were now working on the *Rollright Ritual*. Sangreal Press in the USA had printed my *Office of the Holy Tree of Life*, and my literary contribution to the *Images of the Tree*. At last I had very nearly completed my *Rite of Light* which I had been working on for most of my lifetime..."

A Self Made by Magic however, which he attempted to publish privately, is really very poor despite a few similar nuggets of insight, and seems to be more Bill Gray talking off the top of his head than the product of William G. Gray, the ritualist and qabalist. Sometimes, you can almost hear the voice of ENH with his tone of Sound Common Sense. And his large tome *The Talking Tree* is one of the deepest, densest analyses of the Tarot in the light of the Qabalah that has ever been made. Who else but Bill would have noticed that the apparently random markings on the collar of The Fool are actually Hebrew letters? Who else but Bill would have had the learning to be able to tell us what they mean?

Throughout his life he remained fascinated by words and their origins. The following extract from *Evoking the Primal Goddess* is typical of his insight, all of which found expression in much of his work involving 'ritual sonics':

For those able to find significance in sonic values, it should be noted that the three letters of the Hebrew alphabet classified as 'mothers' are A, M, and Sh. Those are all natural sounds that mothers have made to their babies since time immemorial – the alerting or warning 'Ah-ah.' The comforting and companionable 'MMMMMMM,' and the soothing or slumberous 'SSSSSHHHH' – all associated with the sea and the cycle of life connected with waking a baby up, cuddling it, and putting it to sleep again. 'Mum' is usually the first sensible sound a baby makes, so it is scarcely surprising that it means 'mother' in so many languages. The Semitic version is Amah or Umm, and the reverence attached to the sonic OMM in Sanskrit, reputed to be a root-language of so many humans, is well known by those who may not know its matriarchal meaning consciously. We instinctively pay honour to our greatest Mother every time we use the familiar word amen. However far we may grow away from her womb physically, we return to it mentally on more occasions than are generally recognised.

No-one at that time was writing at this level. Few since have even begun to approach it, although a couple have managed – by stretching themselves enormously – to get their fingertips onto his ledge. Yet we have to constantly remind ourselves that Bill's writings were all deeply rooted in his actual experience: he did not, like so very many of the modern writers on occult topics, simply make it up as he went along or rehash other people's work. If nothing else, whatever his personal or literary faults, he was a true original.

And so we have to look, now, at the crucial time in his life when the divergent streams of his eclectic quest through Witchcraft and Earth Magic, high ritual and Qabalah, all began to focus themselves (rather as the energies of Netzach and Hod converge into golden Tiphareth) on one simple primary concept – the Sangreal.

This becomes the story of how Bill Gray, the chiropodist from Cheltenham, found the Holy Grail in the last years of his extraordinary life.

CHAPTER 11
Seeking The Sangreal

"I've been thinking that what we've missed most in this life is a Cause to live and work for with everything we had. In other lives we've always had <u>something</u> we thought worth dying for whether it was a religion or anything else, but in this incarnation what have we had? Nothing I've ever known about. Can you think of anything?"

Joseph Campbell, author of *The Hero with a Thousand Faces*, has expounded on the great root story of the Western psyche that nourishes virtually every other story ever told, from Mother Goose to the Hollywood blockbusters. He tells of the young innocent, driven from the safe but claustrophobic life of his village, often by his Mother, to search for... *something* – whether it be a treasure, a cause, a raison d'etre, or the Holy Grail itself. He meets a wise elder who, far from giving him the answers he wanted, plants in him only more questions to guide him on his way. In Bill's story this cannot have been anyone else but ENH. As we have already seen in Chapter 4 the crusty old Austrian mage empowered him with the words: 'I can give you only one clue ... the key to the Grail Castle is in yourself. It's up to you to find which lock to turn it in. It may take you the rest of your life to discover that'. And so Bill, like all Questors everywhere, necessarily had to travel onward and alone into the dark wood of the psyche, dealing with the challenges and dangers that lay within.

Yet, as any of the spiritualists he often scorned would insist, at times like this you are never really alone, never completely left to your own devices. Allies are sent when most needed. Quite often these are quite ordinary folk, in many ways, but each having a talent of his or her own that can contribute to the Quest. Then it is a simple question as to whether the hero has the initiative, gumption, and sheer balls to seize the treasure, get the girl, gain the Grail – perhaps they're all the same thing – and bring it home to the 'real' world. If we had to identify two people in particular who gave Bill clear and practical help at crucial moments in his own wildwood, then one was Carr Collins, and the other Jacobus Swart.

Carr Collins, whom he first met him in the lobby of the London Hilton, was a tallish, very slim man in his early fifties with artificially whitened hair and a Harvard Business School success smile. Though this Dallas millionaire was a convinced Christian he had, for some reason, found himself strongly attracted to spiritual topics leading elsewhere entirely. As Bill said, 'I have never met anyone who displayed a keener interest in the occult, yet knew less about its intricacies, often to a point of ludicrous or absurd ignorance'. Yet as Basil Wilby has pointed out, it was Collins' money that funded the publication of much of Bill's work. Which is perhaps a more vital contribution to the Western Tradition than many of us could hope to make in all our rites, prayers and meditations. When Bill Gray walked through the door of the Hilton, and doubtless greeted Carr with his notorious firm handshake and challenging glare, he had found another vital ingredient in the bringing together of his life's work.

Carr Collins was the money man. And before we start getting prissy about the place of 'filthy lucre' in spiritual endeavour, we might remember that the manifestation of any idea into physical reality requires the energies of the mundane plane to give it form. What is cash if not just such an energy exchange? Carr walked a strange road. Even Bill, with his in-depth knowledge of odd humans, was quite startled by certain aspects of this man.

"Carr controlled what he called the Sangreal Foundation, and when I made some reference to its meaning he confessed he had not the slightest idea of its significance. I looked at him unbelievingly and asked him point blank how he had chosen that particular term as a name for his fund... He told me that when he was being divorced from his first wife and setting up a fund for her maintenance, he wanted to put aside some special money for the furtherance of his esoteric interests in such a way that she could never make any claims on it. When he was asking himself what to call this Foundation for the specific purpose of advancing the Western Inner Tradition, the word 'Sangreal' just 'slipped into his mind', and he liked the sound of it, so that was the name he chose. He could not be sure if he heard it spoken with a male or a female voice or anything else, but so far as he was concerned it served his purpose perfectly, and so it was selected. Questioned in depth he could not remember where he had read the word, and he was fascinated to hear my explanations. They were quite new to him and most relevant. To say I was astounded at his information would be putting it mildly."

As we have seen, there were very few books on Magic being published at that time, and most of them were reprints of classics by Crowley, Dion

Fortune, Papus and others long since dead. The plain fact was, as Neville Armstrong, the editor-in-chief of Spearmans occult publishers pointed out to Alan Richardson: 'Books on magic just don't sell. I don't know why, but they just don't'. With the injection of some hard cash into the process, however, it made it possible for the tiny company of Helios Books to launch Bill onto his unremunerative but enormously influential career as a writer. Under the aegis of the Sangreal Foundation, Bill was also awarded an Honorary Doctorate; he hung it in his toilet.

The second person to enter his life and influence it deeply, many years later, was a young South African who found himself casually browsing through the occult titles in a London bookshop, doubtless suppressing inward groans at the various titles promising instant adepthood and power. His eye was drawn to a slim red booklet entitled *The Rite of Light* and bearing the symbol of the Cosmic Circle Cross. This was Jacobus Swart, whose name in English, as Bill pointed out, meant James Black. He was a professional musician and a keen Qabalist who had received training at Safad in Israel, which is a sort of official home of the Lurian School of Qabalistic thought. After studying the small red book carefully he went home and showed it to his 'Teacher', an ex-Jesuit who promptly told him to get hold of the author if he possibly could, because that man would be capable of guiding him wherever he wanted to go. What Jacobus didn't realise at the time was that he was to be a catalyst in taking the author, William Gray, somewhere that he deeply needed to go … South Africa.

The invitation from Jacobus came after a year or so of letters to and fro on the intricacies of Qabalah and the Western Tradition. Jacobus would pay for the air ticket so that Bill could help him to plan out a temple on Western esoteric lines. Bill would also get to meet his group and visit the tourist sights for himself.

"Jacobus and I greeted each other like long parted bloodbrothers. I liked Gloria his wife too…" And by every interpretation of his words, he fell *deeply* in love with South Africa.

Together, he and Jacobus constructed a Temple. "We went from one second hand shop to another picking up likely items… A couple of newspaper cardboard centre rolls which made ideal pillars, with beach balls for their tops and squares of chipboard for their bases. Small kerosene lamps of different colours to mark the Quarters. An ornamental Sword for the East. A plain wooden circle which could be made into a Shield for the North. A special lamp to be stood on a stand in the South with a plain Rod on the wall behind it painted half black and half white. In the West a suitable cupboard to make an altar. Half a dozen chairs and lots of different coloured paints and brushes. Jacobus worked like a fiend... And when we had done all we could in the allotted time, I initiated him in the simplest rites of the Western Mysteries."

It is a testament to their craftsmanship that people who have seen photographs of the temple were convinced that they were looking at a room which had been bankrolled by very rich people indeed, whereas nothing could be further from the truth.

But Bill's African adventure was not finished here.

"There was much more. When initially encountering an entirely fresh environment I do not sleep well for a while because my mind is so full of thoughts that consciousness is stretched to its limits and reaching in all directions for issues arising from this new material. The impact of South Africa and Jacobus combined awakened an entirely new Concept in me, and I named it the Sangreal Concept. The word itself simply means Blood-Royal with a very sacred connotation. By linking this with the legendary Star-people supposed to have visited this planet many millennia ago and begun to breed with the native race of humanoids, I could now see clearly what the Holy Grail was, and why it had to be Quested for until 'achieved'. The Holy Grail, or Sangreal, was factually our capability for bearing this 'strain' of 'Blessed Blood' in ourselves and evolving all the noble and one might say Divine characteristics which it brought so long ago to our chromosome, and had not yet completed on this earth. That Sangreal trace in our genetics had implanted all the possibilities for perfection of our species as spiritual beings. The implications of this happening were so vast and far reaching that they kept me awake almost an entire night thinking about them with awed amazement.

"At last, after nearly a lifetime, I had seen the Sangreal as clearly as if it had appeared in physical form. It was indeed an actuality. The actuality of ourselves being blest by the best blood within our own veins. We ourselves were the vessels which contained this priceless power. Everything in the old-time legends fitted in. Nowhere was the Grail known as a cup, but specifically a Vessel, which could be a container of any kind. It was the principle of containment which was signified, and the Blood-Royal was always considered as a very special inheritance handed down genetically from the earliest times to our days which was said to confer kingly characteristics on those who bore even the slightest trace of it. Since Western mankind had become so widely inter-related, it seemed clear we nearly all had *some* trace of the original strain in ourselves, however slight. All we had to do was to find that and follow where it led. The Kingdom of Heaven literally was within ourselves."

Bill returned to Britain with a fire in his belly, voraciously imbibing every mention he could find of the Sangreal in history and legend. As to the meaning of the word, Jacobus recalled:

> During our research of the Sangreal literature, Bill and I preferred the breakdown 'Sang Real,' because in this division the 'Sang' means Blood, and in case some Etymologists feel differently, I may point out that the word 'Sangria' in Spanish means blood; the French 'Sangre' means blood; 'Sang-de-boeuf' means bullock's blood, and 'sang-froid' means cool blood. The English 'sanguification' means the conversion, by digestion, of food into blood, and so in all these words, as well as many others, SANG means 'Blood'. In turn, the word 'Real' means belonging to the thing itself, that it is existing as fact, substantial, actual, authentic, genuine, and that it is in fact true. 'Real' further means that it is sincere and worthy of the name, that it is complete, not merely apparent and transitory, but that it is permanent. 'Real' also implies that it has an absolute and necessary existence, and 'Real' is the Spanish 'Royal,' coming from the Latin 'Regalis' meaning Royal or Regal. Thus, Bill understood the Sangreal to be our Rightful Royal Blood personified as the Spirit of the West.

"He did come up with another possible origin of the word Sangreal. The French phrase 'a son gre.' That is 'at his pleasure,' 'desire,' etc. I believe this is where the English word 'agreeable' comes from, signifying to be in accord with, and so forth. In that light the Sangreal would be regarded as some kind of Talisman, which brings people into agreement or harmony with each other, or one individual into harmony with all aspects of themselves. I liked it as an alternative or supportive significance, although it certainly does not carry anything like the full meaning of Blood Royal. A parallel suggestion Bill made was that the *Lapis Exilis*, or Stone (Jewel) of Banishment, should have been written *Lapis ex coelis*, Stone (or Jewel) of Heaven, in the sense of descending from Heaven to Earth as a spaceship might have done, or as Lucifer-Satan was supposed to have done. Also, one could render 'a son gre' as: 'as Thou wilt' I suppose. In the end anyone can read anything out of anything, and make meanings out of whatever they will just for the fun of it. Perhaps someone later might do a book entitled *Esoteric Etymology*, giving all the implications of quite ordinary wordings."

Really, you have to gasp. The scholarship and sheer application of Bill and his pupils was just in a different league to that of anyone else in this business of Magic.

So once the definitions were sorted out Bill went on to simplify, refine and cross-reference until the whole was distilled into one profound essence. An excellent example of this is in the Catechism of his *Sangreal Ceremonies and Rituals* which is a series of 110 deceptively simple questions and answers beginning: 'What is the Sangreal' and ending with 'Where do we go from here?' But a crucial question comes fifth: 'How did all this originate?' The answer being: 'Esoteric teaching says that it began with interbreeding between anthropoid humans and a far superior race from another solar system many millennia ago.' It is an answer which is thrown in matter-of-factly but which is quite startling in its implications. This is the crux of modern best-selling books such as *Bloodline of the Holy Grail* and *Genesis of the Grail Kings* by Laurence Gardner, which approached it all from a very different angle yet reached the same conclusions. And earlier still when *Holy Blood, Holy Grail* by messers Baigent, Leigh and Lincoln was published to staggering acclaim and turned orthodox belief on its head, a few of us were muttering that Bill Gray had been saying all this for years...

Nevertheless, star-seed apart, the Sangreal is not an easy concept: it either clicks or it doesn't. In trying to clarify it, Jacobus recalled Bill's thought processes thus:

"He told me that 'It is an optimum that any of the human race may reach in search of spiritual progress and development toward Divinity' and is linked to blood because 'blood was seen as the life-bearing fluid communicating all characteristics through every human generation, and is therefore a constant between the beginning and end of our existence'. I learned from him that the Sangreal is really the objective one is looking for during one's whole lifetime and that, strictly speaking, it is one's own identity within the identity of one's ethnic identity, within the identity of humanity itself, and that again within the identity of all Life throughout the entire Cosmos. A life inside lives which as a whole again is another life, and so on ad infinitum. He compared it to those Russian 'Matrushka' dolls made of wood one inside the other. So in our understanding, the Sangreal is a constant and continuous process of self-discovery".

The Sangreal then, is a composite concept which, while stirring deep recognitions at the heart level, can remain intellectually elusive. This *ne plus ultra* of the Western Tradition has become a euphemism for any virtually unattainable objective of a non-material nature, and a symbol for our Western spiritual quest as a whole. Bill's great achievement was to put this into terms accessible to modern people, to try and clear away the accrued dust of ages around a concept that links us with our earliest beginnings.

Bill believed he had made a real start with a liberating spiritual concept and that all that was needed now was its following up and expansion into something closer to credibility. This aim was furthered by Carr Collins who had been hoping for some time that he would write a complete correspondence course on the Western Inner Tradition in fifty lessons, and was offering to produce it if Bill would put it into writing. For several years, Bill had resisted these demands because he felt correspondence courses on esoteric topics to be futile, despite, or maybe because of, the course he had himself undertaken with the Inner Light. "One might impart information but that was all", he said. "One might as well try and teach moral integrity or honesty by correspondence". Overcoming his reservations, he produced a couple of simple lessons, and soon found that he was writing more than one a week, sending them over to Carr as soon as two or three were ready.

As it turned out, it was not as a correspondence course but as a series of four volumes that these lessons appeared. It had occurred to Bill that here was an opportunity for focusing the whole 'Sangreal Project' under a single heading. It was a series that in some way seemed to amalgamate the breadth of Bill's work on the Tradition. Volume One, *Western Inner Workings* dealt with the history and diversity of the Tradition, from high magic to nature witchcraft. The second, *The Sangreal Sacrament*, was an explication of the Grail story within a re-working of his magnum opus *The Rite of Light*. *Concepts of Qabalah* modernised and clarified the complex workings of the Tree of Life. In the fourth volume *Sangreal Ceremonies and Rituals* he put together all the ceremonies that he had composed at the request of several people for the working of a Sangreal Temple.

And it was thus that the idea of a 'Sangreal Sodality' was born. 'Sodality' may seem to us an archaic and obscure term, but to Bill, as an amateur etymologist, it summed up exactly what he wanted to say. It derives from the latin 'sodalitatem' meaning 'companionship'. No implication of sex or status, merely a friendly fellowship.

"It had to arise more or less spontaneously from readers' reactions with the published material and consist of small and close groupings of Western individuals seeking the Grail within themselves and their association with each other. There must be no central control from a fee-gathering oligarchy out to make money from the concept. Every group had to be self-supporting and autonomous, yet in fraternal communication with others of the same or similar ideology".

Bill was very clear that that the Sangreal Sodality was not a religion or sect of any kind. He was not interested in organisational structures, grades or external trappings, stating that: "You may have initiation certificates from all the recognised (and unrecognised) occult societies and brotherhoods in this world; enough robes and regalia and jewels to stock a shop... Not one single item will make you an iota more or less what you are without any of them."

Likewise the Sangreal itself is seen as a living entity quite separate from the trappings we place upon it: "It is always the same unique 'Spirit of the Western Way' however it presents itself in whatever happens to be the clothing of the current century. It appears under a different disguise in every form of culture we innovate or preserve. We have named it by many names and none of them alter its nature but only our understanding of it. It still remains the Single Soul of which we are all integral parts".

The Sangreal then is a concept that unifies the Christian, Pagan, Qabalist and every other branch of the great Western Tree. It has no exclusivity or monopoly of the truth. It is just one way of 'Being with the Blood' of the Tradition.

Bill in fact always stated that he did not feel the Sangreal Sodality and the concepts behind it would be instantly popular, or that he would ever live to see it really take off. He was told by one psychic that it would only be after his death and when someone discovered how to make money out of the idea that it would begin to have any impact. Nevertheless, it was not long before the seeds he had scattered with the 'Sangreal Sodality' volumes began to show signs of small shoots around the world. Apart from South Africa, correspondence began with groups in Japan, New Zealand, and as we shall see later, in America.

Yet Bill was often perplexed at the lack of response from the Western European heartlands of the Tradition, especially Britain. In many ways though it made great sense that the most urgent recognition of the need for connection and identity came from the 'diaspora' of Western peoples around the globe. The bustle of Americans, Canadians and antipodeans in Edinburgh's Royal Mile searching for clan tartans and family history bears testament to this drive. How symbolic too, on a more profound level, that it was in Africa, a continent that many now believe to have been the earliest home of our species, that Bill made his breakthrough.

He was to return there as Jacobus' guest on several occasions, and though its traditions were not his own, it was to teach him much about the links between humanity and spiritual traditions at source. It was during one of his visits to South Africa that Jacobus witnessed the other, gentler side of Bill that many of us glimpsed, were occasionally touched by, and generally knew was there even if he kept it frustratingly well hidden for much of the time. We can't do better than give his account in full:

"I am not sure if it was during Bill's second or third visit to South Africa that I came up with something very special for him. Since I grew up amongst the Basuto tribes in the foothills of the Maluti mountains on the border between the Orange Free State and Lesotho, I am very familiar with Sotho culture and naturally know the area very well. Nearly two centuries ago the Augustinian Fathers set up a mission station at a place called 'Modderpoort,' and their original church was a small cave. The property they occupied is very sacred to the Basuto, and the cave church itself was originally the home of a great medicine woman, who was one of the advisors to the 19th century King Moshweshwe I. This king waged quite a war against the Afrikaner farmers and the British troops. I seem to recall that one of the reasons why the cave was converted into a church was to 'sanctify' this pagan abode for Christianity, which would have put the missionaries in close contact with the native populace. The local custom amongst the Basuto was, and still is, to raise altars of stones in front of sacred sanctuaries, and several could be seen in the open field adjacent to the cave church. The usual custom is to place a few coins on the stones while making a wish with your abeyances.

"I thought it would be wonderful to arrange with the Augustinian fathers for Bill to hold a Rite of Light inside the sacred cave, and duly wrote them a letter asking for permission. They gave their consent naturally, since they knew me when I was a child and remembered me very well. I introduced Bill to the fathers when we visited the area, and they told Bill how only recently some of the locals were using the cave church and, before the fathers could do anything about it, the populace had sacrificed a sheep in front of the cave. Bill's belly shook as he giggled, and I thought how good it was that the cave returned to its pagan ancestors.

"The following morning, as the sun was rising over the Maluti mountains (part of the Drakensberg mountain range), Bill, myself, my wife and a friend held a Rite of Light in the cave church. As there was no place to robe up, and we did not have to worry about prying eyes, we were all in our robes as we arrived at the cave. As we approached the property and opened the small gate leading to the cave, I thought Bill was particularly silent and deeply withdrawn into himself. On the mountain side of the little pathway, there was a very tall hedge comprising a local cactus which was covered in beautiful lilies, which was exuding the most wonderful perfume. Bill paused without saying a word. He stood looking at this beautiful sight, then looked across the open vista on the other (eastern) side, at the dawn of a very beautiful day. It was truly magnificent, as daybreaks in Africa often are, but all of us knew that there was something most extraordinary taking place. Bill was making contact with this extraordinary land, and it was acknowledging his tribute in a most magnificent way. We silently went to the cave, the entrance of which is exactly east, with the sandstone altar directly opposite in the west. Bill paused in the door, turned around and looked at the rising sun. Then he went into the small sanctuary. I busied myself placing candles and the eucharistic symbols on the altar, plus water and salt, matches, also preparing the thurible I brought along for use later on in the rite, and so forth.

"Bill appeared to be in a state resembling a trance, and we were standing around waiting for him to commence the Rite. We waited a while, and when he did not respond, I lightly touched his arm to signify that I finished the preparations. He nodded and commenced the rite with the 'dark silence,' which started a ritual I shall never forget as long as I live. As Bill was reading particularly slowly and seemingly hesitantly, I thought he was struggling to see the text. I held a candle close to the copy of the Rite of Light in his hands, and inadvertently was dripping hot candle wax on his left hand. By the time I realized what I was doing, the palm and side of his left hand was covered in red wax. Bill appeared to be completely unaware of this, and was still reading as hesitantly as before, and going through the motions of the rite in slow motion, as it were.

"He served each one of us the bread and wine with the greatest outpouring of love I had ever known. At that moment the Presence in the cave was so amazing and incredible, that one just wonders how it ever got into this unhappy, mixed-up world. I could understand it OUT of the world, but it seems as incongruous here as an oasis at the north pole, and I think I understood then what Gibran meant when he said: 'Love lies in the soul alone, not in the body, and like wine should stimulate our better self to welcome gifts of Love Divine.'

"When the rite finished, I started to clear up and collect our ritual equipment, while the rest of our company left the church. My wife came back into the cave and silently but urgently asked me to come outside. I stepped out of the church, and Bill was walking towards one of the stone altars in the area where an elderly black man had just placed a couple of coins and was standing looking at the altar. He noticed the white man in the red robe walking towards him, and he must have thought Bill was one of the Augustinian fathers, because he started making all sorts of greetings and humble abeyances in Bill's direction. Bill smiled, put his hands together, and made a small bow in his direction, then turned to stand next to him facing the stone altar. Bill pulled up his robe on the one side, and fished out a few coins from his pants pockets, and placed these on the stone altar. I thought the black guy would drop dead in shock. I knew that he had NEVER before seen a white man honouring the spirits of his ancestors. As you are probably aware, in the tribal religions of Africa, the people mainly revere the elements and are conscious within a border realm between the living and the dead, where they generally invoke and worship the spirit of their forefathers. Now, the only difference between that old black gentleman and his white counterpart was, that Bill did not so much worship the deceased forebearer, but is conscious of the ancestor through the blood record which separates us naturally into families, tribes and races, and which also evolved us into our present state of awareness. In this consciousness we can recognise our Inner Tribal relationships with our own Inner Blood records, so that we may live, move and have our being in that Inner State of existence.

"Each race carries its own unique record of superphysical and subjective phenomena through its bloodstream, and these memories constitute our fables, legends, gods, heroes and what have you. They cannot be forgotten because they are locked within our genes as a blood record. I fully agree with Bill that a brotherhood of a specific Tradition is not going to work for all races, but only for those who carry its legends and past within themselves. I believe the most mystical tie to be the blood tie – the Blood Soul. This Blood Soul can only be communicated to those who possess it, and all the members, with their respective connections to this Blood Soul, become like one man, one great soul – the Sangreal in our case. Members of any brotherhood, such as the Sangreal Sodality, should be Inner Blood brothers regardless of physical family ties. They must realise a common consciousness, knowing that when you wrong your blood companions, you wrong yourself, your soul and your Tradition.

"Bill made it very clear to me that by no means all people born in the West actually belong to Western Traditions, and many born elsewhere in the world do. Same applies with other Traditions these days. In fact, he maintained that it gets more and more difficult as the world changes. He did however stress that as far as he could see, it was important that all those claiming to belong with a Tradition should be Inner Blood Brothers, whether there are physical family ties between them or not, and even when one feels one genuinely belongs, one should go forward carefully and take care to move step by step, earnestly and diligently, avoiding spiritual indigestion.

"Anyway, to finish the story of Bill in the cave church, he was silent for the rest of the day, but before we left the terrain adjacent to the cave, nature had a nice surprise in store for him. Lying on the ground was what we termed "manna" when we were kids. Though not entirely rare, it is not so abundantly and readily available. I believe it is some sort of secretion from insects, white as snow, with a taste reminiscent of honey, but absolutely unique. I picked some up from the ground, and offered it to Bill. He looked at the stuff in his hand, and looked at me quizzically. I picked up some in turn, handed it to my wife, who stuck it in her mouth with a smile. Bill hesitantly nibbled at it, and the look of childlike astonishment on his face nearly had me off crying again. Fuck, I was so bloody emotional! I still am! I told him that we call it 'manna,' and that it was probably secreted by insects. He promptly picked up as much as he could find in the area, and folded it in a tissue to take home. I later saw him putting the 'manna' into a small plastic bag, and he took it back with him to the UK.

"Anyway, we returned to the home of my grandmother, where we were staying during our visit to the area, and she had cooked one of her great lunches. I think Bill was a bit overcome by it all, including the wonderful hospitality. In the car, on our way back to Johannesburg, he turned to me and said: 'You know Jacobus, your granny is a good Christian witch. She's the kind of person I would like to share heaven with, and I would not want to go there if I knew she wasn't there.' I was sufficiently moved to remember those exact words to this day. My Father-brother honoured my ancestors as well.

"On our return to Johannesburg, I arranged for Bill to meet Credo Mutwa, the famous Zulu medicine man, I mentioned previously. They got on like old friends, and remained so for many years until Bill got too old to travel. He is the author of that sentence: 'Man will never amount to anything until he knows who he is,' which he said to Bill and I quoted in the previous letter. We felt that to be a very profound saying. Mutwa is the author of, amongst others, the books *Indaba my Children* and *My People*. Both works created an immense stir by showing that the Black people have Inner Traditions of their own, and do not need White Traditions imposed upon them. Like Bill, I too believe one of the worst things that whites ever did to blacks was to inflict Christianity on them, an alien set of concepts they did not understand. They had their own Tradition, suitable to themselves, which Mutwa is trying to reclaim, and fundamentally it is much the same as the Sangreal Concept as applied to their race and ideology. Bill and I made a very clear decision prior to our visit to this remarkable medicine man, that we would show respect for his Tradition rather than try to invade or negate it, and that we expect him to do the same for ours. As he said, Credo Mutwa is trying to do for his people exactly what we are trying to do for ours, and that is to preserve and propagate their own Inner Tradition. His English is classic, and I believe he was Jesuit educated. Thank heaven there are still a few African and Australian tribes who have managed to retain a lot of their own traditions, despite the destruction the White Man has brought them. It is a good thing to know there are a few left in this world who value their native traditions enough to try desperately to keep them going."

It is a deeply moving account that, and says a lot on many levels. It would be nice if all those today who brand William G. Gray as an aggressively racist, anti-Semitic, neo-Nazi could have been present at that meeting, or could see the book that Credo Mutwa inscribed to him. It also shows Bill on many levels too and confirms the individual experiences of the present co-writers, both of whom caught frequent glimpses of a very dear and oddly simple man who could be (and often was) enormously generous and sympathetic, and who was often kinder toward two young know-it-all empty-headed fellas than they probably deserved. We who are not anti-Semitic, neo-Nazi, homophobic or racist to any perceptible degree, loved the man – old sod that he was.

Another person deeply touched by the persona of William G. Gray was Marcia Pickands, whom Bill was rather inclined to believe was Dion Fortune reborn – although he treated her just the same as anyone else. His books first came to her attention in 1986, when she and her husband Marty owned and ran the 'The Far Country Book Store' in Albany, NY, which had an especial emphasis on the subjects of mythology, mysticism, metaphysics, the occult, and the various systems of martial arts – in which Marcia is both expert and renowned. As she tells it, one of her regular visitors to the book store was a little old man of indeterminate age who was obviously well read in their specialist subjects and loved to come in and talk. Books always tended to jump off the shelves as he went by and they often used those titles as the topics of conversation. One day they were discussing Dion Fortune's works of fiction and this little elf of a man asked Marcia if she had ever read anything by William G. Gray. She hadn't, but she found in Samuel Weiser, Inc's latest catalogue a new listing for something called The Rite of Light which was sold for $1.50 retail at the time.

"I read that little pamphlet of a book and knew I had found exactly the ritual that I was looking for. It fitted with my personal belief system beautifully. It could also be made useable by almost anyone who truly believed in Deity and other Beings of a greater than Human variety so long as they were willing to commit themselves to the service of both Divinity and Humankind.

"That was part of the Rite of Light's beauty. I was often asked to host and lead rituals for people that had 'alternative/unorthodox' religious/spiritual beliefs and that ritual really did the trick in one form or another for most of them. There were, of course, those who found it a bit too reminiscent of the Christian format for worship. That was OK though. I just took what worked for them and re-wrote the ritual for them so that it sounded and felt a bit more Neo-Paganish…"

Naturally, she had to contact him.

In keeping with the man, most people have their own stories about how they stumbled upon him in vaguely wondrous and quasi-miraculous ways. Marcia wrote to him c/o the address on the *Rite of Light* pamphlet, which was Helios Book Service, 8, The Square, Toddington, nr Cheltenham, Glos. England. In fact at that time Helios had been out of business for 25 years, yet the letter somehow still managed to find him.

"Bill and I were both 'high' on what felt like a bit of Divine Intervention designed to get us together. From that moment of first contact we both behaved as if we were destined to accomplish something important together (I think we managed that rather nicely, and the Work continues to this day). We both tried to take things slowly and practically, but the result was that we did things together from the start that neither of us would ordinarily have done with anyone else without several years of relationship building first."

At this time Bill was in his early 70s, and not in the best of health; in these sort of matters, time was not on his side. Risks and unusual procedures were clearly necessary, and he was obviously well impressed by Marcia, and the potentials she offered. Then again there was the fact that, being half-American himself, he felt that they had many things in common. Some twenty years before he ever met her, he opined that if he ever *had* to reincarnate, then he rather hoped it would be in America. As it turned out, he would later tell a number of people exactly where in America he *would* be reborn, giving specific details that have – apparently – been fulfilled – although it is not the business of the present authors to go into that. Growing up is hard enough anywhere, in any circumstances:

growing up as the recognised reincarnation of William G. Gray would be a cruel burden to impose on any child, no matter how extraordinary.

Marcia went on to describe how, in the first few months that they knew each other, Bill offered her a full initiation into the Sangreal Sodality in a very experimental manner.

"He sent me taped materials and directions. We arranged to both go through the ritual together at the same time while separated by distance. Bill used a coat rack with my name hung on it to represent me as he did his part in Cheltenham and I had his voice in my household chapel in Delmar. I called him just before I was about to start (ring 3 times hang up and then ring again) so that we could synchronise our consciousness as precisely as possible. It was a marvellous experience for both of us… That initiation was the single most powerful 3 way spiritual contact I had ever experienced up to that point in time and I have yet to experience anything that could top it. Bill later brought me the lamp with my name on it that he had used during the ritual. It's still 'buzzy'!"

During her association with Bill they worked together many times both long distance and in person when they could get him to visit at Delmar NY. They had plenty of opportunity to see his delightfully human sides, and weren't afraid to have fun. Once, as they were working on the Temple, her husband Marty came through the house with a freshly painted pillar on his shoulder. As he passed Bill who was sitting in the living room Marty said that when he had been in the US Army he had been taught to march in a column. Bill did a full body grimace and said, 'Bobbie would kill you for that!' For all Bill's interest in word meanings, he really didn't much like puns and apparently his wife detested them. "So, of course, Marty had to continue them. So a bit later Marty came through the Living Room with the other freshly painted pillar and looked Bill in the eye and said, 'Column of twos!' Bill outdid the earlier full body grimace and actually growled at that one!"

They also observed his tendency to deny being particularly psychic.

"We had a large spirit cat in the house named Growler… Bill didn't know this when he came to visit us the first time; however the next morning when he got up he asked us if we had a really big brown tabby cat (we didn't have one in the flesh at that time, big or little) because he had seen one at the end of his bed and then it was gone and he wondered how it had gotten through the closed door of his bedroom. At that point we told him about Growler and our theory that he was a type of elemental that needed to interact with humans for some reason. Bill changed the subject very quickly. He really wasn't very happy about seeing something that wasn't 100% physical."

Of course they didn't always agree on things, especially his 'racialism', but she knew that their energies always produced very strong results. Just as many people, thirty years earlier, didn't hesitate to alter his *Seasonal Occult Rituals* in order to match to their own propensities, so Marcia and her own chapel did similar with his Rite of Light and other works. That might have exasperated him, but he knew it was inevitable. As he said in one of his first letters to her, dated 29th April 1986: "I'm extremely glad to hear you mean to get ANOTHER Sangreal Temple going, but do remember they aren't all supposed to be rubber stamps of the same thing, but collections of *individuals* all seeking the Sangreal in their own way. Remember it will be in no sense *my* Temple, but entirely *yours* in the sense that you will all have to decide how and what you are doing in it, who's going to pay for what, and all the rest of it. I'm sure you'll succeed in the end because you sound so sensible and methodical about it."

It did succeed. So the magic did spread, even if the process was slower than he might have liked. Temples sprang up in several countries throughout the world, each with a Warden interpreting the Sangreal concept in his or her own way.

And it is a very flexible concept. One of the present writers, Marcus Claridge, is very much involved in the Sangreal as defined by Gray himself and has no problems with the concepts. The other, Alan Richardson, still cannot begin to understand it. Yet once he was working on a notion of his own involving what he saw as the 'tribal' nature of all magic, and sent the definition to the old sage to ask for his comments. It read:

> All magic is essentially tribal. This tribe can best be visualised as a circle (or even a sphere). Half of it is in the otherworld, half in the earthworld. It is a circle which links past, present and future and makes no distinction. The tribe contains souls which are incarnate, souls between lives, souls which have ceased incarnation, plus beings which have never been and never will be incarnate.
>
> Each tribe has a succession of leaders in the earthworld. Their job is to bring through the Magical Current. In their turn they are overshadowed by tribal leaders from the otherworld – what are termed the 'Secret Chiefs.'

In fact, if we can, think of that as being in the sense 'Chief of the Clan McDonald,' or 'Chief of the Clan McGregor.' The tone and the style of the tribe alters according to which Chief and which earthworld priest or priestess is predominant at the time. The tribe might grow, change, or contract, but the centre will remain the same.

When a newcomer links with the tribe he can tap the collective wisdom of the tribal mind. Often when this happens he has visions of what may appear to be past lives but which are more nearly tribal visions, or points of collective experience down through the ages. These are not always to be taken personally.

Sometimes the newcomer will feel him/herself overshadowed by a tribal member from the otherworld. A mistake can be made here by believing him/herself to be an actual incarnation of that entity.

Tribes can, do, and should overlap. The Chiefs and the earthworld leaders come and go, but their essence remains within the tribe. The Chiefs, therefore, are not meant to be worshipped, for they are points of contact between the worlds. They are part of us as we are part of them. Each member of the tribe is part of one corporate whole. We cannot worship them for we would be worshipping ourselves.

Whatever intellectual output might result is less important than the personal sense of contact with the otherworld, and linkage with the collective consciousness of the tribe.

Bill's comment was: "That's it! That's the Sangreal *exactly*, using different terms of reference. Now what exactly are you going to DO about it?" The comment was gratifying, but he still cannot see the connection. If others can, and find some allusive insight into the Sangreal of William Gray, then they are welcome to make of it what they will.

In his final years he initiated others into the Sodality, and enjoined each one to go out and *do* something with the magic. Some did, and still work the rites, and mighty well; others apparently disappeared without trace. At first we considered listing all those Temples and contacts which were extant at the time of writing but then we thought as Bill himself would have thought: Each person must find out for him or herself. If they have not the wit or ingenuity or the interest to do so, then they would never amount to much in any case. The most we need say is that there are indications now, some twenty years or so after Bill's death, that the magic of the Sangreal is touching people in many different ways. His work was never in vain.

CHAPTER 12
Returning to Nothingness

"This seems to be the single Great Truth we all of us have to find out for and by ourselves. Namely that we are all part and parcel of the same BEING, however different we may seem to each other or how deeply we may appear to be opposed to each other's viewpoints. In the end it is those very differences which should unite us, and when we learn to do that successfully, this world is going to be a much better place to live in. This is an essential and vital part of Sangreal teaching, and why it is so important that our humanity should recognise and realise it before we wreck everything we have already won."

[penultimate paragraph of WGG's Autobiography, 1991]

There is a statement in Magic that 'the planes are separate'. They don't segue from one level to another, blending qualities on the cusp like in astrology. They are sharply defined. Whether this is spiritually true or not, it at least enables us to explain how some people (like Mozart, Dylan Thomas and Aleister Crowley) can produce such sublime work on spiritual levels while having severely flawed personalities on the lower plane. Some have argued that William Gray certainly had a severely flawed personality, and that his comments about Arthur Chichester, for example, could just as well have applied to himself. Others, seeing the softer side, have elected to think that he was just a bit crotchety, as many true individuals tend to be.

Certainly, in his last days, Bill fell out with just about everyone else that was left to fall out with. Then again he was driven by the sense that his life's work showed no real signs of taking off at all, as he had hoped. His wife Bobbie (a life-long heavy smoker) was clearly dying of throat cancer which she faced with astonishing courage, refusing more chemotherapy but determined to outlive Bill – for Bill's sake. While on top of this he was plagued by age-related problems of increasing severity exacerbated by his chronic arthritis. Had he been able to take his life legally, he would have done so. As it was, he tried to do so in hospital by tying his belt around his neck, fastening it to the bed frame, and throwing himself out onto the floor. The nurses caught him each time. It was not the cry for help of a weak individual: it was the ingenious attempt of a lion-hearted soul whose body was failing him rapidly, and who wanted to do something about it.

Sandra West felt that Bill was suffering from what we now know as Alzheimer's disease, although it wasn't diagnosed as such then. She commented in a letter: "Bobbie described one of Bill's suicide attempts as, 'he seemed to have a seizure of some kind'. I suspect that this was Bill trying to get out of his body. The hospital saved his life and kept his heart beating but they couldn't keep his spirit inside the physical body. British law doesn't prevent a spirit walking out of its physical body. Bill knew how to leave his body and he left it. Bill's spirit was moving house, so to speak."

She also added some words which – in more senses than one – capture the spirit of Bill Gray better than most:

"Within a few minutes of Bill's death, the news reached me that his heart had stopped beating. I was alone in the house at the time and I went upstairs to do a requiem mass. I began with a meditation, trying to contact Bill's spirit. At first I couldn't see it at all and I couldn't understand how Bill could have got so far away from earth so quickly. After a while I had to conclude that he had left his body much earlier. I finally managed to contact his ghost in what seemed to be a mountainous landscape. He seemed to be walking along quite cheerfully. There was no one else with him.

I eased myself into his sight and said, 'Bill, is it really you?'

Bill looked at me and said suspiciously 'Who are you?'

'Come on, Bill. I'm Bobbie's friend, Elizabeth. You remember me. You used to teach me Qabalah.'

'Oh,' Bill said. 'Am I dead?'

'Your heart stopped beating an hour ago.'

'Well, I didn't think much of that incarnation anyway,' he said, turning to go on his way.

'Bill, I am doing a requiem mass for you now,' I said. 'Do you want to come back and observe as I work the ritual?'

'I suppose I should,' he said rather ungraciously. He appeared in my small temple. He watched the ritual and uttered, 'Not bad,' and then he vanished. I have not seen his ghost since…"

The late William G. Gray has left us a large number of books dealing with a wide variety of related topics in completely original ways. He would expect us to build upon the work he did, and make every attempt to better it. The more mundane Bill Gray has left a vast correspondence scattered among hundreds and possibly even thousands of individuals world-wide, each letter filled with – at his best – superb prose enlivened by occasionally wondrous spleen. Someday someone will try to correlate it all, and what a task that will be! On top of that he left behind also dozens of people who regarded themselves as pupils in the formal sense, or who were (quite incidentally) taught by him at some very deep level, and who remain determined to be as innovative in their Work as he always was. His legacy is rich, and still to be fully assessed. One of the main aims of this book was not to provide a comprehensive warts-and-all life story, but to inspire wonder, and provoke intrigue. There is much much more to the reality and legend of William Gray than we have given here. Go out and search the rest for yourself, and understand more about what lay behind the man, and what lies within yourself.

Let us not, finally, cast him aside simply because a few people have branded him a racist. Let him who is without sin… etc etc. Hate the sin but love the sinner.

In 108 years' time (to give a magical but purely arbitrary number), every reader of this book will find him or herself judged by their grandchildren. We who might sit quite comfortably with our characters and spiritual correctness, will be astonished to find ourselves pilloried for attitudes and practices that they will find abhorrent but which we never even considered to be offensive at the time. Our only defence can be that we didn't know any better; we didn't have the insight; everyone else was the same. And our shades must have the decency to blush, take the stick, and vow to learn.

As he once advised Jacobus Swart, you don't learn anything from your heroes by stepping in their footprints: you look at their mistakes, and improve upon their path. Very often our parents have qualities that we can find repellent. If we have any originality, any courage, we challenge them right hard, and/or vow never to make the same mistakes. But do we stop loving them? Do we reject everything else about them utterly and completely? Not if we are human ourselves.

Bill had many faults. Instead of dwelling on them, learn to look at the positive sides of this multi-talented magician. Or better still, use the magic he taught to look within yourself and try to Quest further than he ever did.

That is the task of the *real* magician.
That is the quest of the Sangreal.

APPENDIX

Robert John Stewart is known today as one of the leading writers and teachers of the Western magical traditions. R J was born in Scotland, lived in Bath, England for many years, and now lives in the USA, where he was admitted as "resident alien of extraordinary ability", a status awarded only those of the highest standing in the arts or sciences. He is author of 41 books translated into many languages worldwide, and founder of the Inner Temple Traditions, a network that teaches and mediates sacro-magical spiritual arts. He is also a composer and musician, with many film, television and theater productions to his credit. R J first received Qabalah from W G Gray in the early 1970s, and works in the lineage of Gray, Dion Fortune, and Ronald Heaver, through writing, teaching, and direct spiritual transmission. His books on the faery and underworld traditions have transformed many aspects of modern magic and pagan spirituality, and he is author of a seminal series of books on the figure of Merlin in Celtic tradition, and of two influential books on contemporary magical arts. His most recent book is *The Sphere Of Art*, describing a unique method of sacromagical practice for the 21st century. For further information on books and CDs by R J Stewart, go to www.rjstewart.net and for classes and workshop information, go to www.rjstewart.org

Gareth Knight is internationally known as a teacher and writer of many books on the Western Esoteric tradition. Trained in Dion Fortune's Society of the Inner Light from 1953 to 1964 he met up and worked magically with W. G. Gray from 1965 to 1968, and as a director of Helios Books brought him public recognition by publishing his first important works *The Ladder of Lights* (1968) and *Magical Ritual Methods* (1969), and later the remarkable *The Rollright Ritual* (1975) and associated audio-cassettes. More details of his life and work can be found on his website, www.garethknight.net

Marcia Pickands is Warden of the Sangreal Sodality in Elsmere, New York.

Marcio Braile is Warden of the first Sangreal Temple which was founded by Antonio Delfino in June 1982, and known as *Colegio Capitular Pitagoras*.

The Society of the Inner Light is a Mystery School within the Western Esoteric Tradition, founded by Dion Fortune.

Its principle work is the expansion of consciousness into the psychic and spiritual realms, commonly known as "the inner planes". This extended experience is not regarded as an end in itself, or a means to personal power or knowledge, but as a way of dedicated service to God and all evolving life. The work is necessarily demanding and requires sustained application, whole hearted commitment and a capacity to learn and apply spiritual principles to active life in the world.

We train in the use of the Tree of Life as expressed in our Study Course textbook *The Mystical Qabalah* by Dion Fortune. Beyond that the work consists of group meditation, symbolic visualisation and ritual. Its symbolic structure is derived from the myths and legends at the root of western civilisation, particularly those of classical Greece and ancient Egypt, and also those that form part of the cultural heritage of the British Isles, such as the Arthurian legends and traditions associated with sacred sites such as Glastonbury. Our religious orientation is Christian.

We are not a social club, a religious sect, an alternative medical treatment centre, a leisure interest, a self-help commune, psychical researchers, nor specialists in advice on "psychic attacks". Unless you are genuinely seeking self-regeneration, hard work, and service to the greater good you will not find what you want in this Group.

Other activities of the Society

The Society encourages and assists the continued publication of the works of its founder Dion Fortune. It also publishes a quarterly journal – available on subscription.

The Study Course is available, unsupervised, to anyone, such as those resident overseas, who does not wish to seek full membership. Cost for the whole unsupervised course is currently £20. Students can take a correspondence course which can lead to membership.

Application forms and a copy of the Society's WORK AND AIMS are available from The Secretariat, The Society of the Inner Light, 38 Steele's Road, London NW3 4RG, England. See also www.innerlight.org.uk

The Sangreal Sodality has temples in many countries around the globe. Further information on the Sodality or contact details of Wardens can be found at www.sangrealsodality.com

INDEX

CPSIA information can be obtained at www.ICGtesting.com
Printed in the USA
BVOW02s0627231015

423469BV00003B/210/P